CONTRACT THEORY

The Evolution of Contractual Intent

CONTRACT THEORY

The Evolution of Contractual Intent

Larry A. DiMatteo

Michigan State University Press
East Lansing

♾ The paper used in this publication meets the minimum requirements of ANSI/NISO Z39.48-1992 (R 1997) (Permanence of Paper).

Michigan State University Press
East Lansing, Michigan 48823-5202

04   03   02   01   00   99   98   1   2   3   4   4   5   6   7

Library of Congress Cataloging-in-Publication Data

DiMatteo, Larry A.
    Contract theory : the evolution of contractual intent / Larry A. DiMatteo
        p.   cm.
    Includes bibliographical references and index.
    ISBN 0-87013-486-8 (cloth)
    ISBN 0-87013-444-2 (alk. paper)
    1. Contracts. 2. Declaration of intention. 3. Contracts—Philosophy. I. Title.
K840.D56   1998
346.02—dc21   98-20606
                                                                CIP

Ex Gratia

To my loving wife, Colleen,
my parents, and MJM

CONTENTS

Preface   xi

1. Introduction   1

2. Morality, Promise, and the Objective Method   7

   Ex Gratia to Mansfield, Holmes, Fried, Atiyah   7
   The Transformation from Subjectivism to Objectivism   11
      Limitations of Language   13
      The Dominion of the External   14
   Gilmore's Duality: Questions of Fact and Questions of Law   16
   Cardozo's Objective and Subjective Change   17
   Symmetry of Form and Substance   18

3. Actual Intent versus Apparent Intent   21

   The Internal as *Representation* of the External   21
   The Objective Theory of Contracts   22
      The Reasonable Person Standard   23
      The Twin Pillars of Contract: Bargain and Reliance   25
      Reliance Theory   26
      Reasonable Reliance: The Realm of Expanded Liability   27
      The Frontier of Contracts: Comfort Instruments   28
      The Presumption of Intentionality   31
   Promisor-Promisee Objectivity   33
   Communal Objectivity and Detached Objectivity   36
      Llewellyn's Duality: Specific Assent and Blanket Assent   38
      The Implication of Consent: Barnett's Second-Order Problem
         of Knowledge   42
   The Subjective Theory of Contracts   45
   The Modified Subjective or Intersubjective Approach   49

4. The Reasonable Person Standard 51

    The Parties 53
    Totality of the Circumstances 56
    Custom and Trade Usage 60
        Custom as Supplement 64
        Language as Custom 65
        Main Purpose Rule 66
    Manifestation of Intent and Its Manipulation 68
    Relational Consent 72

5. The Dialectic 75

    Religious Foundations 75
    Philosophical Foundations 79
        Durkheim's Objectivity and the Just Contract 82
    Philosophy and the Reasonable Person 83
    The Psychological Dimension 85
    The Judicial Mind and the Reasonable Person 88

6. Law of Satisfaction 91

    The "Law of Satisfaction" and the Objective Theory of Contracts 91
    Freedom of Contract and the Presumption of Reasonableness 93
    Subjective Satisfaction and Objective Dissatisfaction 94
    Kant's Conception of Law 96
    The Doctrine of Substantial Performance 98

7. The Reality of Intent 101

    The Infancy Law Doctrine 102
        The Objectification of the Infancy Law Doctrine 103
        The Judicial Assault 103
        The Legislative Assault 106
    Law as Evolution 107
    The Case of Economic Duress 109
    The Undue Influence Duality 111
    The Externalities of Contracts 112

8. Analogues   115

  Criminal Law: Mens Rea   115
    Circumstantial Evidence and the State of Mind Requirement   118
    The Criminal Law's Reasonable Person Standard   121
  Law of Agency: Implied and Apparent Authority   121
    Reasonableness and the Law of Agency   123
  The Deontological-Teleological Dialectic   124
  An International Comparative: The CISG   126

9. The Inner Experience of Contract Law   129

  Jural Rudiments and Human Values   129
  The Subjectivity of Judgment   133
    Discretion as the Touchstone of Subjectivity   134
  Dialectic as Synthesis   136
  Law's Inner Experience   138

  Summa   141

  Notes   145

  Bibliography   199

  Index   207

PREFACE

My law school training began with an indoctrination into the lore of contracts. The sacred scrolls of contract unfolded the nomenclature that has remained with me throughout my career. The metaphysical melting or meeting of the minds was proffered as the paradigm of contractual obligation. The perfection of the paradigm was soon modified by the second order discourse represented by the objective theory of contracts. Despite its displacement by the objective theory, the subjective theory continued to surface in judicial rationales. Moreover, this subjective-objective dialectic surfaced elsewhere in my legal studies. The state of mind or mens rea requirement in criminal law, the reasonable person standard in tort, the notion of apparent versus actual authority in the law of agency, and the duality of objective-subjective morality in the realm of legal ethics are but a few examples.

Elsewhere, the realm of subjectivity continued to be a forceful presence. For example, the law of satisfaction is inherently pulled toward the subjective pole of the dialectic. Despite interparty agreement on a subjective standard of satisfaction, the courts have often tried to recast the parties' expressed subjectivity into the mold of the objective reasonable person. They have done this covertly by the use of creative interpretation and judicial fictions in determining what the parties "actually" meant. They also have more overtly recognized the subjective element but have proceeded to cloak it in a subdoctrine of objectivity. A party's satisfaction can be made subjectively personal but that subjectivity is tempered by an implication of a duty of good faith or of genuine and honest dissatisfaction. The implication of good faith in the exercise of the right of dissatisfaction results in a convergence of the dialectic. The gauge of dissatisfaction is not to be achieved by analyzing how the reasonable person would have measured the performance. Instead, the gauge is the genuineness or honesty of the rejection of performance. The rejection may be objectively unreasonable as long as it is honest and genuine. This clearly engenders a study of the subjective motive or intent of the rejecting party.

Paradoxically, the standard of good faith is generally construed as one of objectivity. The *Second Restatement* and the *Uniform Commercial Code* have codified the objective standard of good faith and fair dealing. The quandary facing the courts is how to preserve freedom of contract's mandate of enforcing expressly agreed upon or bargained for subjectivity without rendering its decision based solely upon the external manifestations of the rejecting party. The answer may be in restricting the domain of the reasonable person to that of interpreting the objective manifestations as a way of interfacing with the subjective. The bias of the objective person toward a reasonable result must be disregarded if a court is to be true to a contractual mandate of personal satisfaction.

It is this dialectic that continues to intrigue me. My research into various areas of contract doctrine, such as express satisfaction clauses, the assignability of personal service contracts, the infancy law doctrine, and the enforceability of comfort instruments through reliance theory has continued to reveal the dialectic at work. This book reviews the evolution of the objective-subjective dialectic in contract jurisprudence. First, we look at its relationship to some of the theoretical bases of contractual obligation including contract as promise. Second, we will flesh out different formulations along the objective-subjective spectrum including objectivity from the perspectives of the promisor, the promisee, and the detached perspective of a neutral third party. The neutral third-party arbiter has generally been framed by the notion of an objective reasonable person. A look at the factors used to fabricate the reasonable person will help set the parameters for its use as an objective tool. The subjective pole will be analyzed by an analysis of the traditional subjective theory of contracts and by way of an intersubjective model.

Next, in order to understand the current state of the dialectic, a review of its historical foundations is needed. The dialectic will be viewed from three potential lineages: the philosophical, the religious, and the psychological. Hopefully, this genealogy will provide insight into the common law's flirtation with one or the other pole of the dialectic. It is within this framework that we will better understand the common law's selection of the objective fork in the roadway of twentieth-century jurisprudential thought. A view of the judicial mind's continued focus on the mystical meeting of the minds can be understood better in the context of this historical tug of war.

The book then shifts from the general meanderings of theory to the application of the dialectic. This part will study specific areas where the tension between the two poles of contract is most apparent. The study includes a review of the law of satisfaction, the law of contractual capacity, and the doctrine of economic duress. The former studies the interaction of the objective and subjective notions of satisfactory performance of contract. How does the objective theory of contracts confront the express adoption of a subjective standard by contracting parties? The second studies the use of per se rules to preempt the objective analysis of capacity to contract. The third entails a review of a contracting party's submission to the coercive act of economic duress. Finally, a comparative analysis of areas outside of contracts will be undertaken for guidance in understanding the dialectic. This includes a brief stroll down the avenues of agency and criminal law. The area of ethical theory provides an interesting dialectic of its own. The teleological and deontological theories will be applied to the objective-subjective dichotomy.

The importance and the implications of the dialectic to the future of contract law will conclude the exploration. Has the dialectic and the resultant objectification of contracts brought the common law system to the brink of strict liability? Can the inner experience of the law be brought into better focus through the vehicle of the dialectic? This understanding may be available if we can look at the law of contracts through an objective-subjective gaze. Since the beginning, the coinage of contracts has been cast with the subjective on one side and the objective on the other. Both poles of the dialectic are necessary to fully understand the rationale and binding force of contracts. Aristotelian logic and Hegel's dialectic counsel that the two poles of the dialectic can be brought together into a conceptual whole. Hegel's theme in his *Phenomenology of Mind* asserts that "the object known can never be separated in any way from the knowing subject."[1] The goal of this book is twofold: first, to understand the interrelationship between the subjective and objective elements of contract law; second, to challenge greater minds to further investigate the dialectic both by way of legal historiography and by way of both practical and theoretical discourse.

Three disclaimers are offered at this point. First, I have naively used the words consent, assent, and intent interchangeably. My only defense is that for purposes of examining the dialectic I believed that such differentiation would be at best semantic and, at worst, unduly confusing. Second, it is my hope that the work is more descriptive than argumentative or normative. It is not my intent to be an advocate. Third, I have borrowed extensively from English case law. Hence, this work can best be described as a study of Anglo-American law. Finally, I wish to thank the superb editorial assistance of Colleen F. DiMatteo and Nadim Habib, along with the able research assistance of Scott Mussak. Also, I would like to thank those at Michigan State University Press especially, Martha Bates for her faith in my work and Julie L. Loehr and Annette Tanner for ushering it through the editorial and publication process.

THE EVOLUTION OF CONTRACTUAL INTENT

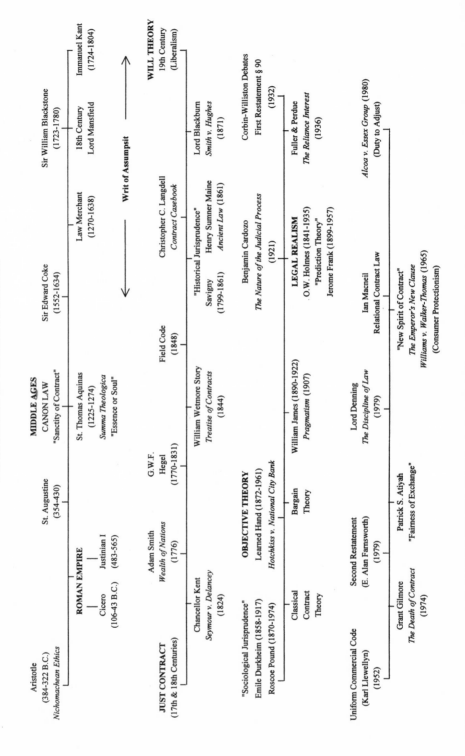

1

INTRODUCTION

Legal rules exist not for their own sake, but to further justice and convenience in the business of human life, *dialectic* is the servant of their purpose.[1]

"**M**odern descendants of Archimedes are still looking for the fulcrum on which they can rest the lever that is to move the whole world."[2] There has been a similar search for the fulcrum that triggers and explains contractual obligation. Numerous pages of contract scholarship have been written in the hope of providing the law of contracts with a unified theory. The intent of a party or the communal consent of the parties as the basis for contractual obligation has spurred a number of different contract theories including contract as promise,[3] law and economics,[4] and libertarianism.[5] Such consent-based theories have a variety of philosophical underpinnings.[6] Their philosophical bases include the morality of promise, promise as social convention, efficiency of contract, and contractual autonomy. These theories do possess a strong degree of commonality. They can be said to be party-based, and they premise contractual enforcement on the freedom of the parties to formulate their own private law. Professor Charny stresses the autonomic nature of consent as the major characteristic of consent-based theories. "In autonomy-based contract theories, obligation arises from the *express consent* of the parties. The basis of obligation is the act of choice."[7] These consent and autonomy-based theories of contract will be used to flush out the continued relevancy of the objective-subjective dialectic in contract law.

Intention has long been the touchstone for the juristic act known as promissory or intentional obligation.[8] Lord Mansfield in the mid-eighteenth century "emphasized basic fairness and the *intentions* of the parties as governing principles."[9] It was with Mansfield that contract law began to be transformed from a limited scope of action to the use of the parties' intentions as the device for granting a general contract remedy. The nineteenth-century's bequest to contract jurisprudence has been the need to discover the

1

intent of the parties in order to grant contractual relief. Most definitions of contract contain the elements of intent and assent. Hence, most issues of contract law involve the determination of the "acts the parties must perform in order to express their intentions and the legal relationships that flow from expressions of assent."[10] Professor Atiyah suggested that this "heritage has led us to place undue emphasis on the extent to which contractual obligations depend upon intentions and the voluntary assumption of liability."[11] Whether undue or not, the finding of either subjective or objective intent has been at the center of the law of contracts.

The courts have been delegated the task of discovering contractual intent. The purpose of their investigation is twofold: first, to determine if there can be found a general intent to create a legally binding obligation; second, once general intent is uncovered, specific intent is needed regarding a specific contractual term or issue. In the face of ambiguity or to fill in missing terms, specific intent was eyed through a process of contractual interpretation and construction in order to salvage the general intent of the parties. Specific intent focuses upon the parties intention as to a particular matter of contract. What were the parties' specific intention regarding the meaning of a specific term or regarding a missing term? Both types of intent are largely contextual. For example, a general intent to create legal relations can be implied by the context of the communications. "In the commercial sphere the intention to create legal relations is readily assumed in such circumstances."[12] Businesspersons are thought to engage one another with the idea of consummating a legally binding transaction or exchange.

Two approaches have been championed in common law jurisprudence as proper methods in the making of these determinations. The subjective theory of contract focuses on the actual intent or *consensus ad idem* of the contracting parties. The objective theory of contract centers on the parties' manifestations of intent. This approach in its purest form holds that a party's actual, provable intent or meaning is irrelevant. Its standard-bearer, the figurative reasonable person, has the duty to inquire into the meaning of the words and acts implored by the parties.[13]

Anglo-American contract law's most dominant theme in the nineteenth and twentieth centuries has been the objectification of its rules and doctrines. "No metaphysical theory has prevailed to prevent the steady march of the law and of juristic thought in the direction of an objective doctrine of legal transactions."[14] In *Barclay v. Spokane* the court defined the objective approach to contracts. "In interpreting a contract our purpose is to ascertain the intent of the parties, but that does not mean that we are to be guided by the unexpressed subjective intent of a party. Rather we are controlled by the objective manifestations of intent expressed in their writings."[15]

The transformation of Anglo-American law from the subjective to the objective can be seen as part of a larger philosophical debate. Modern thinking has periodically moved between the extremes of objectivity and subjectivity. The current shift in contract law from the internal to the external has been widely accepted and generally overstated. Professor Corbin succinctly states that the "law of contract can not be explained by either of these theories standing alone."[16] This book will analyze the illusory triumph of the objective theory over the subjective theory of contracts. This triumph can be premised by the notion that a party is to be bound by her expressions and conduct as interpreted by a fictional third party, the reasonable person. The promisor's actual or subjective intent is thus rendered meaningless. The reality of this generally accepted premise is less than clear. Conceptually, the subjective meeting of the minds approach continues to influence the law of contracts. The "specter of *consensus ad idem* still haunts contract law in the form of an assumption that to make a binding agreement, one must want to make such an agreement."[17] In practice, the *actual* intent of the parties has not been disregarded as a test of contractual liability.[18]

Contract doctrines that provide an excuse or defense to enforcement illustrate that the law of contracts is still heavily influenced by the subjective theory.[19] In the case of *Ouachita Equipment Rental Co. v. Trainer*[20] the element of subjectivity was central to the court's decision to invalidate a contract despite the mistake being objectively of inconsequential importance.[21] The importance of a mistake is based at least partially on subjectivity. The courts exhibit a wide range of discretion by examining "the conduct, profession, and experience of the mistaken party, together with the party's state of mind."[22] The first part of this examination can be brought within the objective umbrella of a totality of the circumstances analysis.[23] The state of mind part of the analysis is inherently subjective. It can be compared to the mens rea requirement found in the criminal law.[24]

Traditionally, the objective and subjective theories of contractual intent have been viewed as a dichotomy. Professor Muris examined the tension between the *objective cast* of contract law and the reality that agreement is subjective in nature. We will view the evolution of contractual intent through the perspective of an ongoing subjective-objective dialectic. The traditional notion of a dichotomy is too limiting given the vagaries of objectivism and subjectivism.[25] Often only the parties can fully appreciate the needs and desires that led to a contract or fully understand the meaning of what transpired in its negotiation. Consequently, tension exists between the subjective nature of the exchange process and the law givers' need to rely on objective criteria to evaluate that process.[26]

The relativeness of objectivity and subjectivity can be represented by viewing contract law along an objective-subjective spectrum.[27] Professor Birmingham quantified four formulations along the objective-subjective spectrum. The most objective formulation, being syntactical, premises contractual liability upon congruency of language tokens.[28]

3

The parties syntactically said the same thing even though they may have meant two different things. At the opposite end of the spectrum is the psychological which affixes liability only if the two parties meant the same thing. In between are two objective-subjective hybrids, referential and meaning-based. The former is a semantic-based analysis. The parties adopt identical linguistic symbols which reference the same thing. The latter represents the use of language which combines intent with the semantical. The language symbols used by the two parties "have the same patterns of references across possible situations."[29]

Professor Eisenberg explains the objective-subjective spectrum of contracts as a movement from the observable to the internalized. "A principle of contract law lies at the objective end of this spectrum if its application depends on a directly observable state of the world, and at the subjective end if its application depends on a mental state."[30] Contractual issues may be found throughout this spectrum. One such placement will be attempted. An examination of express satisfaction clauses will allow us to extrapolate implications for the general law of contracts.[31] The placement of a single issue or term of contract, such as a satisfaction clause, is itself an oversimplification. Each court will vary in its placement of a particular clause along the spectrum. This ongoing spectral oscillation can be simplified into a single dialectic of contracts. It is a view that both objective and subjective elements are present in every issue of contract. The dialectic acknowledges that objectivity and subjectivity in contracts are inseparably bound together.

This dialectic varies among the different legal systems. The objectification of Anglo-American contract law should not be considered as an inevitable consequence of modern commercial transactions. The French Civil Law tradition is proof that the evolution of the objective theory of contracts was neither inevitable nor is it irreversible. "In French law there is no objective test for establishing what the parties are contracting about—the contract being an *agreement* between the parties."[32] Under both the common law and civil law traditions, *consensus ad idem* is the theoretical foundation of contractual obligation. Their approaches to contract formation and interpretation, however, have gone in different directions. The common law has focused upon the notion of bargained-for exchange. It allows for the *objective determination* of the contractual subject matter. In contrast, proof of a party's intent that is in variance with an objective determination will render the prospective transaction a noncontract in French law. "It is the consensus between the parties which constitutes a French contract."[33] Both legal systems employ the dialectic but have placed contract law differently along the subjective-objective spectrum.

We will explore the various formulations along this spectrum. The exploration will begin with the objective theory as viewed from the perspectives of the promisor, promisee, and a detached third party and conclude with an examination of the subjective theory and a variant, the intersubjective model.[34] Next, we will focus on the fabrication of the reasonable person as the device for the application of the objective theory.[35] It can be argued that the use of the reasonable person standard has broadened the sweep of contract law.[36] Instead of needing to prove the actual intent of the promising party, one can imply such an intent through the perspective of the reasonable person. Lord Denning referred to the "officious by-stander as the god who is let down on the stage so as to resolve every problem of an implied term . . ."[37] The officious by-stander is used to imply what the parties would have agreed if made aware of a contract term by the by-stander at the time of the formation of the contract. It is for the courts to determine what type of evidence will be admitted to construct an officious by-stander or reasonable person.

The relative importance of objectivity and subjectivity will be the focus of our undertaking. Hopefully, the journey will lead to a better understanding of the interplay of subjectivity and the use of objective standards in the law of contracts. One textbook author frames his coverage of the entire law of contracts with a challenge to the reader to detect the dialectic at work and to judge its relevancy. "As the course progresses, keep the objective and subjective theories in mind and ask yourself which of the theories the courts are applying in individual cases, if indeed either of the theories is being used."[38] The intent of this book is to review the evolution and continued relevancy of the objective and subjective theories of contract from this perspective.

2

MORALITY, PROMISE, AND
THE OBJECTIVE METHOD

In the discrete contract the content comes from the promises of the parties, but the obligation comes from the promise-enforcing *external* god.[1]

EX GRATIA TO MANSFIELD, HOLMES, FRIED, ATIYAH

The underlying jurisprudence of contract has long embraced the sanctity of the promise.[2] Mansfield's reaction to Blackstonian restrictionism and the limitations of the common law's writ of assumpsit[3] provided the launching pad for the obligatory force of modern-day contract. Mansfield advocated an expansive view of contract premised on the notion of moral obligation and the use of the conception of morality as a general test of enforceablity.[4] More recently, Professor Fried has championed the cause of promise as the moral foundation of contract enforcement. Fried frames the enforceability of promise as the necessary result of the autonomous use of moral or social convention. "There exists a convention that defines the practice of promising and its entailments. . . . By virtue of the basic Kantian principles of trust and respect, it is wrong to invoke that convention in order to make a promise, and then to break it."[5] The inherent moral force of promise has been one of the primary foundations for the enforcement of contract.[6] The morality of promise as a basis for its enforcement can be traced to natural law theorists such as Grotius. In the eighteenth century Lord Mansfield attempted but failed to make morality of promise the basis for contractual liability. His doctrine held that "no promise made as a business transaction could be *nudum pactum*."[7] Instead, something more was required to elevate a promise to the level of a contractual obligation. That something more became enshrined in the need to have intended a contractual exchange and to have that intent supported by consideration.[8]

Etymologically, something that is contractual in nature is something that rises to the level of a legally binding obligation. Professor Finnis defines an obligation as something that "relates particularly to the binding force of promissory or quasi-promissory commitments."[9] Despite clear contract doctrine that states otherwise, the line between legal and moral or contractual and gratuitous promise is not well defined. Karl Llewellyn argued that there was a strong judicial preference to enforce promises of all types. "Rules of law are twisted out of shape in the efforts of courts, despite the rules, to enforce any explicit promise in which the nonlegal obligation is given form enough to be laid hold of."[10] Holmes argued that the separation of morality and law is only temporary. The morality of the community is translated over time into law.

> While the law does still and always, in a certain sense, measure legal liability by moral standards, it nevertheless, by the very necessity of its nature, is continually transmuting those moral standards into external or objective ones, from which the actual guilt of the party concerned is wholly eliminated.[11]

Thus, the fault or culpability concept of the civil law[12] is made implicit in the common law by way of the objectification of morality. The rules of contract can be seen as the external manifestation of the community's moral code.

The entire task of the law of contracts has been to find the appropriate dividing line between the morally binding and the legally binding promise. The bindingness of promise varies among the perspectives of morality, religion, and culture.[13] (The essence of contract law is the determination of which of life's many promises are not to be recognized as legally enforceable.) Professor Fried argues that the placement of this line should not obscure the fact that enforceable contracts find their basis in the morally binding nature of promises. "By promising we transform a choice that was morally neutral into one that is morally compelling. The obligation to keep a promise is grounded in the respect for individual autonomy and in trust."[14] The restraint of contractual obligation allows people to expand their economic options by allowing them to negotiate and bind others to perform future tasks. Professor Burton explains the autonomy justification of contract law as the empowering of "people to make and receive enforceable promises when they communicate decisions to act or refrain from acting in some definite way in the future."[15] An alternative formulation of the autonomy norm is that it allows the promise recipient to act in ways that she would not have but for the receipt of the promise.[16] Contract is thus an autonomic device that expands individual freedom. Freedom *to* contract is the praxis of greater individual freedom to grow both personally and economically.

Professor Atiyah, in contrast, has focused not so much on the promise principle but the consequences of promise as the basis for contractual liability. Atiyah traces the reliance basis of contract to the work of the seventeenth-century's natural law theorist,

Samuel Pufendorf. "Pufendorf argued that the tendency of promises to be relied upon, of men to place their faith in promises, was the principle justification for treating them as binding."[17] Promise is not a necessary condition for a legally binding obligation.[18] Instead, any action, promissorily based or not, that induces a reasonable reliance may result in the imposition of liability.[19] One need not imply a promise in every situation in order to trigger a contractual remedy.[20] The backward reaching nature of this search was exposed by Professor Atiyah. "Both in law and in moral discourse we appear to determine whether there should be an obligation first, and then decide how the language should be construed afterwards."[21] The judicial mind is biased in the interpretation of the facts and the affixation of meaning to those acts. The objective implication of intent is at times a most subjective, creative judicial act.

Professor Eisenberg focuses on the role of objectivity in the common law's rule-making process. Objectivity allows the courts to bring the rules of law into congruence with the moral beliefs of society and to provide systemic fairness to all who seek recourse in the law. Under the rule of objectivity a person must be held accountable for the reasonable consequences of her statements and actions. This is one formulation of the task of the reasonable person standard. The notion of the reasonable person as a neutral arbiter does not mean that she is morally neutral. In fact, the reasonable person often uses morality as a measure for the determination of the reasonableness of a party's conduct. This view of the reasonable person is premised on the belief that one who uses words carelessly is acting in a morally unacceptable manner.[22] He should be held accountable for another's reliance upon those words. It is within this reliance framework of legal obligation that the objective theory plays a different role. The objective method of contract is generally defined as the finding of contractual intent by the objective analysis of a party's outward manifestations. If, however, the basis of liability is that of reliance, then the use of the objective method is not in the finding of intent but in the determination of whether there has been a reasonable reliance. Professor Atiyah grounds his logic in the finding of a contractual obligation despite proof that such an obligation was not actually intended. Thus, the *finding* of intent based on manifestation and in disregard to actual intent cannot be reconciled to the promissory basis of contract.[23]

The objective theory applies to both the finding of intent and the finding of reasonable reliance. Reliance theory and contract as promise are often discussed as two divergent schools of contractual obligation. Although these two interpretative issues may lead to different conclusions regarding the existence of an obligation, most often the two interpretations will lead to the same result. The clearer the manifestation of intent, the more likely it is a reflection of actual intent, and the more reasonable will be the reliance. "If the promisee's reliance is reasonable, it is likely also to be within the reasonable contemplation of the promisor."[24] Reliance can be seen as the flipside of intent.

In fact, intention and reliance are most often directly connected. The dialectic's role is twofold—the implication of contractual intent and reliance-based recovery.

In *High Street House Limited,* Justice Denning applied reliance theory to find a contract despite the lack of consideration. Two parties had entered into a long-term lease arrangement. Due to the conditions of war, the parties agreed to a reduction of rent retroactively to the commencement of the lease.[25] Upon the end of war conditions, the lessor notified the lessee that the rental amount would be increased to the level as stated in the original lease. The lessor argued that since the modification of the lease payment was not supported by consideration, the agreement to reduce the rent was never legally operative. Denning ushered in a new area where reliance, along with traditional consideration, could be used to uphold an otherwise valid agreement. He framed reliance in terms of contractual intent. "A promise intended to be binding, intended to be acted on and in fact acted on, is binding so far as its terms properly apply."[26] Denning found the modification to be legal and implied that it was intended to operate only for as long as the conditions that precipitated it continued to exist. This intent cannot be found in the express modification agreement but is implied by the recognition of the surrounding circumstances at the time of its formation.

The 1871 case of *Smith v. Hughes*[27] illustrates the relationship of promise and reliance within the framework of the objective theory. Two parties of different trades contracted for the sale of oats as indicated by a sample. The purchaser acted under the belief that he was purchasing seasoned oats when in reality the oats were of a newer harvest. The lower court judge proposed the following resolution regarding the issue of enforceability: if the seller "believed the purchaser to believe, or to be under the impression, that he was contracting for the purchase of old oats, then there would be a verdict for the purchaser."[28] Does this interpretation entail an objective or subjective approach to intent? The lower court found that the seller did not possess such a belief. Under the subjective approach there would be no meeting of the minds as to the quality of the subject matter in the transaction. Nonetheless, the contract was enforceable under the objective approach. Even though the two parties were not in agreement as to the age of the oats, they were in agreement that the transaction involved a specific batch of oats. If the seller knew of the purchaser's illusion as to age, then he could be made accountable based upon reliance theory.[29] Since this was not the case, the purchaser was held liable on the contract because "whatever a man's real intention may be, if he so conducts himself that a reasonable man would believe that he was assenting to the terms proposed by the other party, the man thus conducting himself would be bound."[30]

The evolution of a general remedy for breach of promise required the finding of more than a mere promise or *nudum pactum* to warrant judicial intervention.[31] For example, the civil law system often requires the finding of *culpa* or fault as a prerequisite for imposing liability for a breach of contract. In contrast, "English law regards liability for breach of contract as absolute."[32] The issue becomes solely that of what constitutes the contract. Classical contract law[33] required mutual assent initially framed as the subjective meeting of the minds.[34] This will requirement can be traced back into the English common law archives.[35] Actions in covenant dating back to the thirteenth century were premised on the notion of mutual assent.[36] In the early part of this century the will theory[37] of contract required an enforceable promise to have been generated by an *intent* to create a binding obligation. The influence of nineteenth-century laissez faire economics[38] and freedom of contract[39] on the development of the will theory was pronounced. "Two of the finest flowers of nineteenth-century *subjectivism* were an attitude which modulates smoothly into a theory of untrammeled autonomy of the individual *will* and thence into the idea of unrestricted freedom of contract which was surely one of the master concepts of nineteenth century thought."[40] The finding of the individuals' free will as expressed by mutual assent became the core requirement for the formation of a contract in Anglo-American jurisprudence.[41] Mere promise, however, is not considered enough under common law contracts.[42] Objectivity is that additional requirement that converts mere promise into a binding obligation.

THE TRANSFORMATION FROM SUBJECTIVISM TO OBJECTIVISM

The evolution of the requirement of mutual consent is not without challenge. Roman contract law was structured more upon formality than upon notions of consent or intent. "During the formalistic period of Roman law only completion of the proper formalities, rather than consent, was determinative."[43] The Anglo-American legal tradition is filled with formality such as the sealed instrument, livery of seisin, and the statute of frauds. Behind such formality, however, is the belief that contract is the domain of private law. It is the role of the courts to enforce this private law as agreed upon and formulated by the parties. The essence of contract is agreement as determined by the mutual consent of the parties.

The seeds of objectivity as formulated in the notion of the *manifestation* of mutual assent can be found in the predecessors of contracts. The religious and ritualistic foundations of contract measured contractual obligation against the standards of ritual formality and theological morality. The symbolism of the blood covenant, the Roman *stipulatio,* the giving of a thing or *arles* in Germanic Law, the sacredness of giving a promissorial oath, and the giving of *sacramentum*[44] to a deity in Rome were all objective means upon which enforceability or punishment were handed out. "These ceremonies gave an objective character to the word and the resolve of the promisor."[45] The notion of manifestation of promise as symbolic of an intent to create a legally binding obligation

11

can be seen as the modern substitute for the ancient ritual's objective role. Émile Durkheim asserts that today's words of promise and consensual undertakings provide the same objective measurements as did the sacred formalities of ancient times.[46]

The interrelationship of subjective intent and manifestation of intent, of a court's authority to imply intent, and of the ultimate power of a party to prevent such an implication were discussed in Professor Ferson's 1924 article, "The Formation of Simple Contracts."

> The fact [sic] that juristic acts do at times belie the subjective state of the actor, that such acts are sometimes ambiguous, that courts sometimes for practical reasons generalize by assimilating acts of a given kind with seeming disregard of the particular actor's mind, do not disprove the rationale or principle that a person may, by an act symbolic of his consent, subtract from his legal position.[47]

Professor Macneil acknowledges that "two of the underlying norms of contract are the implementation of planning and the *effectuation of consent*."[48] The subjective meeting of the minds or *consensus ad idem* proved too difficult to manage, from the standpoints of both judicial administration and substantive fairness. First, the inherent inability of a court to determine subjective intent soon revealed the charade of the will theory.[49] Second, the ability to induce another to act or forbear and then deny any intention ex post facto provided unfair sanctuary for the unscrupulous. The lineage of those who saw the need for an objectification of law reaches back to Socrates and forward to Coke, Langdell, and Holmes.[50] Justice Holmes saw legal development as the inevitable movement toward objectivity. "The law moves from the *subjective* to the *objective*, from the *internal* to the *external*, from the informal to the formal."[51] Actual thought was replaced by manifested thought.

The evolution of the mailbox rule can be seen as a somewhat idiosyncratic move toward objectivity unique to the common law. "French law requires acceptance to come to the knowledge of the offeror."[52] The United Nations Convention on Contracts for the International Sale of Goods states that an "acceptance becomes effective at the moment the indication of assent reaches the offeror."[53] These noncommon law rules are more consistent with the notion of mutual assent and the will theory of contract. The acceptance upon dispatch or the mailbox rule is firmly planted within the objective theory of contract. The state of mind of the offeror, his or her knowledge of the acceptance, becomes immaterial. The court needs only to objectively determine if the acceptance had properly been dispatched. In fact, the state of mind of the offeree is also immaterial. Objective manifestation, the dispatch, replaces the state of mind inquiry needed to prove an actual meeting of the minds.

12

The continued importance of the subjective element in the law of contracts, however, should not be overlooked. One view of objectivity is that it is merely evidence of the subjective understandings of the parties to a contract. This view made the transition from the will theory of contracts to the objective theory of contracts more palatable to the subjectivists of the early twentieth century. However, the use of the objective reasonable person standard to provide insight into the subjective was soon exposed as a convenient fiction.[54] Morton Horwitz explained the fallacy of viewing the objective theory of contracts as an attempt at approximating the subjective intent of the parties. "What once could be defended and justified as simply a more efficacious way of carrying out the parties' intentions came eventually to be perceived as a system that subordinated and overruled the parties' will."[55]

The divide between the objective and subjective theories reflects the inability of two parties to convert subjective understandings into a clear, objective memorial. The problems of reducing precontractual negotiations to a complete and comprehensive written accounting are well documented.[56] Professor Macneil described the fragmentation of promises resulting from the inability of the human mind to focus upon all the complexities implicit in contractual relationships.[57] The shortcomings of human discourse and its role in contractual interpretation was aptly noted by Justice Cardozo in *Wood v. Lucy, Lady Duff-Gordon*.[58] "A promise may be lacking, and yet the whole writing may be instinct with an obligation, *imperfectly expressed*."[59] We now turn to the limitations of language and their impact on the formation of mutual assent.

Limitations of Language

This problem of converting the subjective to the objective is compounded by the difficulty of transforming promises into words, oral or written.[60] Psychologists inform us that this problem is endemic to the fact that language is essentially nonnotational. To be notational linguistically, symbols need to have a single meaning or interpretation.[61] Notational symbolism is not characteristic of language.[62] Karl Llewellyn saw legal rules as a series of such nonnotational symbols. As such, these rules were infused with the flexibility inherent in word symbols. "What a word symbol signifies can extend beyond that which has already occurred or been conceived of only in a normative sense, not in a descriptive sense."[63] The indeterminacy of words and their meaning provide both limitations and opportunities. The limitation of words precludes contracting parties from meeting absolute agreement. The limitation is that words have no meaning in themselves but are infused with meaning based on the particular experiences of the user of the words. Words also offer law and those who apply the law "an immanent expansive capacity"[64] that allow for the fitting of new fact patterns into existing legal constructs.

The fragmentation of promises caused by human and linguistic shortcomings creates a divide between what is subjectively understood and what is *presentiated* [65] in the objective form. It results in "nonmutuality ranging from subtle to gross differences in understanding."[66] This nonmutuality is at the heart of the subjective-objective dialectic. "The promise made is never exactly the same as the promise received. Every promise is always *two* promises, the sender's and the receiver's."[67] This inherent quality of contractual exchanges and interpersonal communications is the source for the judicial search for interpretive guidance. This guidance has taken a number of forms including community standards, custom, trade usage, and prior dealings.[68] These forms make up the clan of the external, reasonable, and objective world.

The Dominion of the External

It has been forcefully argued that the modern objective theory of contracts is unconcerned with the intention of the parties. This may be due to the difficulty in proving actual contractual intent.[69] The reasonable person is, instead, used to interpret contracts based on community standards of custom and fairness. Doctrines such as duress, unconscionability, good faith, and fair dealing have been used by the courts to advance their concerns about fairness in the exchange. "Since the application of these doctrines depends on a court's judgment of fairness, it seems as if contractual relations depend not on the *will* of the parties but on externally imposed substantive moral judgments of what the relations between the parties should be."[70] Professor Atiyah describes the inner tension between the concerns of freedom of contract and fairness in the exchange.

> The extent to which courts and the law are prepared to go in treating promises . . . merely as prima facie rather than conclusive evidence of the fairness of an exchange, is determined by the degree of paternalism which commends itself to . . . the judiciary in question. A society which believes in allowing the skillful and knowledgeable to reap the rewards of their skill and knowledge is likely to have a higher regard for the *sanctity of promises* than a society which wishes to protect the weak and foolish from the skillful and knowledgeable.[71]

Courts have found contracts where uncertainty of terms could have led easily to the opposite conclusion. They have implied terms to fill the gaps in otherwise inchoate contracts. The mechanism for this contractual salvage effort is the default or gap-filling rules of contract law. The rationale behind these court-imposed rules is that the courts are merely extending the subjective agreement of the two parties. In his work on default rules, Professor Barnett states that, "when parties fail to exercise their power to alter the law of contract for their transaction, their silence has a normative consequence as well."[72] The normative consequence of their silence is consent to the implication of the existing default rules. Barnett dismisses the realist claim that much of contracts is societal-judicial imposition. Instead, he argues that the imposition is consent-based. "A manifested intent to be legally bound is what justifies a court in enforcing default rules on parties who made incomplete commitments."[73]

Oliver Wendell Holmes discounted this metaphysical extension as fiction. "The law has nothing to do with the actual state of the parties' minds. In contract, as elsewhere, it must go to externals."[74] These *externals* are not to be found in evidence of what the parties intended. Externals are to be found in the judicial mind-set of what community standards and customs perceive as fair and reasonable. Professor Corbin refers to the externals upon which the law imposes a contractual obligation "as based upon principles of justice, policy, and right, and not on the expressed will of the parties."[75]

The judicial preference is decidedly in favor of objective standards to determine the terms of a contract, the measurement of performance, and their remedial repercussions. The subjectivity of these determinations can be explored to better understand the objective-subjective dynamic at work. The implication of terms and the measurement of performance are generally accomplished by the fabrication of the objective reasonable person. The reasonable person has been utilized to define ambiguous terms, to imply missing terms, and to determine if performance has been adequately rendered. Generally, the court does not have to look far to find the reasonable person. The gap-filling provisions of the *Uniform Commercial Code* provide the courts a ready-made guide for finding the terms that would satisfy the reasonable person standard.[76] The issue of incorporating subjective elements into the objective reasonable person remains unresolved. How can one "include in the objective world a mental substance having subjective properties?"[77]

Beyond the realm of intent and the reasonable person lies the nebulous area of court-imposed standards. It is gap-filling but not as originally rationalized in the reasonable person as the personification of contractual intent. Instead, it is gap-filling by way of default or immutability, as a device for imposing socially acceptable terms. Professor Patterson labels this gap-filling dichotomy as *interpretive* incompleteness and *substantive* incompleteness.[78] Interpretive incompleteness is the reasonable person front and center. An open term is filled by juxtapositioning the reasonable person into the shoes of the contracting parties. The contract itself is used to help solve the mystery of what the parties would have agreed to if the open term had been fully negotiated and integrated into the contract. The court weaves a conclusion of implied intent by examining the *essence* of the contract within the context of the contracting. In contrast, substantive incompleteness is one in which the openness is not amenable to the fiction of the second-order intent of the parties. The circumstances and the contract do not provide sufficient guidance for the implication of intent. The party-specific *ad hoc* reasonable person is discarded in favor of a community-based standard. The courts simply imply a term that conforms with commercial or community standards of fairness and reasonableness.[79] The court becomes a third party to the contract by imposing a solution that is more a product of judicial modification than a result of the contractual bargaining process.

Can the parties to an agreement preempt the courts' use of the reasonable person and community standards? The notions of freedom of contract [80] and sanctity of contract [81] dictate that the parties are free to avoid the *default rules* [82] provided under the reasonable person standard. The interplay between objectivity and subjectivity in contract law can best be illustrated by examining instances where the parties have agreed to a subjective standard. This interplay can be found in the law pertaining to the use of contractual satisfaction clauses.[83] The judicial discomfort with the subjectivity inherent in satisfaction clauses can be seen as the cause for the evolution of the doctrine of substantial performance.[84] The historical place of the subjective-objective dialectic in the law of contracts is evidenced by doctrinal developments in the law of satisfaction and in the doctrine of substantial performance.[85] This microcosmic view of the dialectic will be examined in chapter 6, "Law of Satisfaction."

GILMORE'S DUALITY: QUESTIONS OF FACT AND QUESTIONS OF LAW

Professor Gilmore's summary of Holmesian jurisprudential thought shows the law as a process of evolution from a subjective moral base to an external, objective law in practice.[86] The genesis of contract law can be found in the realms of moral subjectivity and public policy. Over time there is a severing of the rules and law from their subjective underpinnings. This severance of the rules from their moral content is labeled as the process of objectifying the law. The illusion of the objectification of law does not detract from the fact that the objective rules of contract stemmed from a subjective beginning. The beginning consisted of the affixation of culpability to a certain fact pattern. Over time the courts, once recognizing a certain fact pattern, simply applied the rule associated with that fact pattern. The judicial discretion was in the labeling of the fact pattern, not the application of the rule. Over a greater period of time the substantive rationales were left behind as part of legal history.

This conversion of the subjective to the objective was reconfigured by Professor Gilmore as the conversion of questions of fact into questions of law. Through the vehicle of stare decisis the courts "accumulate precedents about recurring types of permissible and impermissable conduct." This categorization of fact patterns results in the conversion of original issues of fact into precedential issues of law.[87] The subjectiveness of the factual inquiry is replaced by the objective application of a rule of law. The categorizing of a given fact pattern is all that is needed for a finding of contractual liability. The intent of the defendant is irrelevant in this realm of permissible and impermissible conduct.

CARDOZO'S OBJECTIVE AND SUBJECTIVE CHANGE

Contract doctrine has traditionally had a fetish for symmetry of form and substance. That symmetry is evident in the common law doctrine of stare decisis. Symmetry can be seen as the underpinning of much of contract's doctrinal development and resultant formalism. Certainty, predictability, and generality as the impetus for rigid rule application can all be brought under the symmetrical umbrella. The operational system needed to maintain the symmetrical application of contract doctrine is the objective theory. The objective theory provided the software upon which the courts were able to maintain the precepts of contract without blemishing them with concerns of injustice in the particular case. The need to maintain the symmetry and generality of law was discussed by Justice Cardozo within the framework of his *method of philosophy*. The precepts of his philosophy are adherence to precedent, induction, and analogy.[88] Behind these precepts are the basic postulates of legal reasoning and custom.[89] These precepts and their underlying postulates lead Cardozo to conclude that a judge's "standard must be an objective one."[90] An adherence to objective standards, however, should not be confused with the formalistic application of doctrine. Doctrine may be reformulated and objective standards modified in the event that changing times render such rules and standards outdated. Cardozo harkens back to James and Jhering when he states "that the juristic philosophy of the common law is at the bottom the philosophy of pragmatism."[91] The objectivity of certainty and generality must be tempered by a need to keep contract law functional and responsive. The deontological slant of rule application must be tempered with a teleological eye toward the consequences of generality and its application.

In the end, Cardozo, fully aware of the subjective elements within the law, remains a strong advocate for the generality and objectivity of law. His homage to consequential sensitivity is clearly systemic in scope. His conception of the law remains embodied in the importance of the generality of law. Generality of law should not be violated in order to do "justice in the instance." His reference to Jhering's teleological conception is supportive of the notion of jurisprudence as a *method of sociology*. Precedent and doctrine are not static concepts but provide a direction of growth in order for law to remain functional over time. Law is a living process that is responsive to custom, innovation, and pragmatic concerns. The hardware is constantly upgraded but in a way that maintains continued certainty and generality. The constant is the operational software that provides access to the law's hardware. Cardozo concludes that this software needs to be objective in nature.[92]

Cardozo believed that objectivity is the foundation for the generality of law, however, and that subjectivity leads to a deconstruction of the law. Law must always be measured against external standards to prevent it from degenerating into sentimental ad hocism.[93] His conception of law as based on objective standards is not absolute, however. First, he recognizes the human inability to devise and implement a truly objective system. The concept of the legal process as coldly objective and impersonal is merely a goal.[94] Second, although it is the duty of the judge, as an objective administrator of *generality of law,* to ignore case-specific injustice, it is also the duty of the judiciary not to ignore repeated occurrences of injustice caused by the application of a doctrine or rule. It is the duty of the judge to change doctrine in order to conform to changing customs and mores. Cardozo distinguishes this failure to adhere to precedent and the type involving "every instance of the individual sense of justice."[95] Inherent in this distinction is the role of subjectivity in defining nonadherence as an "end to the reign of law"[96] and what is needed to maintain the functionality of the law. Quantifying this distinction is ultimately a matter of judicial discretion. Implicitly, the subjective element is present in recognizing the mores and customs of the day, conforming the rule of law to them, changing the applicable precedent, and modifying the objective standards that such change requires. In the end, both types of change are embodied in the paradigm of a single judge dealing with the facts of a case at bar. Within this paradigm, the notions of objective change and subjective change are likely to become blurred.

SYMMETRY OF FORM AND SUBSTANCE

Professor Lon Fuller differentiated two aspects of the doctrine of consideration: the formal and the substantive. His analysis of consideration lends itself to a wider application. It has meaning for the law of contracts in general and to the dialectic of contracts. The use of form in contract law can be seen as a way of truncating judicial analysis. "In this aspect form offers a legal framework into which the party may fit his actions. It offers channels for the *legally effective expression of intention.*"[97] The parties' intentions are thus channeled through recognizable instruments and forms of law.[98] The selection of such an instrument or form provides strong evidence to the court regarding the parties' intentions to enter into a contractual obligation. This formalization of intent has been called the *specialty principle.* It is the acceptance that some formalized ritual will be taken at face value to create a legal obligation without further inquiry. The specialty principle has been defined as the making of a promise in a "form recognized by law or custom as sufficient for the creation of a power in the promisee."[99] The now archaic common law seal was such a formalization. Today the channel for the formalization of intent is provided through the instruments of custom and usage. Fuller acknowledged that such formalization was limited by the transient nature of meaning and the importance of context to both form and meaning. "There are few words which are not capable of taking on a nuance of meaning because of the context in which they occur."[100] Nonetheless, it can be argued that there is some direct relationship between formality and objective intent. The requirements of formality, be they the statute of frauds or the expression of intent,[101] force the parties to think and memorialize their intent regarding a pending transaction or relationship. Formality requires the parties to deliberate on their intentions and to *canalize* them into objectively recognizable forms.[102]

Formality serves to memorialize the intention of the parties. "It tends to effect a categorization of transactions into legal and nonlegal."[103] One can also argue that formality leads to an increased likelihood of congruence between objective and subjective intention. Formality is a deliberation-inducing device that "will tend to make apparent to the parties the consequences of their actions."[104] The more that a party is *forced* to deliberate the greater will be the interconnection between inner intent and the outer expression of that intent. It is this connection that works to unify the objective and subjective elements of intent. The objective theory becomes the simple agent of the subjective or will theory. The semantics of the dialectic are apparent in Fuller's exposition that the will theory was never truly subjective. The will theory is only a *figurative* way of expressing the principle of freedom of contract or the notion of free will to contract.[105] Objective manifestation has always been the evidence for proving subjective intent. The theoretical importance of the two theories comes into play when the objective expression can be proved to be in conflict with a party's actual intent. The objective theorists would hold the party liable based on the manifestation of her intent. Fuller asks, "What justification can there be for such a view?"[106] He believed that evidence of subjective intent should have a place within the objective theory.[107] The importance of Fuller's analysis for the present discussion is that objective manifestations of intent play a vital evidentiary role within both the subjective and objective approaches to contract. This should be kept in mind when reviewing the different formulations of objectivity and subjectivity in the law of contracts.

3

ACTUAL INTENT VERSUS APPARENT INTENT

For it is in the realm of subjectivity that the battle over the fountainhead of the legal process will ultimately be fought.[1]

T he movement from the subjective to the objective view of contracts has been a relatively universal phenomenon. Australian law in "the nineteenth century regarded a contract as resulting from the true meeting of the minds. The modern tendency is to determine the existence of agreement on a more objective basis."[2] This objectification of law was forewarned by Henry Sumner Maine in his often quoted *Ancient Law*.[3] Maine saw the consensual contract as a natural progression in an evolutionary process.[4] The evidence provided by the objective method of external manifestation is to be used to prove the consensual contract.

THE INTERNAL AS *REPRESENTATION* OF THE EXTERNAL

The use of the external to prove the internal is not a new revelation or one confined to law. Psychologists and experts in perception have long studied what is referred to as representation.[5] Perception is the internalization of external objects or, more correctly stated, the internalization of some *representation* of the external. "It is not the objects of the world that are internalized but only some representation of them."[6] Despite the human limitations in correlating internal representations "with the objects attributed to the world external to the perceiver," our law has increasingly looked to the external and its inner representations as a vehicle in assigning contractual liability.[7] Professor Gilmore noted the malleability of the objective approach. "The objective theory of contract became the great metaphysical solvent—critical test for distinguishing between the false and the true."[8] The objective standard was applied to an increasing variety of contractual issues.

21

One needs to distinguish the notion of reasonableness from the development of the reasonable person standard. Both notions can find grounding in the works of Aristotle and St. Thomas Aquinas which held that reasonableness can be found within each person. They believed in the "existence of natural virtues which incline men to act in accordance with right reason."[9] Aquinas defined this innate reasonableness in his concepts of *conscience* and *synderesis*. Aristotle's political notion of law as a neutral and impersonal arbiter[10] can be seen as a metaphysical predecessor to the reasonable person. His view of the inherent generality of law can be seen as a philosophical support for the objective theory. "In being impersonal, the rule of law can claim to be objective and incorruptible. It is a mean and neutral authority, like Adam Smith's *impartial spectator* or a Kantian regulative idea."[11] The notion of reasonableness has been a part of our common law tradition since the days of Coke and Blackstone.[12] The creation of the reasonable person has a more recent lineage to which we now turn.

The *First Restatement's* adoption of outward manifestations as the standard for mutual assent was not without detractors. Professor Whittier advocated the continued use of actual assent and not the manifested intent of the objective theory of contracts. He advocated the test of actual assent as *communicated* by the contracting parties. He went further by arguing that holding a party to her manifestations of intent and not her actual intent could conceptually be placed within the realm of tort. "The liability for carelessly misleading the other party into the reasonable belief that there was assent might well have been held to be in tort."[13] Whittier's objection to the objective theory is based on a number of premises. First, in the vast majority of cases manifestation of intent and actual intent are present. Thus, the actual intent as mutually communicated best serves the meeting of the minds principle of contracts. The relatively few cases where actual and manifested intent are at odds can be more efficiently handled in tort as *misrepresentation* of intent. Second, the objective theory as stated in the *Restatements* is by necessity filled with serious exceptions. These pockets of subjectivity are often cloaked in objective garb. For example, the acknowledgment that silence can be a basis for acceptance is a reflection of objective reality but is not an objective standard.[14] Although Professor Whittier's critique has lost its following over the years, the vitality of his arguments is relevant to a discussion of the dialectic.

THE OBJECTIVE THEORY OF CONTRACTS

Professor Corbin defined the objective theory of contracts as agreement by expression.[15] "A valid contract is created by *agreement in expression*, the subjective intent of the parties being immaterial."[16] The agent for determining the meaning of the expressions of contract became embodied in the mystical reasonable person.[17] A reasonable person would need to be constructed on a case-by-case basis to reflect the characteristics of a particular contracting party. This substitute contracting party would possess the intellect, sophistication, and good faith demeanor of the average, reasonable person. The issue in dispute would then be offered to this juxtapositioned reasonable party. The subjective intent of the parties is discarded in favor of the intent of the reasonable person applied *ex ante*.

Professor Slawson coined the term *laws of meaning* to refer to a narrow preemption to the objective theory of contracts. There are a few rules of contract that act to *give* meaning to a contract as opposed to the *discovery* of the parties' meaning through the interpretive device of the reasonable person. These rules provide a meaning that is different than that provided under the reasonable person standard. Slawson gives section 234 of the *Second Restatement* as an example of a law of meaning.[18] It dictates that if a contract is silent as to the order of performances and the performances are susceptible to simultaneous rendering, then there shall be a simultaneous ordering of performance. This preemption of the objective theory is of conceptual interest but is an exceedingly rare occurrence. Most of the gap-filling provisions of the *Uniform Commercial Code* [19] and the *Second Restatement*[20] are premised on the use of the objective theory to custom design a term based on the totality of the circumstances. Contractual interpretation and implication of meaning is essentially a contextual phenomenon.[21] The modern device for the determination of meaning in contracts' infinite number of contexts is the reasonable person.

The Reasonable Person Standard

Judge Learned Hand wrote the coming out announcement for the objective approach to contract in the 1911 case of *Hotchkiss v. National City Bank of New York:* [22]

> A contract has, strictly speaking, nothing to do with the personal . . . intent of the parties. A contract is an obligation *attached by the mere force of law* to certain acts of the parties . . . If . . . it were proved by twenty bishops that either party, when he used the words, intended something else than the usual meaning which the law imposes upon them, he would still be held . . . [to what] would have such meaning to *ordinary men*.[23]

This objectification of contract has had a profound impact. First, the evidentiary mindset has been shifted from the personal to the external.[24] Contractual intent, ambiguous terms, the implication of missing terms, and the measurement of performance are to be judged based on community standards and evaluated against communitarian values. Second, the equating of contract with promise has been forever shattered. Increasingly, the consequences of contract have become the center of focus for contract enforcement and interpretation. "Normatively speaking, it seems clear that it is impossible to affirm that *all* promises *ought* to create moral or social obligations, without any regard to the reasons for the making of the promise, or the consequences which have ensued from its being made."[25] This shift from the deontological mind-set that one has a duty to honor one's promises to a teleological approach is compatible with the shift from the internal to the external.

In the 1974 case of *Storer v. Manchester City Council*[26] Lord Denning discarded the need for the actual exchange of a formalized contract to consummate the sale of a home. He noted that a letter offering for sale to tenants of government-owned houses envisioned a simplified scheme minus the standard legal formalities of real estate sales.[27] Lord Denning restated the external focus of contract law. "A contract is formed when there is, to all *outward appearances*, a contract. A party's intention is to be found *only* in the outward expression which his letters convey."[28] The discarded formalities in this case are the types of manifestations that courts have traditionally looked to in determining contractual intent. For example, the lack of formalities may indicate that a contract had not yet been formed. The evidentiary and channeling functions of formalities have long been recognized. In his seminal work, "Consideration and Form," Lon Fuller argued that the use of legal formalities serve to aid a judge in determining if a contract had been formed.[29] Formalities include the use of the operative words of contract,[30] the expression and communication of intent, the requirements of the statute of frauds, the use of recognized forms of contract, and the formal exchange of consideration. Legal formalities provide objective "evidence of the existence and purport of the contract."[31] The selection of a recognized transactional form, what Jhering called the *legal alphabet*,[32] allows the parties to channel their dealings into a legally binding agreement. Legal history is filled with such forms. Examples include the Roman *stipulatio*,[33] the medieval livery of seisin,[34] and the common law's seal.[35] The litany of acceptable forms has grown to include the mortgage, the lease, the guaranty, the promissory note, the security interest, and the bill of sale to name a few. Such forms offer "a legal framework into which the party may fit his actions. It offers channels for the *legally effective expression of intention*."[36] The traditional importance of such formalities was acknowledged by Lord Lawton in a concurring opinion in *Storer*.[37] He notes, however, that the general inference to be drawn from the lack of a formal exchange can be rebutted. "Other evidence may rebut the inferences which are normally drawn as to the intention of the parties when there are negotiations for a contract of sale carried out between solicitors with the attendant formalities."[38]

It should be clearly stated that a shift from the subjective to the objective is not the same as the replacement of one for the other. Most doctrinal and theoretical shifts in the law of contracts transpire in a matter of degrees over a prolonged period of time. Tendencies may change, underlying factors and norms may be more clearly restated, and old fictions laid to rest, but the overarching framework for decision making varies only slightly. It would be incorrect to state that the objectification of contract has exiled the subjective component to the distant land of noncontract.

The Twin Pillars of Contract: Bargain and Reliance

The objectification of contract seems to fit nicely into the consequentialist slant. Much of the expansion of contractual liability can be attributed to the prevention of unjust consequences through reliance theory. Whether a contractual obligation was intended and whether such an intent may be disproved is of little significance. Liability will be forthcoming if another has reasonably relied.[39] One may argue that intention is immaterial if there has been reasonable reliance. The law of tort provides the rationale for such a premise. A person owes a duty to all those in a position to be influenced by his statements or actions not to negligently induce reliance upon such manifestations. Alternatively, statements or conduct falsely intentioned may be viewed as a sort of misrepresentation that should not go unpunished. This argument was adopted in *M.J. Oldenstedt Plumbing* where the court connected the notion of nonintention with misrepresentation. "Assuming for the sake of argument that the party had no intention of agreeing to the contract, he certainly undertook both words and conduct which amounted to a misrepresentation."[40] Thus, unintentional manifestations to contract yield a notion of culpability that justifies a finding of liability.

In other situations, where there has been no such reliance, liability may still be affixed based upon the sanctity of promise. This is the land of the wholly executory exchange of promises. The morality of keeping one's promises provides a strong metaphysical base upon which to enforce such exchanges. The *Second Restatement* has codified this branch of contract into what is most often referred to as the bargain principle.[41] The common theoretical thread for affixing contractual liability to both the wholly executory promise[42] and the *unreciprocated promise* (reliance) is the construction of the reasonable person. In a bilateral exchange of promises the reasonable person would determine if in fact there had been a manifestation of mutual assent.[43] Often, however, the manifestations produce an *objective ambiguity*. In reality, the objective theory does not generally uncover the true mutual assent of the contracting parties. Instead, it is likely to reflect the intention of one of the parties. "The application of the objective test of contractual intention will generally have the effect of according predominance to the intention of one of the parties on the basis of the evidence of the negotiations leading to the contract's conclusion."[44] This will generally be the intention of the more expressive and successful negotiator. If the objective ambiguity is a product of two equally competent negotiators, then the court would most likely give greater sway to the party's manifestations that more closely resemble community standards.

In the case of an unreciprocated promise, the reasonable person standard is applied to determine if there had been reasonable reliance on the part of the promisee. Agreement or mutual assent, the lifeblood of classical contract theory, is no longer required to affix liability. The will theory's meeting of the minds or the bargain theory's exchange remain solid foundations upon which to rest a decision, however, they no longer serve as meaningful limitations in the face of the remedial charge of reliance recovery. "The trend in contract law is to compensate *any* detriment reasonably incurred by a plaintiff in reliance."[45] A closer look at contracts' foundational shift from bargained-for exchange[46] to reliance-based recovery is warranted.

Reliance Theory

If the reasonable person is viewed as a law-giver, then reliance theory is her creed. Reliance liability in contract has a relatively short lineage. Its pedigree is often traced to the landmark works of Lon Fuller and William Perdue. Some commentators may take issue with the statement that their work signified the birth of twentieth-century contract theory. Few would argue with the statement that their two articles, "Reliance One"[47] and "Reliance Two,"[48] represent a watershed in American contract theory and jurisprudence. The voluminous size of reliance literature[49] and the growing importance of section 90 of the *Second Restatement*[50] attest to its central place in current contract theory. Section 90 characterizes the focus of reliance recovery as the prevention of injustice. The avoidance of injustice requirement is further qualified by "the reasonableness of the promisee's reliance"[51] and the relief to be granted as "measured by the extent of the promisee's actual reliance."[52] This poses some interesting questions. Can the requirement of reasonableness and the injustice avoiding requirement result in different conclusions regarding reliance recovery? Professor Corbin believed that the two requirements were interconnected and would point to the same remedial direction. "If all other requirements of the stated rule are satisfied, does not justice always require enforcement of the promise?"[53] Professor Corbin reached an affirmative conclusion. If the promisee's reliance is reasonable, then enforcement of the promise will always be required to prevent an injustice. Corbin's status as the major proponent for the placement of section 90 within the *Restatement* gives his opinion authoritative weight.[54]

The litmus test of section 90 is something of a hybrid. The perspective in application is clearly that of the promisee. The promisee's perspective is filtered, however, through the prism of the reasonable person. The reasonable person plays two roles in the reliance recovery equation. First, the promisee's reliance has to be reasonable. Second, the reliance "must be of such a kind as a reasonable person in the position of the promisor would have foreseen when making the promise."[55] Objectivity from the perspectives of the promisee and the promisor is accounted for in this analysis of reasonableness. Along with the promisee's reasonable reliance, an element of fault on the part of the promisor is also required. The promisor must have acted intentionally or negligently.[56]

Reasonable Reliance: The Realm of Expanded Liability

The twin pillars of contractual liability are intent and reliance. They are represented in sections 75 and 90 of the *Second Restatement* as the principles of bargained for exchange and promissory estoppel. The latter has been recognized as a residual category to be used by courts as a last resort in the fight against injustice. In their famous work on reliance, Fuller and Perdue saw it as a necessary tool to elevate certain transactions to the level of contract, despite promissorial shortcomings.[57] The rise of reliance in twentieth-century jurisprudence is a further product of the objectification of contract. The subjective notion of mutual assent need not be given lip service in a reliance analysis. The analysis of Fuller and Perdue is firmly planted within the objective theory of contract. Their statement poses a number of issues that are to be answered by the reasonableness of the objective person: What is serious reliance? Is it the reliance that a reasonable person would consider to be legally significant? How is the court to determine the seriousness of the promisor's reliance-producing behavior? The answers to these questions are to be found in the reliance-producing factors that are to be distilled from the circumstances surrounding the relationship in question. The courts are given a variety of tools in this search for liability. The surrounding circumstances[58] are found in the prior dealings and relative sophistication of the parties, the course of the dealing in question, and with the customs and the trade usages of the specific business being conducted.

The realms of promissorial intent and reliance are often intertwined. If a party speaks words of promise, then the reasonableness of the reliance is likely to be increased. Alternatively, reasonable reliance is a strong indication that the promisor possessed legally significant intent to create an enforceable obligation. The use of terms of art may form the basis for the implication of contractual intent and for the determination of reasonable reliance. Most areas of law, be it real property, trusts, or contract, make use of operative phrases "whose meanings and effect have long since been determined."[59] The use of such terms is evidence that a party possessed a state of mind for which contractual liability may be affixed. Another factor a court looks to in determining the existence of the intent-reliance poles of contract is the level of contextual detail existing, whether written or verbal. The greater the expressed detail of an activity or relationship, the stronger the case for finding that the language supports a finding of either promise or reliance. These examinations come within the scope of a subjective-objective framework of analysis.

Reliance theory is modern contract law's response to the pure objective theory as embodied in classical contract's bargain principle. It was a response to the rigidity of the strict rule application found in the bargain principle. Reliance theory acts as an equitable counterpoise to pure contractual objectivity.[60] An analogy can be drawn between this rule-fairness dichotomy and the objective-subjective dialectic. The subjective inquiry can be analogized with the inquiry into the fairness of the exchange analysis. Both require case by case examination involving factors with which courts are uncomfortable. Modern contract's shift from rule to standards application[61] is the seed that has allowed the subjective pole of the dialectic to reassert itself. One basis for this assertion is the argument that reliance theory is fairness-based. Promissory estoppel provides a mechanism whereby a court may mollify the injustice in a particular case by allowing reliance recovery. The threat of expanded liability is due to the unshackling of the courts from the limiting norm of mutuality of promise.

The reliance determination will at times require a subjective inquiry. For example, the reason for the use of a noncontractual transactional or relational vehicle may be crucial in determining reliance. Why did the parties choose the instrument, words, or conduct they used as opposed to other options? A recent court held that the underlying reason or intent "cannot be said to be irrelevant."[62] A bona fide reason for not using a more formal contractual instrument, coupled with actual reliance, would make a pervasive case for promissory estoppel. If the words or conduct of an exchange fail to clearly manifest intent, a court may imply intent by finding reasonable reliance. It is the subjective side of the dialectic which can provide greater insight into these issues.

The Frontier of Contracts: Comfort Instruments

At the frontier of contractual obligation are instruments that are imbued with an internal repugnancy. Such instruments are found in most areas of business and finance. Examples include the attorney opinion letter, letters of intent, accountant certifications, letters of support, letters of responsibility, and letters of assurance. They have no recognizable nomenclature, no generally accepted definitions, and are generally considered to be *ex territorium* to the field of contractual liability. For want of a better term, they will be referred to as comfort instruments.[63] Comfort instruments are generally given to assure another party contemplating a contractual obligation. The assurance is given with the intent of not incurring a legal obligation. If, however, the litmus test of reliance is used, then it is conceivable that these instruments may rise to the level of enforceable obligations.

The potential for contractual liability lies in the internal inconsistency of many of these instruments. The prototypical comfort instrument tries to provide a guaranty-type of assurance without the resultant guaranty-type of liability.[64] The 1923 English case of *Rose & Frank Co. v. Crompton*[65] is one of the earliest instances of a court coming to terms with a comfort instrument's internal repugnancy. The court expressly recognized the doctrinal inconsistencies in the language of the letter. It weighed the assurance language with the disclaimer language, ultimately deciding that the latter was the more dominant. It determined that the operative phrase in the letter was that it was a *contract of honour*,[66] the word contract being a misnomer. "If the parties manifest an intention that only a moral obligation is undertaken, the agreement is not binding."[67] Comfort instruments seem to exist in a doctrinal gray area between inchoate expectation and legally enforceable reliance. From a theoretical and doctrinal basis this line between contract and non-contract has not become fixed. The question of enforceability provides a framework for analyzing the twin pillars of contract—promissorial intent and promisee reliance.

In *Chemco Leasing Spa. v. Rediffusion plc.*, Judge Vaisey sarcastically frames the issue of comfort instrument enforceability. It is a "gentlemen's agreement which is not an agreement, made between two persons neither of whom is a gentlemen, whereby each expects the other to be strictly bound without himself being bound at all."[68] If this is true, then there is little ground for enforcement under either express intent or reliance. On its face the instrument's ambiguous nature would make it difficult to find the requisite intent either subjectively or objectively. The recipient of the comfort instrument would be hard-pressed to prove justifiable reliance.

Internationally, courts have been more likely to enforce such instruments. This is most likely due to the fact that the dialectic has evolved differently within the jurisprudential frameworks of other national legal regimes. The civil law system, for instance, seems to place less weight on the semantic labeling of instruments when determining the existence of a legally enforceable obligation. The objective viewfinder is broader in scope than the one found in the common law system. The lack of dependency on legal literalism, both in the labeling of instruments and in the words of art used within the instruments, allows for greater flexibility in the affixation of contractual liability. For example, in the Federal Republic of Germany "there are no specific provisions in the Civil or Commercial Codes concerning contractual guarantees."[69] This legal informalism provides not only judicial flexibility in the objective interpretation of contracts but also gives the parties a great deal of flexibility in the formation of their contractual enterprise.[70] The parties are at liberty to customize legal hybrids in the structuring of their business relationships.[71] The expansiveness of the objective realm is evident in French jurisprudential thought. French law approaches the issue of contractual intent in a direct, commonsensical way. "The creation in the commercial world of a meaningless instrument is unthinkable."[72] Why would two commercial entities create unenforceable instruments? Anglo-American contract theory would hold that such instruments are unenforceable because they lack clear contractual intent. French jurisprudence renders a contrary presumption that the objective person would presume that such commercial instruments possess an implied intent to be binding *obligations de faire*.

The objectiveness of the German law approach is more than a difference in the degree of formalism or scope. The objective effect of the judicial interpretation plays a major role in the implication of intent. The objectivity of result is intimately connected to the objectivity of intent. One goal of contractual interpretation and construction is to give effect to the purpose of the instrument. This teleological or purpose-oriented approach is less focused on the literal, objective meaning of the language of contract. Rather than restricting themselves to a "literal interpretation of the wording of a contractual term, they tend to consider the purpose of the contract and to interpret it in the way best suited to meet that purpose."[73] The focus of the objective inquiry is shifted away from the specific manifestations or intent of the promisor. Instead, the court looks to the purpose or essence of the contract to project a result in accord with that purpose. This approach has surfaced from time to time in the common law. In *Steller v. Thomas,* the court states that the intention of the parties is "not to be determined exclusively from the mere language of the contract, it must be construed in the light of the *nature,* subject, and purpose of the contract."[74] This forward-looking approach is not without historical precedent. Thomas Aquinas spoke of the *essence* of contract as the vehicle for defining contractual obligation.[75] Purpose and intent can both be seen as tools to be used in the finding of contractual liability.

The common law has long espoused the belief that the proper focus of the judge is to look backward to the genesis of the contract. Contractual intent as it existed at the formation of the contract is the only true guide to defining the contractual obligation. This narrow, backward-looking objectivity was the major justificatory force existing at the time of Williston's *First Restatement.* Judicial decision making anchored in the bedrock of contractual intent has since passed. The Willistonian expectation that the judicial decision maker must affix blinders so as not to see the consequences of enforcing the parties' private law does not reflect the reality of modern contract law. Fairness concerns have become an overriding force in the implication of contractual terms. The immutable rules of good faith, fair dealing, and unconscionability are far removed from the specific contractual intent of the parties.[76]

The Presumption of Intentionality

Earlier discussions noted a divergence between the civil and common law systems regarding the formalism of intent. The latter system requires a more formal stating of intent to create legal obligations as a prerequisite to enforceability. This proposition should not be overstated. In fact, it may be stated that the common law system, through various techniques of construction, often arrives at similar enforceability decisions. A presumption of intentionality can be deciphered from both systems. The presumption is grounded in the belief that parties generally do not intend to create meaningless contractual-type documentation or nonchalantly partake in contractual-type conduct.[77] The civil law approach assumes intention up front while the common law's reverence for mutual assent results in it entering from the back door. Justice Hirst noted the constructional presumption in favor of enforceability. "It is for the party who claims there is no such intention to create legal relations to disprove it, and the onus is a heavy one."[78] Another rule of construction that favors a presumption of intentionality is *contra proferentem*. This rule holds that "in case of ambiguity when all other rules of construction fail, the doubt is removed by construing the document adversely against the writer"[79] This construction results in a finding of an intent that is favorable to the recipient of the writing.

In his study of the evolving doctrine of commercial impracticability, Professor Halpern noted the courts' continued deference to the notion of contractual intent.[80] The notion of presumed intent has been used by courts to reconcile the principle of mutual assent with excuses of performances that were not foreseen by the parties. The presumption is based on the fiction that if the parties are retrospectively made aware of the unforeseen occurrence, then they would have reasonably intended a way of dealing with that occurrence. The illusion of implied objective intent as an indication of actual or subjective intent is thus discarded. Nonetheless, the presumption of intent maintains the illusion that the courts' decisions are still premised on the notion of mutual assent.[81] Objective intent in the second-order form of presumed intent allows the court to *interpret or imply* the requisite excuse into the contract.

The notion of presumed intent in the area of excuse can be seen as an attempt to align the law of excuse with contracts' general theory of objectivity. The presumption of intent has been anchored in objective foreseeability. If such an occurrence is deemed to be unforeseeable by a reasonable person, then an excuse of performance may be justified. The risk or occurrence under consideration must not only have been unforeseen by the actual parties, it must also be reasonably unforeseeable. Professor Halpern argues that the *Uniform Commercial Code* [82] and the *Second Restatement* have adopted a subjective approach to the excuse of impracticability. Instead of focusing upon objective foreseeability, the code and the *Restatement* focus on whether the prospective excuse is directly related to a *basic assumption* of the contract.[83] The focus shifts to a more subjective inquiry into what the parties believed would be the performance-related events or occurrences.[84]

The presumption of intentionality also plays a key role in the construction of instruments that are highly negotiated and ambiguously worded. In the field of comfort instruments the problem is compounded by internal repugnancy. The instrument possesses equally clear language and operative phraseology that support both findings of intentionality and nonintentionality. They often possess disclaimer-type language at the behest of the promisor and language that is contractual in nature in order to appease the promisee. It ultimately falls to the subjective determination of the court to decide who was the successful negotiator. The classically inclined jurist will look to the ambiguity of consent and hold that there is no contract. Modern jurisprudential leanings are toward enforceability. For those who believe it against reason for two reasonably sophisticated parties to pursue negotiations over the wording of a nonlegal instrument, a presumption of intentionality will be an attractive device. This can be seen as an expansion of the American fetish for implying intent and the English doctrine of presumed intent.[85] The key point of interest is the potential utilization of the presumption in the face of language not clearly reflective of mutual assent. The presumption of intentionality is a factor to be weighed by a reasonable promisee. "Under the objective theory of contracts the test is whether a reasonable person in the position of the receiving party would conclude that the sending party had made a commitment."[86] The parameters used in the construction of this reasonable person are likely to be pivotal in the judicial decision-making process.

In the 1875 case of *Phillip v. Gallant,* the court applied the presumption of intentionality to two distinct areas of contract law—formation and breach. The defendant was a French national not fluent in the English language who entered into an agreement to construct a building. The court applied the reasonable person standard in the finding of a contract despite the defendant's lack of understanding of its terms due to language difficulties. "Where one party to a contract conducts himself as to lead a reasonable man to believe that he understands and assents to its terms, and the other party so believing executes it, the former is precluded from asserting that he did not so understand and assent."[87] Elements of both the subjective and objective schools are evident in this statement. First, the reasonable person standard is applied in determining that the defendant manifested an intent to enter into the contract. Second, the court found that the understanding was not only that of the reasonable person but also that of the actual, subjective state of mind of the plaintiff. The phrase "and the other party so believing" indicates that it was important to the court to find that the understanding was not only that of the reasonable person but was the actual understanding of the plaintiff. These two findings lead to a conclusive presumption of intent on the part of the defendant.[88] The presumption of intentionality was also applied to the issue of breach. The issue is whether the defendant intentionally and willfully departed from the terms of the contract. Such a finding would prevent the defendant from claiming the benefit of the equitable doctrine of substantial performance. The court stated that the intentional departure from the terms of the contract is a "question of fact that although it was not in terms found at least it could be *presumed*."[89]

PROMISOR-PROMISEE OBJECTIVITY

The common law has generally framed its objective theory of contract from the perspective of the promisee. Pollock's treatise on contracts defines the test of liability as "what expectation the promisor's words would have created in the mind of a reasonable man in the *promisee's place*."[90] The notion of different views of objectivity was discussed by Professor Gardner. Gardner defined the terms *actual promise, apparent promise, power predicted*, and *power asserted* in his discussion of the anatomy of promise.[91] Embedded in this terminology was the notion of promisor-promisee objectivity. In analyzing the famous case of *Raffles v. Wichelhaus*,[92] he explained that there are "two distinct assertions, the one uttered and the one heard, and legal consequences may be predicated on either or both."[93] Objectivity can thus be viewed as a duality involving the promise understood by the promisor (actual promise or power asserted) and the promise understood by the promisee (apparent promise or power predicted).

The key issue in granting a contractual or quasi-contractual remedy[94] is generally whether the promisee reasonably relied on the conduct or promise of the other party. From the perspective of the relying party, was her interpretation of the import of the other party's contractual actions reasonable? Was her reliance that which an objectively reasonable person would have relied upon? In discussing manifestation of intention, the *Second Restatement* (section 200) acknowledges the importance of the meaning attributed by the maker-promisor to the promise or agreement. It qualifies the subjectivity of this rule of interpretation by noting that "the expectation and understanding of the other party must also be taken into account."[95] Section 2 adopts the objective standard in defining the notion of manifestation of intent. "The phrase *manifestation of intention* adopts an external or objective standard for interpreting conduct; it means the external expression of intention as distinguished from undisclosed intention."[96] The subjective standard of actual intent is rejected in favor of external manifestation or the objective standard. In the final analysis, the *Second Restatement* places a stronger emphasis on promisee interpretation, expectation, and reliance than upon the promisor's subjective intent.[97]

The growth in the popularity of promissory estoppel is a strong indication that American jurisprudence continues to evolve in the direction of promisee objectivity. The entire notion of justifiable or detrimental reliance renders the meaning attributed by the promisor of minor importance. Promissory estoppel as a ground for contractual obligation has been *codified* in section 90 of the *Second Restatement*. It is generally viewed as a vehicle to protect the expectations and reliance of the promisee. The objectivity of the promisee's reliance and not the culpability of the promisor is the benchmark to recovery. There is a competing school of thought that holds that objectivity within the realm of section 90 should be viewed from the promisor's perspective.[98] Professor Williston, a staunch advocate of the promissory basis of contract, viewed section 90 as simply enforcing promises that escaped the reach of the bargain principle as stated in section 75 of the *First Restatement*. The liability and remedial issues still revolved around the expectations of the promisor and not the reliance per se of the promisee. The litmus test of contractual reliability was the foreseeability of the promisee's reliance from the perspective of a reasonable promisor. The viewing of foreseeability from the perspective of the promisor also managed to satisfy Holmesian concerns that the promisor was knowingly assuming the risk of her promise making.[99] The line between foreseeability and intent is indeterminate at best. The proceedings to the *First Restatement* illuminates this school of thought. "We have confined section 90 to the case where a reasonable person would say that the promisor expected the man to do just what he did or that he ought to have expected it."[100] More recently, Professor Fried has championed the promisor perspective as the gauge of section 90 liability. The granting of a remedy for promisee reliance is merely an attempt to fill a gap in the general regime of promissorial liability.[101] Subjectively, what did the promisor expect to happen when executing the promise? Objectively, what would a reasonable promisor expect to result from the making of the promise? This focus on the promisor is at the heart of Fried's thesis of contract as promise.

The focus on promisee objectivity has been closely associated with the tortification of contracts as advocated by death of contract theorists. "*Ex delicto* seems to be well on the way toward swallowing up *ex contractu*."[102] Professor Gilmore explains this as a process of *syncretism* or union of the different theories of obligation—contract, tort, and restitution. He discusses the duality of section 75's bargain principle and section 90's reliance principle as inconsistent. Unlike the dialectic, he argues that "in the end one must swallow the other up."[103] If true, this will alter the use of the dialectic as applied to contracts. When the promisor or the promise itself is the focus of the judicial inquiry, then the dialectic in some form will be the tool used in the determination of relief. However, "if we assimilate contractual obligation to the law of torts, our focus shifts to the injury suffered."[104] For purposes of studying the efficacy and relevancy of the dialectic, an assumption in favor of Professor Fried's work will be made that despite the increasing remedial congruency of contract and torts,[105] promissory obligation remains the fundamental basis of contracts.

The balkanization of objectivity into competing perspectives was concisely analyzed in two articles appearing in the *Law Quarterly Review*.[106] The authors discussed the notions of promisor, promisee, and detached objectivity. William Howarth asserts that the notion of promisor objectivity is an equally plausible paradigm for affixing meaning and liability to prospective contracts. He aligns promisor objectivity with the legacy of the nineteenth-century's subjective theory. Promisor objectivity focuses on the understanding of the promisor as to how the promise *would be* received by the promisee. How the promise was actually received or the actual intent of the promisor is irrelevant. It is unclear how one can realistically distinguish the promisor's intent and "the promisor's subjective apprehension of the sense in which his promise would be received by the promisee."[107] Promisor objectivity is more understandable if Howarth's premise is modified to replace *would be* with *was*. *Would be* seems akin to intent. How the promise was received by the promisee from the perspective of the promisor is easier to objectify. A reasonable person can be transplanted into the place of the promisor to determine the perceived impact or effect of the promise. This shifts promisor objectivity away from subjective intent and further into the realm of objectivity. Promisor objectivity as an alternative paradigm calls into question modern contract's focus on the reasonableness of the promisee's reliance as the test for contractual liability. Howarth concludes that either perspective is a viable approach within the theory of objectivity. Both focus on the parties to the agreement and are more likely to result in an interpretation in alignment with the notion of mutual assent.[108]

The traditional rationale for the promisee perspective of the objective theory is that the aims of contract enforcement and remedies are to protect expectations reasonably caused by a promise. J.P. Vorster argues that such a rationale is fundamentally flawed. First, in the paradigmatic bilateral exchange the distinction between promisor and promisee becomes blurred. Each party is both promisor and promisee. The exchange of promises should thus be viewed in their entirety from the perspective of both parties acting as promisors and promisees. Second, the underlying *negligence* rationale for the promisee perspective of objectivity is also conceptually flawed. The rationale argues that the promisor should be held responsible for not ensuring that his assertions are presented and understood in the way that they were intended. Vorster argues that it is equally reasonable to place a similar onus on the promisee. Just as the promisor has a duty not to mislead, the promisee has a duty to communicate his expectations and his understanding of the promisor's promise.[109] The use of evidence to verify either perspective is persuasive. A contract is the "product of a joint creative effort."[110] It is the result of the give-and-take process of hard bargaining. As such, neither the promisor's nor promisee's perspective alone can adequately define the conclusion of that process.[111]

The adoption of promisor objectivity can be seen as a resurrection of the subjective theory of contract. Vorster cites Lord Blackburn in the 1871 case of *Smith v. Hughes* [112] for the premise that any analysis of the reasonable beliefs of the promisee focuses on her understanding of the subjective mind-set of the promisor. "A reasonable understanding or expectation of the promisee presupposes a subjective expectation on the part of the promisor."[113] This logic seems somewhat strained given the fact that the objective theory holds that the subjective expectation of the promisor is to be discarded in the face of conflicting promisee objectivity.

Vorster's analysis that there are in fact four perspectives based on the different views of objectivity offers more promise. He premises his four-step model on the rationale used by Lord Diplock in *Hannah Blumenthal*.[114] Lord Diplock declares that contractual liability should be affixed when the "intention of each of the parties as it has been *communicated* to and *understood* by the other should coincide."[115] Vorster's four perspectives combine both the subjective understanding of both parties and the objectivity of the reasonable person in the position of both the promisee and the promisor. The first step of his model finds a contract if both parties had the same subjective understanding of intent and subject matter. The fact that a reasonable person would find otherwise is irrelevant. The reasonable person standard is only applied when the subjective understandings of the parties are in conflict. Subjective conflict would lead a court to the final three steps in the paradigm. If both the promisor and promisee perspectives are reasonable, then there is no contract. Alternatively, if both perspectives are unreasonable, there is still no contract. Cases involving mutual mistake would be handled by the application of these two steps. Finally, if the reasonable person is in agreement with only one of the party's perspectives, then that party's subjective understanding would prevail. This model incorporates the different party-focused theories of contractual intent. The next section complicates the viability of this model by looking at the notion of contract as community-based and not party- or intent-based. This school of contract recognizes that contract interpretation is often a vehicle for court-imposed notions of fairness. Contract as the sole creation of intent is discarded as a judicial fiction.

COMMUNAL OBJECTIVITY AND DETACHED OBJECTIVITY

The basis of the objective theory is somewhat schizophrenic due to the existence of party-based and community-based perspectives. Traditionally, the objective theory has been party-based. It was positioned to attempt to determine what the parties reasonably intended to accomplish. Professor Atiyah's notion of the fairness of exchange illustrates that much of modern contract law cannot be reconciled with the paradigm of consensual obligation. The courts have increasingly fabricated reasonable *interpretations* that are not supportable by contractual intent, whether objectively or subjectively framed. "The courts may, in the interests of justice as *they* perceive it, sometimes impose solutions in the teeth of the contracting parties' intent."[116]   Promisor-promisee objectivity revolves around party-focused intent while detached-communal objectivity becomes the code words for judicial interventionism.[117]

Detached and communal objectivity are essentially different shades of the same color. The former focuses the issues of interpretation and enforcement on what an objective observer would have interpreted the parties' manifestations to mean. The observer is a fictional witness to the operative acts[118] of the contract. She is familiar with all available information and has been exposed to the totality of the circumstances[119] surrounding the formation of the contract. It is from this fully informed eyewitness that the intention of the parties and the meanings to be attributed to contractual terms are to be discerned. The notion of communal objectivity acknowledges that this observer may not be unbiased. The observation of the acts of contract is clouded by a communal mind-set preconditioned to view such acts from the vantage point of community and commercial standards of acceptability.

This communal reasonable person's view of reality is likely to be distorted by certain externalities. These externalities are the standards of fairness, justice, and reasonableness that the reasonable person brings with him to the role of observer. The result is an interpretation which may not be so much rooted in the discovery of intent but in the search for a fair and reasonable interpretation. Communal objectivity can be seen at work in the 1834 case of *Britton v. Turner*.[120] The case involved a contract for labor for a period of one year. The contract clearly expressed that payment was due upon the completion of one year of work and labor. After nine months of labor, the worker left the employer's service without consent. The issue is whether the employer owes pro rata compensation for the time served. Under the detached objectivity approach the answer would be negative. The contract clearly expressed that compensation would be due only upon the completion of the one-year period of service. The court, however, elected to apply communal objectivity and rendered a decision in favor of the breaching laborer. "We have abundant reason to believe, that the *general understanding of the community* is, that the hired laborer shall be entitled to compensation for the service actually performed and such contracts must be presumed to be made with reference to that understanding."[121] Communal default rules or custom are used to overcome an injustice that a purely detached objectivity would have dictated.

The importance of these two versions of third-person objectivity is that they can result in different interpretations of the contracting parties' external manifestations.

Lord Denning described these alternative fictitious personages as the reasonable person and the officious bystander.[122] In the area of implied terms the two personages represent the difference between a term implied in fact and one that is implied in law. Denning advocates objectivity as implied in law and not as implied from the supposed intent of the parties. His advocacy of the reasonable person form of objectivity over detached objectivity is extended beyond the gap-filling realm of implied terms. The reasonable person is not to be construed as a residual interpretative tool. Instead, Denning perceives the role of the reasonable person as much more proactive. The reasonable person is to be used as an interpretative device to filter even relatively clear and express contractual language. He rationalizes such an expansive use of the reasonable person as a response to the parties' failure to clearly define their intent and the terms in their contract. Parties are "apt to use words which, taken literally, are wider than they intend."[123] The shortcomings of language as an instrument to communicate unambiguous obligations necessarily result in the need for some interpretive analysis. Denning poses this question: Are the words of the contract "to become tyrannical masters" or should they be qualified in order to bring them within the "true scope of the contract?"[124] The divergence between the spirit of the contract as approved by the reasonable person and the words of the contract as the creation of the actual intent of the parties is to be resolved in favor of the former.[125] An alternative formulation of Denning's premise is that the failure to manifest a clear meaning results in an abdication from the contracting parties to judicial interpretation and the reasonable person. The role of interpreting contractual language or of supplying a missing term is shifted from the actual parties to the reasonable person. And the reasonable person "is no more than the anthropomorphic conception of justice, *is and must be the court itself.*"[126]

Llewellyn's Duality: Specific Assent and Blanket Assent

Karl Llewellyn recognized the courts' use of the reasonable person to "*construe* language into not meaning what the language is patently trying to say"[127] or what the parties intended. Llewellyn analyzed the use of creative misconstruction[128] in the context of a boilerplate-dickered-terms dichotomy. The advent of standard form contracts presented courts with a dilemma regarding the notion of mutual assent. How can the pretense of mutual assent be maintained when a standard form is supplied by one of the contracting parties, often given with a take-it-or-leave-it edict, and with fine print or boilerplate passing unread by the assenting recipient? Llewellyn's solution to this dilemma was to bifurcate the contract into two contracts, the *dickered* deal and the *supplementary* boilerplate deal.[129] This bifurcation of contract is accompanied by a similar bifurcation of the mutual assent requirement into specific assent to the dickered terms and a blanket assent to the remainder. The blanket assent is restricted to reasonable boilerplate terms. Blanket assent is defined as assent "to any *not unreasonable* or indecent terms the seller may have on his form, which do not alter or eviscerate the *reasonable meaning* of the dickered terms."[130]

The *Second Restatement* pays homage to Llewellyn's creation in a comment to its section 211 dealing with standardized agreements. It states that a party signing another's standard form agreement "assents to a few terms, typically asserted in blanks on the printed form, and gives *blanket assent* to the *type of transaction* embodied in the standard form."[131] The notion of blanket assent to a specific type of contract as a touchstone for the implication of intent has been resurveyed by Professor Fried. It is the task of the court to "construct a kind of nonconsensual penumbra around the consensual core."[132] A contract, much like a constitution, allows the courts freedom to imply any term or meaning necessary and proper in carrying out its intent and spirit. The spirit of the contract stems from the fact that the voluntary engagement of the convention of contract commits the parties to a *common enterprise*.[133] It is the consensual core and the notion of common enterprise that provide the justification for the courts' role in salvaging a contract. The specific solution provided by the court may be seen as a reflection of the parties' intent to share the risks and benefits of their common contractual enterprise. The parties remain free to preempt the court's intervention by better controlling "the meaning and extent of their relation"[134] through the vehicle of specific assent.

The courts must determine if the term at issue is material and whether it is within the consensual core or *circle of assent*.[135] If a term is not within the consensual core of an agreement it will be more susceptible to an attack on the ground of unconscionability. The central factor within unconscionability is not unequal bargaining position but lack of real assent. The *Uniform Commercial Code* states that the "principle is one of the prevention of oppression and unfair surprise and not of disturbance of allocation of risks because of superior bargaining power."[136] Two types of assent are needed to remove a term within a form contract from the sweep of the doctrine of unconscionability.[137] First, if the party raising unconscionability had a viable alternative to entering the contract, then her assent was not overpowered by oppression. Her assent can be determined to be real and not the product of duress, undue influence, or oppression. Second, she must have been conscious of the existence of the term in question at the time of the contract formation. If the term had been disclosed, then there was apparent consent. Mere disclosure, however, may not be sufficient to overcome a lack of apparent assent. The disclosure has to be of the type that would inform the reasonable consumer possessing the characteristics of this particular purchaser. The question is "whether the consumer, as a reasonable person, should have been aware of the material risk allocated to him"[138] Only when there is a choice (real assent) and disclosure (apparent assent) can there be a finding of meaningful mutual assent. One may look to the ancient plea of *non est factum* for an ancestral analogy. This plea—"I did not make this contract"—was generally used by the blind or illiterate who had been duped into signing a document. So in the "battle of the forms" the adverse party can be said to be blind to any unreasonable, boilerplate terms in the form contract. The operative question becomes whether the document was "in fact substantially, seriously or fundamentally different in its purport from what the signer believed to be the case?"[139]

This bifurcation of assent presents a problem of rationalization. A traditional adage of American contract theory is that it is not for the court to make a contract for the parties. This notion is often framed within the rubric of certainty of contract.[140] The lack of specific consent to the boilerplate of standardized contracts[141] calls into question the courts' ability to preserve contract as a reflection of intent while at the same time remaining faithful to the adage. Llewellyn makes an attempt at rephrasing the assent problem and venturing a solution in one brief statement. "A court's business is not the making of detailed contracts for parties; but a court's business is eminently the marking out of the limits of the permissible."[142] This solution sees the courts' role as one of paring down the contract mainly through the elimination of unnecessary and unreasonable terms.[143]

Blanket assent is used to conform the standardized contract to the dictates of the classical theory's contractual intent requirement. The certainty of terms problem is resolved within the courts' role as arbiters of the limits of the permissible. The *limits of the permissible* provide for a two-step process. The first step is the conforming of the nondickered terms to the specific assent as expressed in the dickered terms. Second is the conforming of the nondickered terms to what is considered to be fair to a reasonable person. The first requirement is the interpretation of the nondickered terms in light of the specific assent of the parties. The boilerplate should "not alter or impair the fair meaning of the dickered terms."[144] This requirement is based upon the assumption that the blanket assent was given only to terms that were in accord with the fair meaning of the dickered terms. The second requirement is based on the further assumption that the blanket assent was made with an implied understanding that the boilerplate did not contain unfair or unreasonable terms. The terms must not offend the reasonable person standard.[145]

Llewellyn's two-pronged analysis is illustrative of the influence that the subjective-objective dialectic has had on contracts. The specific assent element reflects the actual subjective meeting of the minds. The blanket assent element reflects the objective approach of reading reasonable terms into an agreement under the banner of preservation of contract. The analysis also serves to illustrate that the dialectic is not an either-or proposition. In Llewellyn's blueprint the objective construct is used to preserve the subjective component. Both the subjective and objective approaches to contract serve essential roles. An initial assessment would indicate that instead of being characterized by exclusivity, the subjective-objective elements of contract are intricately intertwined.

Llewellyn's duality can be seen at work in the general approach to liability outlined in article 2 of the *Uniform Commercial Code*. Professor Speidel describes the code's *intention test of liability* as a departure from the bargain paradigm found in classical contract theory. The classical theory rested liability on an affirmative answer to the question of whether there was an agreement as to every material term. The approach of the code centers around the notion that something less than *full* agreement is necessary in affixing contractual liability. The operative question then becomes: "[H]ow much agreement in a bargain is required before a contract will be created?"[146] The focus of the code is on the determination, uncertainty of terms aside, of whether there was a general intent to create a contractual relationship.[147] A sort of Llewellynian blanket assent is preferred to the specific intent of the bargain approach. This approach became operational with the adoption of the gap-filling provisions in the code. The general intent of the parties to create legal relations is used as a springboard to the imposition of reasonableness into private contract. The fabrication of contractual terms through the medium of custom, trade usage, and reasonableness enables the courts to find contracts where none would have been found under pre-code common law. The bedrock of materiality has become nothing but quicksand. Material terms under the classical theory have become immaterial.

The importance of contractual intent has in essence become all important. The need to find assent to all material terms has dissolved into the need to find simple intent to create or enter into an agreement. "The parties' intention, whether clearly expressed or inferred from the commercial context, may create a contract even though there is no express agreement on material terms."[148] The jural foundations for premising contract on general and not specific intent preceded the adoption of the code and its gap-filling provisions. In a 1946 case involving a distribution agreement the court looked to general intent to create a contract to overcome the lack of specific assent to the quantity term. "The lack of specific obligation by one of the parties to a contract will not invalidate it where the whole contract may be instinct with obligation even though imperfectly expressed."[149] It is this imposition of reasonableness that has led judicial scholars to argue the illusory nature of contractual intent. "The tests aimed at discovering the parties' intentions almost invariably lead the courts to *impose* their view of a solution to the dispute."[150] The so-called "intent to create legal relations" test has been exposed as a subpart of the illusion of contractual intent.

Some scholars have argued that nonlegal motivations and sanctions play a greater role in commercial transactions than does the intent to create legally binding commitments. "Many business executives are indifferent whether their agreements constitute binding contracts; business dealings are regulated more by mutual trust and shared conventions."[151] Beale and Dugdale found three types of contractual or quasi-contractual relations or exchanges ranging from highly negotiated customized contracts to highly informalized oral commitments. With regard to the former they concluded that "contracts formed as a result of detailed negotiation were comparatively rare."[152] In between these two poles they found the "majority of firms intended to make their contracts by the use of forms containing standard conditions."[153]

An alternative argument recognizes the importance of trust and shared conventions but argues that sophisticated businesspersons are fully aware of the default rules of contract and their supportive cadre of legal sanctions.[154] There is, however, an acknowledgment that contracts informally entered into are generally formed within a milieu of trust and convention. Within this milieu, specific contractual intent is nonexistent. Instead, such contracts are grounded on the *unexpressed assumptions* of the parties.[155] These assumptions include custom, trade usage, and commercial practice. The reasonable person standard's totality of the circumstances analysis also utilizes these assumptions to meet the evidentiary threshold of contractual intent.[156]

The initial growth of standard form contracts can be seen as the major force in rendering the subjective theory obsolete. The idea of a subjective meeting of the minds over nondickered boilerplate became implausible to defend. "In an increasingly national corporate economy, the goal of standardization of commercial transactions began to overwhelm the desire to conceive of contract law as expressing the subjective desires of individuals.[157] The quest for uniformity and standardization in transactions necessitated a different approach. The legal inquiry shifted from a focus on actual intent toward a concern with reasonable and customary practices.[158] The predictability of reasonableness transplanted the uncertainty of idiosyncratic individual will. The need to legally process large volumes of similar commercial and consumer transactions dictated a legal construct that could be administered quickly and consistently: the objective theory's reasonable person. The objective theory no longer could be considered a device for providing insight into the subjective will.[159]

The Implication of Consent: Barnett's Second-Order Problem of Knowledge

The courts' intervention into contracts through the art of interpretation and construction can take a number of forms. One is the recognition of the default or gap-filling rules (voluntary, permissive rules of contract) that apply to the type of contract or common enterprise at issue. The other is the imposition of the immutable or rules of contract.[160] Immutable rules (mandatory rules of contract) include the duty of good faith and fair dealing, the requirements of the statute of frauds, and the rules of capacity. The former are based on consent, the latter are imposed by the legal system. The existence of widely accepted default rules allows the court to imply consent. The rationale is that the parties can be presumed to have knowledge of the default rules. This presumption of knowledge leads to a presumption of intent. By not contracting out of the default rules the parties are presumed to have intended that the default rules would apply. The terms that the default rules provide "are indirectly consented to by parties who could have contracted around them."[161]

Professor Barnett speaks of an overall consent to enter into a contractual relationship as the basis for a secondary intent to be bound by existing default rules.[162] The framework of Barnett's consent theory illustrates an important point of the dialectic. The dialectic is not generally a conflict between the objective and the subjective. Recognition and knowledge of customary default rules leads to a convergence of actual consent and implied consent. Oftentimes the objective and subjective meanings will share much more common ground than divergence. The greater the knowledge of default rules among contracting parties, the greater the convergence of the subjective and objective meanings of their contracts. Alternatively stated, the greater the recognition of default rules "existing in the relevant community of discourse, then the more likely they are to reflect the *tacit subjective agreement* of the parties."[163]

The problem with knowledge is that it is personal and inaccessible. Knowledge is within the family of subjectivity and thus possesses all of the attendant problems of accessibility. This is the second-order problem of knowledge. "Lacking any direct access to intentions, recipients of contractual exchanges can never be entirely sure ex ante that subjective assent is present."[164] Overcoming the problems of knowledge and communication requires "a better understanding of the functional relationship between subjective and objective consent in contract."[165] Widely accepted manifestations of intent help break down the barriers to actual assent. There is convergence of objective and subjective consent with the use of widely known default rules.[166] The greater the use of commonly and generally understood language, the more likely that manifested intent will approximate the actual intent of the parties. "The concept of consent that is at the root of contract theory is *communicated* consent, though one reason for the centrality of communicated consent is its close empirical correspondence with *subjective* consent."[167] This correspondence is likely to become closer with the use of widely accepted manifestations of intent and clear communication by the parties of their reciprocal knowledge of these customary manifestations. The greater this correspondence, the lesser the second-order problem of knowledge.

The communication of personal knowledge of noncustomary manifestations of intent and of meanings raises an interesting issue within the dialectic—what meaning controls? Does the common meaning of the parties control or the meaning provided by the objective theory of contracts? Under a pure application of the objective theory, the manifestations of the parties as interpreted by the reasonable person would control. The actual, subjective meanings of those manifestations affixed by the parties would be irrelevant. Professor Farnsworth indicates that the greater weight of authority has been to apply the subjective meaning of the parties and not the objective meaning.[168] The 1948 case of *Campbell v. Rockerfeller* echoes this sentiment. "We find nothing in the law which forbids the court to give effect to the actual understanding of the parties."[169] Giving effect to the actual understanding of the parties seems to be the more rational and just approach. It is important because it shows that we do not live under an unfettered objective regime.

Other subjective-objective scenarios can be formulated. The first is a variant of the above scenario. What is the role of the courts when the actual understanding of the parties is not only in variance with the objective interpretation but also brings about an unreasonable result? Should the courts remain faithful to the subjective understanding? The answers, although somewhat discomforting, would seem to be clear. Absent evidence of overreaching or fraud, the contract should be, in the words of Justice Cardozo, "read as business men would read them." If the choice is to read them as the particular parties intended them to be read, then unreasonableness should not be a ground for a reformation of intent.

A second variant is when there is a subjective misunderstanding as to the meaning of the contract along with the ability to objectively interpret the contractual terms in various ways. Should the court attempt to salvage the contract or leave the parties where they are due to uncertainty of contract? This issue was addressed by the court in *Outlet Embroidery v. Derwent Mills*.[170] The case involved a contract for the sale of goods. It contained a provision that prices were subject to change pending tariff revision. It is important to note that this 1930 case far precedes the adoption of the *Uniform Commercial Code* and its gap-filling provisions. A finding of uncertainty as to a material term was generally fatal to a finding of a contract. The argument of the defendant was that the contract was illusory because it was not one in which the price could be made certain. The plaintiff argued that such certainty could be provided by a court's review of the surrounding circumstances. Justice Cardozo sided with the plaintiff by proclaiming that "in the transactions of business life, sanity of end and aim is at least a presumption."[171] In holding that the subject-to-change language was not fatal to a finding of contract, he distinguishes between literal objectivity and reasonable objectivity. Cardozo acknowledges that both of the parties' interpretations were plausible. The plausibility of both parties' interpretations did not void the contract on grounds of misunderstanding and uncertainty.[172] The court concluded that it may still salvage the contract by applying the substantive over the literal; the contract-preserving interpretation over the contract-abrogating interpretation. "If literalness is sheer absurdity, we are to seek some other meaning whereby reason will be instilled and absurdity avoided."[173] A determination that there was a general intent to contract made the defendant's argument of noncontract such an absurdity. The reasonable, contract-preserving interpretation won out over the literal, objective interpretation and the intersubjective misunderstanding.

Earlier we saw that the fabrication of the reasonable person is an exercise in knowledge acquisition. It is the imbuing of the reasonable person with the knowledge of what the parties knew and what they should have known. Professor Slawson ventures this definition of the objective theory of contracts. "The objective theory of contracts dictates that a contract shall have the meaning that a reasonable person would give it under the circumstances under which it was made, if he knew everything he should plus everything the parties actually knew."[174] One can argue that the *should know* is the domain of the objective theory. The *actually knew* recognizes the importance of the subjective element in the law of contracts. This duality acknowledges that if contract is to be a law of meaning, then the role of the subjective must play a vital role.[175] We now turn to the subjective approach to contracts.

THE SUBJECTIVE THEORY OF CONTRACTS

Professor Williston noted that the subjective approach to contract was a viable alternative. "The subjective theory seems to have developed and to have had considerable acceptance on the Continent of Europe."[176] Nonetheless, Williston believed that the objective theory best suited the common law.[177] For him an intent to create a legal relationship was not imperative for finding contractual liability. The only intent that was required was the intent to make the acts that constitute the manifestation of assent. Professor Corbin was a good deal more sympathetic to the importance of actual or subjective intent as a requirement for contract formation. He acknowledged, however, the evidentiary difficulties endemic in such an approach. "The actual intent of the one party and the actual understanding of the other party are matters of fact that may be difficult to prove and thus, the meanings that would be given by other reasonable means may be decisive."[178] The twentieth-century's distinguishing feature was the full embrace of the objective theory.

The acknowledgment of the objective theory's triumph does not necessarily exile the subjectivists to the historical dustbin of contract lore. Despite the courts' universal embrace of the objective theory, they have been unable to discard the paradigmatic purity of the notion of contract as a meeting of the minds. A 1983 case illustrates the courts' continued infatuation with both schools of thought. "One is bound, not only by what he *subjectively* intends, but by what he leads others *reasonably* to think that he intends."[179] The notion of subjective intention continues to find at least an interstitial place in contract jurisprudence. The subjective theory is of historical significance and is important to the present and the future of contract. In the present the subjective theory plays dual roles. First, there are areas of contract in which it has not fully released its grasp.[180] Examples include mutual mistake, economic duress, and satisfaction clauses. Second, the subjective slant of contracts provides the backdrop needed to fully understand and appreciate the role of the objective approach. The future of the subjective theory of contract may not be as bleak as one would think. Contract is replete with numerous examples of Lazarus arising from the dead.[181] Contract theory is more cyclical than linear in its progression.[182]

Despite the displacement of the subjectively based will theory,[183] its spirit still plays a role in modern contract law. The terminology of the subjective theory continues to pervade our jurisprudence. Although manifestation of intent is formally adopted in the *Second Restatement*,[184] the importance of actual assent is acknowledged.[185] This leads to a number of potential scenarios that highlight the importance of the subjective-objective dialectic. The first scenario is one in which there is a dispute regarding material differences of meaning attributed to the contract by the two parties. In this scenario one finds a conflict between what one or possibly both of the parties actually intended and the agreement found by the manifestation of their intentions. The issue then becomes one of interpretation for the court. A determination as to the reasonable certainty of the terms must be satisfied. The court is authorized to apply the rules of interpretation[186] in ferreting out a contract from the manifestations of assent. In short, the parties have attached different meanings to the agreement. The court will then determine the *true* meaning by applying widely accepted aids of interpretation. The court will interpret the contractual manifestations in light of all the circumstances[187] with reference to generally prevailing meaning[188] and to technical meaning,[189] along with "any relevant course of performance, course of dealing, or usage of trade."[190] The result will be either an agreement intended by one of the parties or an agreement created by the aids of interpretation that neither party had intended.

A second scenario is more illustrative of the importance of the subjective-objective dialectic. It is one where there is convincing evidence that one of the parties subjectively intended something that is different from what was manifested under the rules of interpretation. This is not the case of one revealing a previously undisclosed intent not to be bound. It is the case of a party or parties intending something in good faith that is construed differently when an objective standard is applied. The answer provided by the objective theory of contract is clear. The person is bound by a contract based on his manifestations. The person's actual intent is irrelevant. A person who can offer proof of actual intent is no better off than a person who may only assert such actual intent. In practice, are courts willing to shun such evidence of actual intent? Or will courts view a defendant's good faith actual intent in a different way than they will view a defendant who asserts actual intent as a rue to avoid the obligations of her bargain?

In *Upton-On-Severn Rural District Council v. Powell*,[191] an English court applied an objective interpretation to counteract the subjective state of mind of *both* parties. The defendant's farm was the scene of a fire. He telephoned the Upton fire brigade believing that his farm was in the Upton Fire District. In fact, the farm was in the Pershore Fire District. The plaintiff's fire district also believed that the farm was in its jurisdiction. "The fire brigade went intending to render a gratuitous service. It was only when it discovered that the fire was in another area that it decided that a charge should be made."[192] At issue is whether Upton can collect in contract for services rendered when both parties initially assumed that the services were to be gratuitous.[193] The court held that despite the subjective belief of the parties, a contractual relationship was created.[194] One may argue that the *Upton-On-Severn* case was one of mutual mistake. But it was not expressly decided as such. Instead the court ignored the import of the mistake. It simply filtered the manifestations of the defendant, the calling of the fire brigade for services, through a process of objectivity.

Mistake generally works in the recognition of the subjective over the objective intent. When a strict application of the process of objectivity to a party's manifestations results in undue hardship, a court will look to the subjective intent of the party in attempt to avoid such hardship. The objective approach is discarded in the interests of justice and fairness. This occurred in the 1939 English case of *Hartog v. Colin & Shields*.[195] The promisor expressly offered in writing to sell goods at a price per pound. Despite the clarity of the language the court held that the promisor had intended to quote on a price-per-piece basis.[196] "The promisee could not reasonably have supposed that the offer expressed the *real intention* of the person making it."[197] The subjective implied mind-sets of both the promisor and the promisee are given contractual life. The objective manifestations of the agreement are discounted by recognition of the promisor's real intent and what the promisee "must have known."[198]

Comment *b.* of section 200 of the *Second Restatement* seems to suggest that at times actual intent may indeed play a role in a court's thinking in the face of manifestations of intent that dictate otherwise. "A party is not bound by a meaning unless he has reason to know of it, but the expectation and understanding of the other party must also be taken into account."[199] An example of where the subjective understanding of the parties becomes decisive involves the case of frolic. Assume A agrees to buy and B agrees to sell an old baseball glove for $500. The glove has a value of approximately ten dollars. They both understand the transaction as a joke. To a neutral observer, the infamous reasonable person, the clear manifestations of intent would lead her to conclude that the parties had entered into a contract. Section 21 of the *Second Restatement* concludes otherwise.[200]

The case of *Blackpool & Fylde Aero Club v. Blackpool Borough Council* provides another example. The Blackpool Borough Council advertised for offers to operate airplanes at the municipal airport. It provided a deadline in which the tenders were to be submitted in order to be considered. The plaintiff submitted just prior to the expiration of the deadline but was not given any consideration. This scenario is most akin to the area of precontractual negotiations and of nonbinding invitations to offer. Nonetheless, the court held that the council actually intended to create a limited contractual relation. The implied contract was not for the use of the airport but to give due consideration to any offer submitted prior to the deadline. The council was not under any obligation to grant rights to the plaintiff but was required to at least consider its tender. The objective theory would likely hold that such an advertisement coupled with complete discretion to refuse any and all tenders does not manifest intent to enter into a contractual obligation. The council's duty was one of simple courtesy. The court recognizes the general rule of not finding contractual obligations during the period of *precontract*. It then proceeds to carve out an exception based on actual, subjective intent. "The circumstances in this case indicate that this is one of the fairly rare exceptions to the general rule." This exception is premised on the finding that there was an intention to create a binding legal obligation.[201]

The use of contractual formalities has long been seen as an instrument upon which intent can be implied. In the sale of real estate a binding contract is generally recognized only when both parties sign and exchange the contractual instrument. In *Storer v. Manchester City Council*, the court held that the lack of such formality may not preclude a finding of actual intent. It accepted evidence to "rebut the inferences which are normally to be drawn as to the intention of the parties when there are negotiations for a contract of sale."[202] The court found that the seller actually intended to be bound despite not signing and returning the contract to the purchaser.[203] A clear objective rule requiring an exchange of a signed contract was jettisoned in the face of evidence of actual intent to be bound.

The strength of the subjective theory as a rationale for the enforcement or the nonenforcement of contracts remains. The triumph of the objective theory is more pronounced in theory than in practice. "While courts tend to speak in terms of the objective theory, there is substantial doubt whether it is applied as often as it is articulated."[204] If a court is not applying the objective theory, then what is the theoretical construct upon which its decision is based? At least three constructs can be offered. First, the court is viewing the expression of intent as truly reflecting the actual, subjective intent of the parties. Second, the court is applying an objective-subjective blend or synthesis. Third, the judge's frame of mind or subjective predisposition is the predominant factor in the implication of intent and of the terms of the contract. These constructs will be examined more fully in subsequent chapters.

THE MODIFIED SUBJECTIVE OR INTERSUBJECTIVE APPROACH

Contract law's adoption of the objective approach has not been without qualification. The ghost of nineteenth-century subjectivism can still be seen roaming the hallowed corridors of the citadel of contracts. Specific areas of contract involving performance contain a purely subjectivist foundation.[205] The area of contract satisfaction is one such example.[206] A modified subjective approach has also been recognized as a dimension within the subjective-objective dialectic. The litmus test is neither the objective approach's reasonable person nor the actual subjective understanding of the parties. Instead, the measuring stick is a communal intersubjective[207] meaning attributed to one of the parties to the transaction. One commentator states this approach in a succinct manner. "The key to the modified subjective approach is not what a person subjectively means, nor what he objectively means. Rather, it rests on inter-subjective understandings and thereby militates against one party exploiting another's known understanding."[208] Thus, at times, a court may attribute a meaning to a contractual term or gesture based on neither the intended meaning of the acting party nor the meaning of the third party objective person, but instead based on the meaning attributed by the receiving party as to her understanding of the acting party's belief.[209] In his 1931 article "What Price Contract?" Karl Llewellyn recognizes an objective-subjective theory of contracts as "the objective expressions of a promisor setting the measure of his obligation, limited further, however, by the subjective understandings of the promisee."[210] This is an example of a hybrid involving both objectivity and subjectivity. Intersubjectivity is a variant of a different color. It is a blend of the subjective beliefs of both the promisor and the promisee.

Some guidance for the notion of intersubjectivity can be taken from twentieth-century philosopher Jürgen Habermas. In his *Theory of Communicative Action* he speaks about a process of social integration by which meaning is given to communicative actions. "Communication is tied to the structure of inter-subjectivity of the lifeworld."[211] The *lifeworld* is the social background or societal default rules by which all communicative acts are given meaning. Often our understandings come from this world of intuition. "Lifeworld designates the horizon of unthematized, intuitive, and assumed assumptions, definitions, and modes of orientation."[212] It is through social integration and socialization that we become fully integrated humans with a shared, social horizon.[213] The lifeworld is acquired throughout our growth and development as human beings living together in a society. We learn the meaning of things *as a matter of course*. This matter of course is generally measured by way of its conformity to its use in a given community.[214] It is from this background or lifeworld that intersubjective meaning is constructed. Intersubjectivity can be seen as a recasting of the dialectic into a different form. It is cast from the entire subjective-objective spectrum. Like the lifeworld, it contains "a cognitively interpreted external reality, a normatively interpreted social one, and an individually interpreted subjective sphere."[215]

It is important to note that this intersubjective meaning may differ from the actual meaning given by the receiving party as to her understanding of a term or gesture. Borrowing from sociologist Robert Young, intersubjectivity is both an obstacle and a bridge in human interaction. "Whereas we may lack direct access to the intentions and meanings of others and we each have our own unique subjective view of the world, we nevertheless share certain subjective definitions of reality that make meaningful interaction possible."[216] An example can be gleaned from the 1871 English case of *Smith v. Hughes*,[217] which has been viewed traditionally as a unilateral mistake case involving the sale of oats.[218] The offeror *subjectively* intended to sell green oats. The purchaser *subjectively* intended to purchase old oats. The offeror realized the purchaser-offeree had mistaken the terms of the offer. Assuming that a reasonable person would have interpreted the offer as one for green oats, should the purchaser be forced to accept the consequences of his mistake? The court held otherwise despite the fact that the mistake was unilateral in nature. Adams and Brownsword explain that the key to the decision was that "the modified subjective factor came into play."[219]

The pivotal factor in *Smith v. Hughes* was the seller's knowledge of the subjective intent of the purchaser. "The seller will not be allowed to take advantage of the buyer's *known* misunderstanding, and this means either that there is no contract or that there is a contract on the terms intended by the buyer."[220] Under a purely objective theory of contract the excuse of mistake would not exist. The purchaser's subjective intent is clearly at odds with the objective manifestations of the agreement. Nonetheless, courts have allowed for the reformation or rescission of contracts where the subjective term was reasonable and the nonmistaken party knew of the mistake. In *Hartog v. Colin and Shields*[221] the price term was mistakenly quoted as a price per pound instead of the standard price per item. "In line with modified subjectivism it was held that the plaintiffs must have realized that a mistake had been made in the offer, and that the defendants were, therefore, not bound to deliver at the quoted price."[222] Thus, one party's error may result in the other party suffering the consequences.

4

THE REASONABLE PERSON STANDARD

Reason is the faculty of the mind by which it distinguishes truth from falsehood, good from evil, and which enables the possessor to deduce inferences from facts or from propositions.[1]

Who is this all-knowing arbiter of good faith known as the reasonable person? Is she the same reasonable person found in tort, the rational person of economics, or the low-income consumer deserving the protection of the principle of unconscionability?[2] Professor Corbin stated some eighty years ago that in the "law of contract as in the law of tort, men are expected to live up to the standard of the reasonably prudent man."[3] How do courts go about creating this contractual mystic? Saint Thomas Aquinas would argue that the reasonable person exists in each and every one of us. He states that "the law that is in us by nature is nothing else than the *reasoning creature's* sharing in the eternal law."[4] In his work on natural law theory, John Finnis, speaks of practical reasonableness as a basic human value. All human beings should seek "to bring an intelligent and reasonable order into one's own actions and habits and practical attitudes."[5] In essence, each one of us should conform our decisions to the reasonable person that dwells within us. The internal reasonable person should conform its influence to reflect the standard of the objective theory's external reasonable person. Both would suggest that its human personage honor his or her contractual obligations.

Professor Prosser notes that the reasonable person of tort is a hypothetical personification of the community idea of reasonable behavior.[6] To this extent the reasonable person is the creation of external, objective standards. However, the second part of the reasonable person analysis in tort seeks to apply the reasonable person standard in the context of a given fact pattern. How would the reasonable person have responded under the same or similar circumstances?[7] Under this ambit of application the courts have taken into account the physical attributes, the mental capacity, the age, and the educa-

51

tion of the particular individual. This adjustment of the reasonable person has opened the door of objectivity to the full reach of the dialectic.

> The courts have made allowance not only for the external facts, but for many of the characteristics of the actor himself, and have applied . . . a more or less subjective standard. Depending on the context, the reasonable person standard may, in fact, combine in varying measure both objective and subjective ingredients.[8]

In fact the inclusion of individualistic characteristics in the reasonable person analysis inevitably blurs the line between objective community standards and subjective-based standards. "For the judge or jury, a completely individualized objective standard would be virtually indistinguishable from a subjective standard."[9]

Although derived from the same family tree as the reasonable person found in torts, the reasonable person of contract is different in her makeup and disposition. In tort the reasonable person is generally a more universalized personage reflective of general duties of care owed to all human beings. The reasonable person in contract is a more specialized creature possessing all of the idiosyncratic features of the contracting parties, along with the specific information of which they *should* be in possession. The reasonable person of contract is often not a reflection of how an ordinary, reasonable person would react to a situation. Instead, he is more concerned with what people actually do in the specific marketplace in which the parties find themselves. The courts look to a number of sources in constructing the reasonable person, such as custom, trade usage, the characteristics of the parties, and the totality of the circumstances. The sources are derived from the context in which a contract is formed. They are the background of common meaning that the parties bring to the contracting process. John Dewey investigated the notion of background in his analysis of conscious and unconscious understanding. "Two persons can converse intelligently with each other because a common experience supplies a background of mutual understanding upon which their respective remarks are projected."[10]

The language of contract is defined within the context of its rendering. It is through the sources of context that a contract is interpreted and given meaning. It is in this context that the reasonable person gives meaning to promises. "What turns a manifestation of intention into a promise has everything to do with the context in which the intention is manifested."[11] The context is especially important in providing the background for second-order intent. Second-order intent is used to complete the spaces of an incomplete contract. Contract terms are either implied through the contract or imposed by law. In such situations where manifested intent is unclear as to a contractual issue, the court is forced to extrapolate a secondary intent from the parties' expressed or primary intent or from its belief of what society *intends* to be the appropriate solution. The possible sources for the courts' extrapolation are the promisor's intent, the promisee's intent, and the context of the promise.[12] If an analysis of the context fails to yield a secondary intent, then the courts are likely to apply community or customary standards to imply a term that is reasonable given the circumstances.

There is a spectrum of intentional states ranging from primary as derived from the parties' expressions of agreement to secondary or second-order intent. The secondary intentional states are derived from what was *implicitly agreed* or from what is "consistent with a *composite* of secondary intentions associated with the community or practice."[13] In terms of the reasonable person standard it is the imbuing of the reasonable person with the knowledge of what the parties knew and should have known. "The objective theory of contracts dictates that a contract shall have the meaning that a reasonable person would give it under the circumstances under which it was made, if he knew everything he should plus everything the parties actually knew."[14] We now turn to how courts determine what a party knew and what she should have known.

The Parties

The courts often look to the characteristics of the respective parties in their implication of intent inquiries. The sophistication of the parties, including their personal or institutional understanding of the meanings of transactional devices, provides a window into the issue of contractual intent. In *Lloyd's Bank Canada,* a Canadian court recognized that the words of contract are not an end but a means to determining intent. "It is not only the meaning of the words but the understanding of the parties of the meaning of the words that is relevant."[15] In the art of contractual interpretation, the *meaning* of the words used in a relationship are persuasive but not conclusive as to the intent of the parties. The sophistication, knowledge, and experiences of the parties are vital factors in the affixation of meaning to the words of their discourse. This party-specific investigation is apparent in a court's reference to a party as a prudent investor[16] or as experienced and sophisticated.[17] In *Hoosier Energy Rural Electric,* the court placed a strong emphasis on the sophistication of the parties to preclude a party from introducing evidence that would have controverted the plain meaning of the contract. The fact that the parties were large, specialized corporations represented by sophisticated law firms that drafted "a complex and detailed fifty-seven page contract" weighed heavily in the court's decision.[18]

The importance of the past experiences of the parties is explained in section 201 of the *Second Restatement*. The past experiences of the parties help form the context in which the words of the contract are to be interpreted. "The context of words and other conduct is seldom exactly the same for two different people, since connotations depend on the entire past experience and the attitudes and expectations of the person whose understanding is in question."[19] Each person's past experiences prior to entering the particular contractual relationship help mold their personal understanding of the contract. The combined experiences of both parties to a transaction are also vital in determining the meaning of their words. Misunderstanding can breed understanding if the relationship is ongoing. The experiences and understandings that each party brings to the relationship are likely to be modified over time by that relationship. "Usages over time, and persons engaged in transactions with each other often develop temporary usages peculiar to themselves."[20] Holmesian objectivism would question the utility of this analysis. A purely objective theory would hold the parties to the generally prevailing meaning of their words and not to any peculiar meaning attached to them by the parties. The Comments to section 201 would indicate otherwise: "The primary search is for a common meaning of the parties, not a meaning imposed on them by the law." The subjective understandings of the parties are the primary focus of this inquiry. It is clear, however, that the objective or prevailing meaning remains the residual means for interpretation. If the peculiar meanings of the parties are in conflict or unclear, then the generally prevailing meaning will be adopted by the courts.

The bargaining parties' levels of sophistication and experience are measured by imputed knowledge as well as actual knowledge. Complicated commercial transactions rarely proceed without the benefit of legal counsel. At times legal representation is procured at the infancy of the contractual negotiations. The timing and the content of such advice have an impact on the knowledge and experience element of each party's contractual makeup. The reasonable person inquiry should focus on intraparty communications as well as on interparty communications. The legal advice received by the respective parties has a bearing on the issues of intent and reliance. A determination of intent or reliance, whether objectively or subjectively construed, is one that can best be defined as a state of mind inquiry. The advice of counsel or of other advisors bears directly upon the party's state of mind as to its understanding of the legal significance of the interparty communications. It is then a small step from the determination of a party's state of mind to the resolution of the issue of intent.

Party-specific characteristics are used to construct the reasonable person for purposes of the implication of intent and the interpretation of meaning. The law of satisfaction summons an interesting point. In *Kennedy Associates, Inc. v. Fischer*,[21] the court poses the issue with regard to whether a subjective or objective standard for satisfactory performance should be applied. The court adopted an objective standard by rationalizing that "it is practicable to apply an objective test in gauging its validity as it cannot reasonably be deemed an *idiosyncratic* decision."[22] Should the court apply a subjective standard if a party possesses truly idiosyncratic characteristics? An analogous prosubjective factor found in the law of satisfaction is the notion of *multiplicity of factors*. In *Weisz Trucking Co.*,[23] the court reasoned that the greater the multiplicity of factors that entered the satisfaction decision, the stronger the argument for applying a subjective standard. Thus, the purely commercial enterprise of obtaining satisfactory leases was held to be subjective in nature.[24] The rationale offered was that "the factors involved in determining whether a lease is satisfactory to the lessor are too numerous and varied to permit the application of a reasonable person standard."[25] In this example, subjectivity plays a role in the objective world of commercial transactions.

An alternative reason for the use of a subjective approach is simply the unavailability of an objective standard. If such a standard were readily available, then the use of the subjective approach would be less likely. In *Misano di Navigazione, SpA., v. U.S.*[26] the court examined a specific incident of the subjective-objective dynamic. The case involved a claim for a wrongful cancellation of a charter. The defendant rejected a vessel supplied by the plaintiff under a charter agreement. He argued that the vessel failed to satisfy reasonable standards of cleanliness. The contract provided for the suitability determination to be made by the defendant's engineer. The dialectic is framed as a choice between the availability of an objective standard and the subjective satisfaction of a professional. The plaintiff argued that the court should impose an objective standard because "the standard for cleanliness is readily defined by industry guidelines."[27] Instead, the court pointed to an exception to the general preference for objective standards. It referenced Comment *b.* of section 228 of the *Second Restatement* dealing with the use of third-party professionals.[28] The court concluded that when a third party is to determine satisfaction "the courts will not rush to apply the objective standard."[29]

Kreis v. Venture Out In America, Inc., illustrates the quagmire that courts have immersed themselves in dealing with contractual interpretation. This quagmire is a result of not coming to terms with the dialectic. "The courts cannot only look to the language of the contract but must ascertain the intention of the parties and make a construction that is fair and reasonable."[30] Conceptually, this statement represents a court that is unsure as to the appropriate approach to contract interpretation. The rudiments of both the objective and subjective approaches are present. The objectivity of the *language of the instrument* is placed on the same plane as the more subjective finding of the *intention of the parties*. The language of the instrument does not prevent the court from straying outside its four corners to find the actual intent of the parties. Both poles of the dialectic are at work in this court's interpretive exercise. A restrictive reading of contractual intent is disregarded. The use of surrounding circumstances to find the *real* intent of the parties is used to *make a construction that is fair and reasonable*. The reasonable person is seen here as a vehicle to impose a construction that is fair but not necessarily a reflection of the parties' actual intent. "One rule of construction is to give effect to the parties' intent in light of all the surrounding circumstances."[31] This element of the interpretive process will be given a closer look in the following section.

TOTALITY OF THE CIRCUMSTANCES

The reasonable person is cut from the fabric of facts. These facts are distilled from the totality of the circumstances[32] in which the contractual undertaking transpired. The facts of this totality analysis are gleaned from any possible source that can provide insight into the intentions of the parties. The totality timeline in modern contracts is much more expansive than the one found in classical contracts. Classical contracts' fixation with the moment of creation narrows the courts' focus to the time of its formation. Modern contract law has liberalized the contractual viewfinder to include any event that may shed light on contractual intent. Its contractual timeline reaches back to custom and trade usage which provide the background for the conceptual and epistemological framework that the parties bring to the contracting process. It is this baggage of custom that often allows the parties to communicate and to speak the language of business. The courts may also look backward to the facts surrounding the prior dealings between the parties and to the precontractual negotiations, and forward to postformation facts including the course of dealing, contractual modifications, and unforeseen events that may have an impact on the continued efficacy of the contract.

The starting point of any inquiry is the contract itself. The language of the contract is looked to as the touchstone of contractual intent and for affixing liability. If the contract is facially clear, then the objective theory mandates that the words of the contract be given their plain and ordinary meaning. The determination of clarity begins from the premise that there is a "strong presumption that a written instrument correctly expresses the intention of the parties to it."[33] This presumption argues against the reading of ambiguity into an otherwise unambiguous contract. The burden is heavy for the party offering an alternative meaning to the one facially expressed in the agreement.[34] This is the objective theory in its paradigmatic essence. As one moves away from the fully integrated, written contract to informal writings and oral contracts, the clarity of the words becomes increasingly suspect. The totality of the circumstances analysis will be needed to differentiate mere puff from contractual statements.[35] The same words may result in different legal consequences depending upon the context in which they were offered.[36]

Often the language is not conclusive regarding general contractual intent or mutual assent regarding a specific term. The courts then must look to the facts of the transaction and to the relationship to determine if such intent existed. In 1918 Justice Holmes stated the nature of this inquiry. "A word is not a crystal, transparent and unchanged, it is skin of a living thought and may vary greatly in color and content *according to the circumstances* and the time in which it is used."[37] The *Second Restatement* acknowledges the inherent shortcomings and resultant ambiguities of human language. "Material differences of meaning are a standard cause of contract disputes, and the decision of such disputes necessarily requires interpretation of the language and other conduct of the parties in the light of the circumstances."[38]

If the correspondence at issue falls short of legally clear intent or legally significant reliance, then a court may examine evidence from other interparty communications.[39] Contextual evidence stemming from prior dealings, precontract negotiations, contemporaneous communications, and course of performance may be used to prove contractual intent.[40] This is an acknowledgment that the parties may have a common experience and understanding unique to their relationship. It is an intersubjective understanding based on prior negotiations and prior dealings. Prior dealings, in effect, become a part of the transaction in question. Through tacit recognition, such parties have imparted a specific meaning to the language used in subsequent transactions.[41] The parties create a unique language for their transactions. In supplying an omitted term, the courts often recognize such common language or the tacit understandings of the parties.[42] The *Second Restatement* expressly adopts the use of prior agreements and negotiations as an aide to interpretation including the determination of contractual intent[43] and the implication of a missing term.[44]

The objective meaning of a contract can be called into question if prior dealings, precontract negotiations, and course of performance show that the parties' subjective meaning was otherwise. "Even though words seem on their face to have only a single possible meaning, other meanings often appear when the circumstances are disclosed."[45] These circumstances include the specific communal meaning affixed by the parties. The *Uniform Commercial Code* defines course of dealing as a "sequence of previous conduct between the parties which is fairly to be regarded as establishing a common basis of understanding for interpreting their expressions and other conduct."[46] The implication of the subjective meaning of the parties is also derived from how the agreement is actually performed. The code acknowledges that the implementation phase of a contract is strong evidence of the parties' subjective intent at the time of its formation.[47] For this reason the subsequent conduct and statements of the parties can be used to appropriate a given meaning to the contract. Such evidence can also be used to determine one party's understanding of the subjective meaning being applied by the other party. The *Second Restatement* concludes that "statements of a contracting party subsequent to the adoption of an integration are admissible against him to show his understanding of the meaning asserted by the other party."[48]

The *Second Restatement* clearly sides with the need to apply the objective meaning in the interpretation of contracts. "The relevant intention of a party is that manifested by him rather than any different undisclosed intention."[49] This verdict in favor of objective interpretation is not without reservation. One of the rationales for the objective approach is an evidentiary concern. How does one prove subjective intent? How does one prevent a person from changing her recollection of intent in order to improve her chances in a dispute? In the realm of general contractual intent, a presumption of intentionality may help ease the problem of the unscrupulous party attempting to skirt her contractual obligations. A more interesting dilemma is where the subjective intent of a party can be proven from a preponderance of the evidence. Must a court ignore such evidence and apply a contradictory objective interpretation? To the strict objectivists, testimony of a party's subjective intent from *twenty bishops* is irrelevant—the manifestations of intent as objectively deciphered must control. A totality of the circumstances analysis would best be served by admitting such evidence. The facts of a party's subjective state of mind is directly relevant in a totality analysis.

The *Second Restatement* does not resolve this contradiction between totality of the circumstances and a purely objective approach.

> When a party is held to a meaning of which he had reason to know, it is sometimes said that the *objective* meaning of his language or other conduct prevails over his *subjective* meaning. Even so, the operative meaning is found in the transaction and its context rather than in the law or in the usages of people other than the parties.[50]

This passage speaks of three meanings: the objective, the subjective, and the operative. The objective meaning is that which a reasonable person would interpret certain expressions and conduct to mean. The reasonable person is further implied in the phrase "the usages of people other than the parties." An alternative notion of the objective theory is not what a reasonable person would imply or discern but what society feels is a fair resolution of the dispute. This alternative notion is referenced by the language "rather than in the law." The delegation of subjective meaning to secondary status is clear: ". . . the objective meaning . . . prevails over his subjective meaning." If so, then why does the passage make reference to something called the operative meaning of the contract? I would submit that it is a step back from the previous sentence's discarding of the importance of subjective meaning. After stating that the objective meaning is the controlling standard, it begins the next sentence with the modifying "even so." The operative meaning "found in the transaction and its context" is the true standard for interpretation. This undefined operative meaning leaves a role for both objective and subjective elements of evidence. It may, in fact, be an unconscious recognition of the role of the subjective-objective dialectic.

The manifestation of intent language used as the cornerstone for the objective approach to contractual intent indicates that manifestation is all that is required to imply the required intent.[51] More accurately, it is the manifestation of a mutuality of assent[52] in which both parties manifest an intent to enter into a contract and both manifestations reference each other. But manifestation alone is not enough to create a contractually binding obligation. A clear subjective element is still apparent within the so-called objective theory. "A manifestation of assent is not a mere appearance; the party must in some way be responsible for the appearance."[53] Therefore, a manifestation, objectively interpreted, is not enough to win the day on the issue of intent. The notion of responsibility brings the state of mind of the manifestor into the scope of the inquiry. "In effect there must be either intentional or negligent creation of an appearance of assent."[54] The subjective element continues to arise from the contractual dustbin.

The sweep of the totality of the circumstances analysis has been the center of much debate. Should the analysis be limited to the circumstances surrounding the formation of the contract? May subsequent events be used as an aid in contract interpretation? Should the courts use subsequent conduct and acts to retroactively determine the contractual intent of the parties at the time of formation? The House of Lords addressed this issue in the case of *Schuler A.G. v. Wickman Tools*. The Wickman Tools case involved a long-term agency contract in which one party was to solicit purchase orders for the other party's machinery. The issue was the construction of a clause that supposedly made the agreement conditional upon the agent party's duty to visit prospective purchasers on a weekly basis. The selling agent's practice varied regarding the frequency of visits over the period of the contract. Subsequently, the manufacturer party sought to dissolve the contract based on the agent's breach of contract. The attorney for the plaintiff argued the case for truncating the totality of the circumstances at the formation stage. To allow evidence of subsequent conduct "would entail the law embarking on a slippery slope on which there is no halting place. It would be the end of certainty in relation to the construction of documents."[55] Lord Reid agreed by stating that "I find no substantial support in the authorities for any general rule permitting subsequent acts of the parties to be used as throwing light on its meaning."[56] The legal document is all that is needed in order to construct the intent of the parties. Lord Wilberforce focused instead on the exceptions to the rule that allow an extension of the totality of the circumstances analysis to subsequent events. "Evidence may be admitted of surrounding circumstances in order to explain technical expressions or to identify the subject matter of an agreement or to resolve a latent ambiguity."[57]

Lord Simon took issue with both expositions of the evidentiary rules pertaining to the admission of subsequent circumstantial evidence in the contractual intent inquiry.

The distinction between the admissibility of direct and circumstantial evidence of intention seems to me to be quite unjustifiable in these days. And the distinctions between patent ambiguities, latent ambiguities and equivocations as regards admissibility of extrinsic evidence are based on outmoded and highly technical and artificial rules and introduce absurd refinements.[58]

This expanded totality of the circumstances approach is more in tune with the uncovering of contractual intent in modern contractual relationships. The long-term, relational nature of many contracts make it necessary for the courts to view all evidence of meaning in order to render a proper determination of intent. Contract formation in the relational context is no longer a single, fixed event. It is only the beginning of an evolutionary process which continuously refines, expands, and modifies the contractual relationship. The cutting off of the evidentiary inquiry may have been conducive to the discovery of intent in the discrete transactional contract but results in a disservice in the context of long-term, relational ones.

CUSTOM AND TRADE USAGE

The reasonable person is not one of static intellect. The courts often look to the customs of the times or of a business in determining the knowledge and skills the contracting parties bring to the negotiating table. "The law of contracts reflects, in an imperfect way, the needs and values of the communities it serves."[59] Savigny's historical school saw law as a mirrored reflection of community custom. "This school saw the law as an expression of the *folk spirit* and it was the task of law to capture what had been exhibited in the freely developed customs of the community."[60] Contract law serves not only a general *community*, i.e., society, but also a number of narrower communities, such as a trade or a profession. In *Larwin-Southern Cal., Inc. v. JBG Inv.*, the court observed that "custom and usage within a trade may properly be used in clarifying what, on the face of a contract, appears to be an ambiguity."[61] Section 1–205 of the *Uniform Commercial Code* states that a "usage of trade is any practice or method of dealing having such regularity of observance in a place, vocation or trade as to justify the expectation that it will be observed with respect to the transaction in question."[62] It is a mechanism that the court will look to in clarifying an ambiguity of intent. "The language used is to be interpreted as meaning what it may fairly be expected to mean to parties involved in the particular commercial transaction in a given locality or in a given vocation or trade."[63] Custom, usage, and practice can be seen as the background of contractual obligation. They are used to clarify any ambiguity of intent existing in the instruments of contract. If such clarity is not forthcoming, then the courts must look to the existing rules of contract law for an answer.[64] It is for the courts to decide whether contract law will provide a recourse or whether the parties are to be left without recourse.

The reasonable person provides the needed flexibility in a system that places emphasis on rule application. There is, in essence, a duality of change. Change may be engineered through a reformulation of the common law rules by way of judicial manipulation or statutory preemption. Alternatively, the personage of the reasonable person may be reinvented to reflect the changes in customs and society in general. In *Lipschutz v. Gordon Jewelry Corp.*, the court acknowledged that "a *custom* is a practice which by its universality has acquired the force and effect of law."[65] Either way there will be enough of an effect on the end result of the judicial process (either through a reformulation of the formal rules of contract or by the reinvention of the reasonable person) to reflect changes in custom and usage.

The imprimatur of the reasonable person approach can be seen throughout the *Second Restatement* and the *Uniform Commercial Code*. It can be seen whenever reference is made to the fact that a party had reason to know or should have known. There is reason to know if a person "has information from which a person of similar intelligence would infer that the fact in question does or will exist."[66] The line between *reason to know* and actual knowledge is often nonexistent. In contrast, *should know* is generally associated with a legal duty to know. "Should know imports a duty to ascertain the facts."[67] Thus, *should know* is relatively unconcerned with actual knowledge. The determination of whether a party had reason to know is accomplished within the framework of the totality of the circumstances analysis.[68] *Reason to know* is a factual determination based on the circumstances and information available to the parties. *Should know* is more a judicial reflection regarding what is reasonable given the parties and the circumstances. The difference is that *reason to know* is a party-specific objectivity. In contrast, *should know* is community-focused objectivity, that is, what is a reasonable interpretation or result as seen through the litmus test of community standards.[69] Modern contract law has witnessed an increasing preemption of the judicial reasonableness inquiry by way of statutory preemption. The English Unfair Contract Terms Act of 1977 adopts a presumption of unreasonableness for indemnity clauses that "by reference to any contract term a party is made to indemnify another party in respect of liability for negligence or breach of contract."[70] For international sales contracts it voids any choice of law clause whose purpose is the avoidance of the Unfair Terms Act.[71] These immutable rules preempt the objective contract theory's search for contractual intent.

A study in microcosm of the relationship between custom and the objective theory of contracts can be seen in section 41 of the *Second Restatement*. Section 41 deals with the lapse of time as a way of automatically revoking an offer. The general rule is that an offeror is the master of her offer. Therefore, an offeror may or may not revoke at her whim anytime prior to acceptance by the offeree. The law, however, limits the reach of the offer to a reasonable period of time. If the offer remains outstanding beyond a reasonable period of time, then a subsequent acceptance is converted to a new offer which the original offeror is free to accept or reject. The issue is what constitutes a reasonable period of time for an offer to remain viable. Reasonableness is an objective determination of fact based on the totality of the circumstances of each case. Section 41 lists a litany of factors to be entered into the judicial analysis, which include the nature of the contract, the purposes of the parties, course of dealing, and trade usage and practice.[72] This raises a supplemental issue of whether custom is part and parcel with the reasonable person. Does the fact that something has risen to the level of custom place an imprimatur of reasonableness upon it? The *Second Restatement* advocates that custom or trade usage does possess a strong presumption of reasonableness. Commentary to section 222 states that "commercial acceptance by regular observance makes out a prima facie case that a usage of trade is reasonable."[73] Custom and trade usage are ready-made arbiters of reasonableness. As such, their place within the objective theory of contract is secure.

Customary law as imputed into the reasonable person provides a stopgap that allows the judicial process to render decisions that reflect objective or commercial reality. This is likely to precede the reformulation of the formal rules to reflect that reality. Custom and usage have often been the vehicles by which the common law has mended itself and amended its rules to accommodate changing times.[74] In the 1842 case of *Jacob v. State*,[75] Justice Turley describes this grassroots metamorphosis: "Common law sources are to be found in the usage, habits, manners, and customs of a people. The common law of a country will be modified, and extended by analogy, *construction and custom*, so as to embrace new relations, springing up from time to time, from an amelioration or change of society."[76] The relationship between law and custom can be seen as reciprocal in nature. Custom is a source of law and law has impact on custom. Aristotle saw law as a vehicle for inducing positive behavioral modifications within the populace. "The foundation of law is to lay down sound and balanced principles of character-formation to *accustom* various kinds of people, each in different ways, to refrain from greed."[77] The reasonable person acts as a receptacle for customary practice. The courts can also use the reasonable person standard more proactively to discourage unconscionable practices and encourage the development of judicially approved standards of reasonableness.

Karl Llewellyn asserted that trade practice provides the interpretative background of contract. "The background of trade practice gives a first indication; the line of authority rejecting unreasonable practice offers the needed corrective."[78] He speaks of a double-barreled objectivity in which the words of a contract are to be read through two lenses. The interpretation of words through the lens of custom and practice provide a baseline. The courts must also look to whether the parties attached a variant meaning. Words are to be interpreted "first in the light of trade usage, second in the light of the common meaning to the hearer and the course of dealing of the parties."[79] In supplying a missing term, the court can use trade practice or usage to imply what "a sane man might reasonably expect to find in the contract."[80]

Trade usage often implies esoteric knowledge to which only those in a particular trade or profession are privy. Generally, the cases revolve around the expert testimony offered by the respective parties in support of their contentions regarding the meaning of the contract. In *Folk v. Central Nat. Bank & Trust Co.*[81] a series of experts were called to give testimony pertaining to the quality of pavement work at a raceway performed under a construction contract. The contractor was suing for contract damages arguing that it had substantially performed the contract. The owner's defense was that defective installation resulted in a material breach. The contractor called a consulting engineer who testified that the asphalt work was in accordance with standard procedures.[82] A road contractor who specializes in asphalt installation testified that the new surface was "nice and tight," indicating a proper bonding.[83] A number of race car drivers were called to testify that the surface was acceptable and "as good or better than other tracks."[84] The defense witnesses included a professional engineer who testified that deviations on the surfaces far exceeded acceptable standards.[85] Another asphalt contractor testified that the workmanship was of substandard quality.[86] Officials of a national racers association testified that it removed its certification of the raceway because of safety concerns pertaining to the track's surface. Two race drivers testified that the new surface was dangerous.[87] Finally, a report from an engineer testing company provided measurements of variations in the track's surface. The determination of usage or practice can be a harried one!

The jurisprudential issues in the above scenario revolve around the complexity of fabricating the reasonable person in the face of such testimony. The complexity of such a fabrication is increased due to the highly technical and specialized nature of the evidence. Is a judge equipped to handle the avalanche of evidentiary concerns pertaining to such testimony? Should we expect a jury of ordinary citizens to be able to decipher commercial and professional evidence and the assorted technicalities in applying the reasonable person standard? Karl Llewellyn was one who believed that the judge and jury are not equipped to handle this extension of the objective theory of contracts.[88] He believed that the notion of reasonableness in a specific trade or profession would best be served through the use of expert arbitrators or the use of a merchant tribunal.[89] The idea of a merchant tribunal to assist the courts in making an informed judgment[90] of mercantile facts was never adopted. If our quest under the objective theory is to find the understanding of the parties or to determine commercial reasonableness, then such expert judging would seem to make a good deal of sense.

Custom as Supplement

The previous section illustrated the use of custom and trade usage as a source of the common law. Its role in the notion of contractual intent can be as pervasive. The courts often look to custom and trade usage in giving meaning to a contract. The implied terms of custom are used to salvage incomplete contracts. The parties are held to intend those practices, usages, and meanings of their business or trade that are regularly used or recognized. "The supplement might even be held to create a contract when otherwise a contract might not have been found."[91] Consent, however, still remains the justification for the use of custom and trade usage as interpretive devices. The fact that the use in question is regularly observed implies that the parties had knowledge of the usage. Contractual silence is then taken as an implied intent by the parties to be bound by the implications of that particular custom or usage. Custom and practice can be seen as providing insight into the subjective intent of the parties.

Subjective intent, however, implies actual knowledge by the parties of the custom or usage. In practice, the reasonable person standard is used to imply such meaning or knowledge as that which a person in the trade or business should have reasonably been in possession. Nonetheless, the subjective element plays an important role in the area of custom and trade usage. The courts initially perform a party-specific analysis to determine if the parties can be rightfully placed within a particular business or trade. A party will not be held to the knowledge or standards of a trade unless he possesses the qualities and experiences of the members of that trade or business. The reasonableness standard should apply only if it is determined that the particular party is indeed a member of that particular trade.[92]

Custom provides insight as to the *is* of what the parties intended and as to what a specific contractual term is likely to mean. Custom also provides a normative function. It provides a barometer for measuring what the community believes the contractual terms *should* mean. Kent Greenawalt asserts that there is a direct relationship "between the interpreter and what is being interpreted and between the interpreter and the community in which he is situated."[93] The interpretive inquiry of the objective theory is inherently normative because it is influenced by community standards of reasonableness. "Those who make the law try not to stray too far from the community's moral sense."[94] At least at the subconscious level, there is an inevitable propensity to conform contractual intent to community standards.

Language As Custom

A customary glaze covers most of human activity. There is little that can be said or performed that is not viewed through the lens of custom. Custom may enforce a finding of contractual liability. It may also play a nonlegal role of connoting certain conduct as immoral or unbusinesslike. "Custom shows that memorializing even a weak legal commitment carries some moral and business weight."[95] Language itself is a creature of custom that developed from an evolutionary process of trial and error reaching back millennia to primordial man.[96] Dewey states that "speech forms are our great carriers: the easy running vehicles by which meanings are transported from experiences that no longer concern us to those that are as yet dark and dubious."[97] The language of the law is the specialized creation of custom and tradition. Lawyers, judges, and scholars communicate in "an inherited and traditional language with marked peculiarities of vocabulary and construction."[98] In the previous section it was seen that the custom or usage of a trade or a profession can imbue words with meanings not apparent to a layperson.[99] This trade-specific narrowing of meaning takes place in a world where words continue to possess numerous connotations.[100]

Aristotle recognized the ephemeral nature of language and its dependency upon context. "Just as each meaning of the word can live and survive in its own context, separately from the rest of its meanings, none is more relevant or essential than any of the others."[101] The fixing of specific meaning to words is often done informally through the socialization of change in the form of usage and custom. "Words are used as conventional symbols of mental states, with standardized meanings *based on habitual or customary practice*. Unless a different intention is shown, language is interpreted in accordance with its generally prevailing meaning."[102] If a court finds that the contract is unambiguous, then the language of the contract is held to yield the intent of the parties.[103] In his *Theory of Legal Interpretation*, Justice Holmes defines ordinary meaning as nothing more than the language of the reasonable person.

> The normal speaker of English is merely a special variety, a literary form, so to speak, of our old friend the prudent man. He is external to the particular writer, and a reference to him as the criterion is simply another instance of the *externality of the law*. . . . For each party to a contract has notice that the other will understand his words according to the usage of the normal speaker of English.[104]

The customary use of language is the *dialect* used by the reasonable person. The intentions of the parties as to the meaning of words become acute when a word has both a common and a technical meaning.[105] "It is incumbent upon the parties to make it abundantly plain that the intended word is to have the technical meaning, or otherwise the court will give the word its popular meaning."[106] The intention to utter words in an idiosyncratic way satisfies contracts' intentionality requirement regarding the general or customary meaning of the words. The analysis of contracts under the objective theory is thus "bounded by the words in which they are made, and the *social conventions* those words invoke—distinct from the subjective intentions of the parties."[107] The language of the law is a "sort of social literature, a way of talking about people and their relationships."[108] Words specifically defined or carefully chosen are required to preempt the law's objective interpretation. To the extent the parties are able to rein in the meaning of their words, the closer will be the convergence of the actual meaning of the contract and the *interpretative meaning* supplied by the courts.

Main Purpose Rule

In the area of breach of contract the courts have to differentiate between fundamental and minor breach. If the breach affects the main purpose or root of the contract, then it is considered fundamental. A fundamental breach allows the nonbreaching party to reject performance and avoid the contract. The same is true for the doctrine of anticipatory repudiation. The anticipated breach must go to the root of the contract. In *Cehave N.V. v. Bremer,* the court dealt with the issue of fundamental breach. The case involved a contract for the delivery of citrus pellets. A portion of the shipment was damaged. The purchaser elected to reject the entire shipment and discharge the contract. The contract provided that the goods were to be shipped in good condition. The issue was whether this provision was intended as a condition that would allow the purchaser to discharge the contract if the shipment did not strictly comply or whether a general test of merchantability would apply. Lord Denning held that the law disfavors conditions and that the issue would be that of merchantability. He then sought the guidance of the *commercial man* on the issue of merchantability. The commercial man would look to the totality of the circumstances in determining whether the goods were of merchantable quality. The factors to be considered include "the purpose for which the goods of that kind are commonly bought," the description of the goods in the contract, the price paid as an indication of expected quality, and whether there is an express clause dealing with the issue of rejection.[109] The court focused on the fact that the goods were resold and used for the same purpose as anticipated in the contract. Based on the resale it concluded that the breach did not go to the *root* of the contract.[110] It can be presumed that the parties did not intend that such a minimal divergence in quality would be a ground for rejection and discharge.

This presumption that a performance that satisfies the essence or root of the contract cannot be rejected is rebuttable. This was made clear in a case involving the purchase of a quantity of one-half-inch wooden staves. The staves that were supplied varied slightly from the contract description. Despite the variations, they were still of merchantable quality. Nonetheless, the court held that the contract was clear enough to preempt the test of merchantability. "The fact that the goods were merchantable under the contract is not the proper test to be applied in determining whether the goods satisfied the contract description."[111] Clear language of contractual intent can limit the chance of judicial constructionism. To be successful in preventing the implementation of the doctrine of presumed intent, the parties must make "no room in their contract for any elasticity."[112]

In *Suisse Atlantique Societe D'Armement Maritime S.A.*, the House of Lords made a similar distinction between fundamental breach and the breach of a fundamental term (the former being court-imposed, the latter being party-imposed by way of express agreement). The parties may elevate what is generally considered a minor term to the level of a fundamental term. If this intent is clearly expressed, then the court must strictly enforce the term regardless of its harshness. First, it must determine if a term was intended to be fundamental.[113] The court may look to a number of factors in making this determination. "A fundamental term of a contract is one which the parties have agreed either expressly *or* by necessary implication, *or* which the general law regards as going to the *root* of the contract."[114] If it is not apparent that a term is fundamental, then the court will perform a totality analysis to determine whether the breach was nonetheless a fundamental one. Lord Reid analogized the use of exculpatory clauses as an example of the need for proper judicial construction. He mentions the rule of strict construction and the main purpose rule as the means to balance freedom of contract with the need to preserve meaningful promissory obligations.

> Such clauses must be construed strictly and if ambiguous the narrower meaning will be taken. Or it may appear that the terms of the clause are so wide that they cannot be applied literally: that may be because this would lead to an absurdity or because it would defeat the *main object* of the contract. And where some limit must be read into the clause it is reasonable to draw the line at fundamental breaches. If some limitation has to be read in it seems reasonable to suppose that neither party had in contemplation a breach that goes to the *root* of the contract.[115]

Lord Reid seems to be proclaiming that there is an implied general intent to require performances that conform to the essence or root of the contract. The fashioning of an exemption clause through specific intent in order to avoid liability for fundamental breach will have to give way in certain circumstances to this intentional essence.

Lord Upjohn rationalizes this preemption of specific contractual intent by the age-old fiction of presumed intent. By the use of "a well-known cannon of construction, words must be so construed as to give business efficacy to the contract and the *presumed intention* of the parties."[116] The parties are presumed to have intended to carry out the fundamental core of the contract. Therefore, they are presumed to have intended that the exemption or exculpatory clause was not meant to cover such fundamental breaches. A literal interpretation would likely reach the opposite conclusion. The main purpose of the contract is interconnected with contractual intent in the process of judicial construction. This principle was stated more than 100 years ago in *Glynn v. Margetson & Co.* A court is to look "at the whole of the instrument, and seeing what one must regard as its main purpose, one must reject words if they are inconsistent with what one assumes to be the main purpose of the contract."[117] The fiction of presumed intent seems magnified in this type of case. Despite the fact that the fourcorners of the contract state otherwise, the courts have justified strict construction upon the grounds of contractual intent. Their rationalization is that the parties could not have intended what the contract clearly states.[118] The written word is thus conformed to the root or essence of the contract. "The principle is that the contractual intention is to be ascertained—not just grammatically from the words used, but by consideration of those words in relation to the commercial purpose of the contract."[119] The type of contract and its essence, and not just the written contract, are used as guideposts to contractual intent.

MANIFESTATION OF INTENT AND ITS MANIPULATION

Once constructed, the reasonable person is used as an interpretive tool in the determination of whether the parties' words and conduct represented a manifestation of intent to contract. It is the task of the reasonable person to decide if there has been a manifestation of intent and not whether there was an actual intent to contract. Upon the affirmative determination of manifested intent, the reasonable person's second-order task is to interpret the manifested intent. Manifested intent as viewed by the reasonable person is used to infuse the contract with meaning. What are the terms of the contract as reflected in the parties' manifestation of intent? The objective theory's focus on manifestation is a twofold analysis. First, was there a general intent to contract? Second, what were the parties' specific intent as to the particulars of that contract? The reasonable person implies both general and specific intent though its objective interpretation of the parties' manifestations. This mandate removes the role of subjective intent from the realms of contract formation and enforcement. The objective theory holds that the reasonable person is to be objectively constructed and objectively applied. Nonetheless, the subjective leanings of the judge play a role in the fabrication of the reasonable person, and subjectivity plays a role in the application of the reasonable person to the interpretation of contractual manifestations.

Professor Macneil notes that subjectivity enters through the back door of the objective theory through its embodiment of the reasonable person. Through the device of manipulation the subjective intent of a party can enter the interpretive equation. The subjectification of the reasonable person transpires in a number of scenarios. First, manifested intent is manipulated to reflect the subjective intent of the parties. The manipulation of manifested intent represents "efforts of the courts to effectuate what it thinks was the real or subjective intention of both of the parties."[120]

Second, a similar manipulation involves conforming the manifestation of intent to the basic type of contract intended by the parties. This is a second-order category of *real intention*. It is not directed at a particular term or issue of a contract but is based on the parties' intentions to enter into a general type of contract. "The court is manipulating manifested intention in order to achieve what *it thinks* were the basic purposes of the parties in carrying on the contractual relationship."[121] The subjectivity shifts from the conscious subjective intentions of the parties in the first scenario to what the court thinks is the *essence* of the contractual relationship.[122] The notion of determining intent from an essence has a long history inside and outside of the law. It is a "philosophical tradition going back to ancient Greece that to explain a phenomenon is to provide its *essential* nature."[123] The courts often look to the contract itself to uncover its purpose or essential character and then use that determination to imply the parties' states of mind at the time of formation.

A third scenario is party-specific intent as opposed to the mutual assent evidenced in the first two scenarios. It is the manipulation of manifested intent which is in contradiction to the actual, subjective intent of one of the parties. It is an "effort to effectuate the real, subjective intention of one of the parties contrary to his manifested intention."[124] Professor Macneil argues that the courts' "consensual notion of justice is the motivating factor. A party's real intent should not be ignored because of her careless and ambiguous use of language."[125] The excuse of mistake is an area where one finds manifested intent at odds with subjective intent. Under a regime of pure objectivity, contractual adjustments for mistake would not be permitted. Pure objectivity consists of the interpretation of external manifestations which are then formalistically applied. Early legal systems, such as the ritualistic system of ancient Rome, are characterized by such an approach. "In the formalistic stage a legal system which has come to enforce contracts will enforce them as made, and will not give relief for mistakes."[126] The common law doctrine of mistake does give relief even though the parties' manifested intentions indicate that a contract had been formed. Relief through reformation or rescission is given in face of the objective theory's mandate to do otherwise. The subjective element is allowed to triumph over the objective in the name of justice. To this, Professor Hoffman Fuller asserts that "under mistake's meaningless shelter a court is free to do as it chooses, set loose to sail on an ocean of *subjectivity*."[127]

A fourth scenario of judicial manipulation of manifested intent is the judicial enterprise of gap-filling. Although not antithetical to the notion of consent, it is clearly of a different order than the first three scenarios. The focus is on events, generally unforeseen, that occur subsequent to the formation of the contract. It is illusory to talk of conscious, subjective intent pertaining to a term or issue that was never contemplated or discussed. A fiction often perpetrated by the courts is that the implication of a term is in conformity with what would have been the intention of the parties had they been aware of the gap. The implication of a contractual term is accompanied by an implication of intent. Macneil offers a subcategory within this scenario where the implication of a term would be consistent with actual, subjective intent. This would be possible if two elements are present. First, the court is willing to move the timeline of intent from the time of formation forward to postformation intent. Second, the parties' view of the relationship has changed and they have exhibited a mutual intent since the formation of the contract regarding the issue in question. Their doing so would be in "harmony with a notion of consent, because their view of the relationship and intent may be thought to have changed as the relationship developed."[128] This metamorphosis of intent will be studied further in the next section on relational intent.

A natural kinship can be seen between the fourth scenario (gap-filling) and the second scenario (contractual essence). Neither manipulation is premised on the existence of actual, subjective intent at the time of contract formation. The earlier scenario manipulates the manifested intent present at the time of the formation to reflect an interpretation in conformity with the purpose of the contract. The fourth scenario manipulates manifested intent to deal with postformation issues. Nonetheless, both seem to find their guidance from a notion that such intent can be implied through an analysis of the *essence* of the contract. The gap-filler is not a reflection of what the parties intended but of what can be implied by the nature or the essence of the contract. In a way, there is an anthropomorphizing of the contractual document. This transference of the intent inquiry from the parties to the instrument that they created was persuasively stated in Arthur Leff's "Contract as Thing."[129] Professor Atiyah connects Leff's contract *as thing* with the classical model of contracts. The classical model views "contract as a *thing*, which has some kind of objective existence prior to any performance or any act of the parties."[130] The *essence* of a contract and contract as *thing* are convenient theoretical devices for conforming judicial gap-filling to the traditional *discovery* of party-specific intent.

There have been other attempts to reificate[131] contracts and to find personal intent by extrapolating it from the contract itself. Lon Fuller believed that contracts and contractual processes have an internal rationality. "Contractual processes have a distinctive inner order of their own—an integrity—to be discovered and respected by those who

70

have responsibility for their functioning."[132] Georg Hegel referred to this notion as the inner rationality of law.[133] One may extend the logic of Fuller and Hegel to the discovery of contractual intent through the examination of the internal integrity of the contract itself. It is their belief that contractual intent should be made congruent with the internal integrity or rationality of the contract documents.

A final scenario represents the greatest attenuation of manifested intent. It is when the courts "manipulate manifested intention to achieve goals *contrary* to the mutual purposes of the parties."[134] This is what Professor Macneil refers to as social adjustment through the "regulation of contractual relationships."[135] The court is in essence reformulating the contract to meet societal goals. These goals have been characterized as the need to adjust contracts so that they conform to notions of good faith, fair dealing, and conscionability. Although such altruism may be necessary, it should not be advanced through the fiction of manifested intent. The adjustment or reformulation is unconnected to the intent of the parties, actual or manifested.

A paradox has developed in the battle of the forms scenario involving the application of the objective theory and the finding of mutual assent. Is there a true consent to all the fine print terms found in the other party's business forms? In reality a party cannot specifically consent to something she is unlikely to have read. One way of upholding these contracts and conforming them to the objective theory is to assert that the receiving party, nonetheless, has a duty to read any form that she signs. The sanctity of a written contract, coupled with the duty to read, truncates the totality of the circumstances inquiry. There is consent based on a four-corners reading when in reality no such consent exists. The totality analysis would consider the following questions. If one party provides the contractual form, is the other party held to have consented to all of the terms of that contract (merchant-consumer scenario)? If both parties provide forms of contract with conflicting terms, which terms will be deemed to have been consented to (merchant-merchant scenario)?

The last question has led to some conflicting conclusions as to the bindingness of so-called additional terms. Section 2–207(2) of the *Uniform Commercial Code* makes the additional terms a part of the contract if they are deemed not to materially alter the contract. It is not unusual to find additional terms in many of the numerous exchanges of correspondence that makeup today's commercial transactions. In such layered transactional exchanges it is difficult to determine which terms are at the consensual core and which are to be construed as additional. The entire concept of a contractual consent to these additional terms is intellectually dishonest. There is no subjective or objective consent to terms that are neither read nor challenged for the sake of commercial tranquillity. The complexity of the tasks involved in fulfilling the mandates of section 2–207 will be at least partially rectified with recently proposed revisions to article 2 of the code. The additional terms terminology is replaced with the more encompassing notion of varying terms. The importance of the sequential order of exchange in order to quantify terms as additional is eliminated. The revisions to the code would exclude all terms unless there has been an express agreement to include them in the contract.[136] This approach brings the battle of the forms more into line with the notion of contractual consent as a reflection of objective reality.

In the event that the form provider is aware of the other party's lack of knowledge of the form's content the doctrine of mistake can be used to correct this informational asymmetry. The mistaken party is usually granted either a rescission or reformation of the contract. The recipient party cannot be said to have consented, subjectively or objectively, to any unreasonable or unique terms in the form. This abuse of form contracts has led the courts into a more interventionist stance. The reasonable expectations of the recipient party are used for interpretive guidance. The reasonable expectations supplant the terms of the actual written contract.[137]

The exchange of forms with fine print would seem to preclude a finding of subjective agreement. A fiction has been used, however, to objectively find contractual intent. It is held that the act of signing a standard form or the exchange of such forms provides the objective mechanics of agreement. A party is held to have intended to accept the terms of a form she has signed or upon which she has acted upon. The totality of the circumstances analysis is shunted and the reasonable person inquiry is ignored. The court simply restricts its inquiry to the fourcorners of each form. In essence, there is a transformation of the agreement from a bilateral to a unilateral contract. The signing or receipt of the form becomes the objective conduct of the traditional unilateral contract. A rational application of the objective theory would recognize the flaw in basing consent on such acts. Objectivity is to be grounded in reality. Reality makes clear that in the case of standard forms the failure to find a subjective agreement precludes the finding of objective agreement. There is no manifestation of intent because there has been no conscious agreement to the unread terms embedded in a standard form.[138]

RELATIONAL CONSENT

The shift from the rigidity of classical contract to the standards-based analysis of modern contract law reflects climatic changes in the contractual environment.[139] Classical contract's paradigm is the discrete, one-shot transactional event. Modern contracts have become increasingly complex multi-event happenings. They are often relational, long-term, evolutionary processes. The openendedness of many of today's contractual arrangements is evidenced by the fact that "most modern agreements will rarely be fully completed."[140] Clear contractual intent pertaining to a specific event in this evolutionary relationship may be difficult to find.[141] The longer the term of the contractual relationship, the greater the likelihood that it will breed trust, cooperation, and informality among the parties.

Misunderstanding is inherent in interpersonal communication. In a relational contract situation the interpretation of another's intent or meaning is often a trial-and-error process. Ambiguity is likely to increase in cases in which a party is unsure of her own intentions. A person's intent and interpretation of meaning may need the sounding board of an interactive relationship in order to crystallize interpersonal transactional consent.[142] This relational informality causes evidentiary problems when a court is asked to intervene in an event-specific dispute. An event encased in a long-term contractual relationship will display different manifestations of intent than one between contractual strangers entering into a one-time exchange. The courts' interpretive analysis is likely to center on the "practices of the actors and on their usages, customs, and interpretations that mediate their patterns of conduct and the formal juridical instruments that are deemed to govern them."[143]

The background of mutual, unexpressed understandings often takes the place of clearly expressed intent in the relational contract situation. Professor Macneil refers to this common understanding as the tacit assumptions of relational contracts.[144] The newness of the parties in the single transaction scenario focuses their attention on expressed manifestations because of a lack of prior, mutual understanding or tacit assumptions.[145]

The notion of mutual assent to a specific event of contract seems archaic given the complexity, duration, and multidimensional characteristics of modern-day contractual relationships. In place of a finding of classical contracts' objective meeting of the minds to a specific incident of contract, a court should look to the historical relationship between the parties to see if there is an overall relational intent to be bound absent specific intent. An agreement needs to be viewed as a single event within a more expansive, complex relationship or transaction. Within such a structure, intent should not be viewed as event-specific. An expanded relational framework is needed to find the required intent to create binding obligations. This expanded analysis is a grander version of the traditional totality of the circumstances analysis. The contracting process in the relational context becomes one of ongoing planning and not the simple effectuation of consent. This broadened perspective makes it difficult to bring relational contract interpretation and enforcement within the classical objective theory of contracts. The objective theory is premised on the finding of manifestations of specific contractual intent. In the relational contract there is at most a general consent to enter into a relationship.[146] The specifics of the relationship will need to be developed and agreed upon as the relationship unfolds. The notion of specific contractual intent pertaining to the multitude of contractual issues and terms is an illusion. Extrapolation from a general relational consent is a more relevant and truthful exercise.

Along with the shift from the notion of specific intent to relational consent, a shift away from viewing consent from a purely human perspective is also in order. The nature of today's contracting parties requires a shift from the individualistic view of intent of classical contract theory to the notion of organizational intent. The fragmentation of promise that appears in even the most discrete transactions is magnified as the complexities of a transaction and of the parties' organizational structures increase. The contract-making process in a large corporate structure is highly fragmented. Those authorized to negotiate, to formalize the negotiations into a contract, to render performance, to modify the contract, and to declare a breach come from different areas of the organizational structure. Contractual intent is severed from the other parts of the contracting process. In its place is a normative framework upon which the open terms of the contractual relationship are given meaning. Philosophically, the "parties will a certain normative relationship" and as such the "terms that govern their contract are not explicitly willed but follow from the relationship."[147] In the organizational setting, the contractual will of an individual person no longer controls the substance of contract.

5

THE DIALECTIC

It is not enough to point out simply that contract is not a branch of theology, for no lawyer *consciously* believes that it is. It is precisely because the notion is buried so deep in the legal psyche that it is so hard to weed out.[1]

I t was once said that "in its origin law is religious."[2] We now turn to the historical roots of the dialectic. Professor Gordley states that the "great elementary conceptions of contract law came out of a Greek philosophical tradition grafted on to Roman law by moral philosophers."[3] Along with the religious, an investigation of potential philosophical and psychological groundings for the dialectic will be studied.[4] In the philosophy of law we will take a look at the rationales given by proponents of the objective and subjective theories of contracts. From the area of religion, a look at the secularization of religious precepts into private and public laws will provide added insight. Finally, the field of psychology will provide insight into the mental processes that convert the external into the internal. A greater empirical understanding of perception, representation, and cognitive reality will help us to better quantify the dialectic.

RELIGIOUS FOUNDATIONS

The interdependence of legal, religious, and philosophical thought can be traced back at least to the twelfth century. Canon law was the preeminent force in juridicial studies in the twelfth century. It was common for "the same person to combine the offices of theologian and canonists."[5] Each of the three disciplines of law, religion, and philosophy borrowed from one another. For example, beginning with St. Augustine, philosophy was used to justify religion as rationally based. The theological "rationalist, made the *dialectical* method the chief one, and placed reason above dogma."[6] A dialectic can be seen forming within the realm of natural and divine law. The natural law was seen as an object of human will that can be found internally in communion with God. On the other hand, it was also based on reason that could be objectively proved. The mystics also believed in a dialectic between the internal and the external but for them the external was the supernatural world. "The mystics delighted in interpreting the visible world as a sign of the supernatural and they used a symbolic method"[7] for this purpose. One can begin to see a possible source for the creation of the dialectic in contracts. The roots of objectivity in contract can be seen in the development of the scholastic method in the twelfth century. It was used to rationally reconcile the *corpus juris civilis* internally and externally with customary law. "Its primary task was the summation of the text, the closing of gaps within, and the resolution of contradictions. The method is *dialectical*, in that it seeks reconciliation of opposites."[8]

The objectivity represented in the notion of the manifestation of mutual assent can be traced to the Middle Ages and its notion of solemn or ritual contract.[9] A contract was formed with the use of formal sacred rituals. The idea of consensual contract was made possible by the sanctifying presence of religious morality. The binding nature of contract was not of individual expectation or reliance but the fear of recrimination from an omnipotent deity. The solemn nature of contract from Roman times to the Renaissance was based on religion. Contract was in essence a type of sacrament much like that of marriage or baptism. It created not one duty but two: one to the other contracting party and, more important, a duty to one's God through the *sacrament* of promise. To breach one's promise was "committing sacrilege, because one was breaking an oath, profaning a sacred thing, and committing an act forbidden by religion."[10] The manifestation of will can be seen as the modern-day counterpart to the solemn or ritual contract. It was the words of the contractual ceremony or oath that provided the vehicle for the creation of a binding, enforceable bond. The sacred formalities were what created obligation. The requirements of consideration, of a writing, or even of mutual assent were formalities still residing in the contractual womb.

Émile Durkhiem asserts that the "value of the contractual undertaking did not come about through the consent of wills but by the formula used. If the solemn ritual was lacking, there was no contract."[11] The rise of modern contractual formalities can be seen as serving the same purpose which the ritual formalities served a thousand years ago—objectivity. Formalism was easier to scrutinize than the will or intent of the parties. More broadly, the objectivity of contract was measured by religious morality. The authoritative texts for the gauging of that morality have varied over time. In the Middle Ages the convergence of canon and secular law was embodied in the rediscovery of the *Codex*, *Novellae*, *Institutiones*, and *Digestae* of Justinian. This idea of the existence of an autonomous device to judge private interaction has intermittently held sway over contract. "The Western legal tradition still stands for the belief that so long as law remains autonomous, so long as it conforms to reason and morality . . . it will continue to be able to resolve individual and social conflicts."[12] The subjective approach failed to satisfy this tradition and its need for autonomous measurement. It was inevitable that objective manifestation would evolve to replace *consensus ad idem* as the touchstone of contractual liability.

A number of fundamental philosophical shifts have led to this secularization of the formalities of contract. A century-long evolution can be pointed to as providing the impetus for the evolution of consensual contract, objectively determined, as the core vehicle for obligation. The "decline in faith lessened the value attached to the ritual formalities,"[13] the secularization of law through the rise of the common law and the corresponding decline of the English ecclesiastical courts, and the resultant separation of church and state all played roles in this evolution. A number of nonreligious developments also helped precipitate the rise of the consensual contract. The dramatic rise of mass production, consumerism, and the modern market economy made it impractical for the parties to come together to perform the ritual formalities of the solemn contract. Practicality in a modern economy required that reasonable expectations in bilateral agreements be secured without the encumbrance of ritual formalities. Roscoe Pound noted that the "more highly specialized the division of labor the more each individual must be secured in the reasonable expectations involved in his relations with others."[14] A closely associated development was the political and economic rise of the importance of individual rights. John Locke and Adam Smith provided the words; the industrial revolution and the revolution of democracy provided the means by which the individual took center stage in the political, economic, and legal arenas.

The legal arena developed the machinery needed to allow the modern economy to function: the consensual contract. Businesspersons in the modern age needed to enter into bilateral agreements quickly with the expectation that they would create mutually binding and enforceable obligations.[15] Durkheim theorized that only something premised on the "psychological factor of the will or intention"[16] would be able to accomplish this need. In the religious reaches of contract it was the formula that controlled obligation. The consensual contract replaced the *rule of formula* with that of human will. Formality was no longer seen as an end but as a means to an end. The end was the finding and interpretation of the consensual wills.

The evolution of criminal law from that of absolute liability to the requirement of criminal intent was also heavily influenced by canon law. "The canonists had long insisted that the mental element was the real criterion of guilt and under their influence the conception of subjective blamesworthiness as the foundation of legal guilt"[17] began to evolve. In the area of contract the English ecclesiastical courts were the first to require the finding of a guilty state of mind in order to uphold the *sanctity of contracts*. Breach of a contractual promise was equated with the notion of sin. The importance of a guilty state of mind in the notion of the breach of contract as sin focused the lawgiver on the reality of the consent.[18]

The unity of religious and legal obligations was at its pinnacle during the Middle Ages.[19] During that period the Chancery Court preceded the common law in granting relief for a breach of contract. The equating of breach of promise to dishonesty in business "combined to give to contracts a measure of *religious blessedness* and to breaches of contract a mark of sinful or unethical aberration."[20] Thus, the ecclesiastical and Chancery Courts had already provided the basis for the evolution of the writ of *assumpsit* in the common law courts. The general premise of the morality of promise was the impetus for the common law's fabrication of a general remedy for breach of contract.

> The invocation of morality had the virtue of presenting a definition which was without a coherent competitor and which could be used to discipline a quantity of refractory precedent. It escaped serious challenge for a generation and was not expelled from the law until the middle of the nineteenth century. It was not surprising that contracts developed a juristic blessedness or halo and were so often regarded as sacred. Their sanctity is directly traceable to their early religious and ecclesiastical associations.[21]

The genesis of the reasonable person can be seen in the law's religious and magical ancestors. Saint Thomas Aquinas saw law as evolving from human reason. "Certain principles imprinted in human reason provide a general standard of measurement for everything human beings do."[22] One can see the reasonable person as the embodiment of human reason which is used as a measure of inappropriate behavior. Aquinas also saw the role of custom in the formation of laws. In *Summa Theologiae* he asserts that "law starts with what nature produces, then by use of reason certain things become customs, and finally things produced by nature and tested by custom are sanctified with the awe and religious weight of laws."[23] This notion of collectivity as reflected in custom imbued early juridical thought with the aura of divine sanctity. It was believed that "the judge transmitted to the people the will of the gods which became transformed into law, and that these laws sanction religious obligations."[24] The members of a community or a society were thought to have a *single consciousness*. The reasonable person can be seen as a modern version of this collective consciousness.[25]

The natural law theorists provide further support to the notion that the reasonable person's genesis was religiously based. Natural law theory holds that God has given all humans the ability to determine the rightness or wrongness of an action. The reasonable person is a reflection of the innate, rational person that exists in all of us. "Natural law holds that human beings are logical and reasonable creatures. Thus, the concept of the *reasonable person* has been a major guidepost for lawyers. Jurists perceive that human beings are autonomous and can choose rationally between courses of action, weighing costs, benefits, and sanctions."[26] The religious foundation of the reasonable person depicts her as not just a passive receptacle of community values. Instead, the religious reasonable person is somewhat of a zealot whose role is to advance legal and community values toward a divine ideal.[27]

PHILOSOPHICAL FOUNDATIONS

It is no surprise to proclaim that the dialectic stems from a philosophical base. Law is generally a product of philosophy. Jhering intimately connected law with that of general philosophy.[28] Much of contract theory has involved the search for a unifying philosophy that can explain and give meaning to all of contract law. A philosophy that objectifies all of contract would place fact patterns into existing decisional constructs. This codification of objectivity was championed in the twentieth century by Oliver Wendell Holmes. "He provided an apparently convincing demonstration that it was possible to reduce all principles of liability to a single, philosophically continuous series and to construct a unitary theory which would explain all conceivable single instances."[29] After the construction of this unitary theory, the courts had only to objectively slot each case into one of the existing constructs.

The objectivists' and subjectivists' battle for control of contract law can be traced to at least the sixteenth century when the "scholastics reorganized Roman Law around the concepts of Aristotle and Thomas Aquinas."[30] The re-examination of these concepts in the seventeenth century resulted in a doctrinal formulation based upon the "will theories of contract."[31] The subjective duty to be true to one's will as manifested in promise held sway until the rise to preeminence of the objective theory of contracts beginning in the nineteenth century. The shortcoming of the will theory had been its inability to explain why the will of the parties justified, by itself, the intervention of the courts. For example, why is the will to exchange morally different than the will to give? If the will as expressed in a promise is the basis for contractual obligation, then why does there have to be a communication and acceptance of that will?[32]

One explanation is evidentiary. The importance of the will in the creation of contracts is accepted by subjectivists and many objectivists. It is the problem of proof that has led to the rise of the reasonable person's reign over the realm of contractual interpretation. At first there was an attempt to reconcile the two approaches. The objective theory was offered as an evidentiary tool for proving the subjective will of the parties. Through a process of reasoning by analogy, objective manifestations could provide insight as to the actual state of mind of the contracting parties. This connection between the mental and the physical is known in philosophical terms as interactionism.[33] The Romans and subsequently Thomas Aquinas made their own attempts to solve the evidentiary dilemma. The Romans abandoned any hope of creating a general theory of contract. Instead, they embarked on the more mechanical effort embodied in the *categorization* of contracts. The Romans fashioned different laws of contracts around each of its different categories. Thus, a verbal contract was made enforceable by the expression of the *stipulatio* and the promise of a public donation, a *pollicitatio*, was also made an enforceable promise.

In the thirteenth century Thomas Aquinas categorized agreements based on their essences. This provided a vehicle to fill in the gaps in agreements through the implication of terms in order to conform the contract to its *essence*. A rationalization took hold that although the parties had not willed certain terms, they had willed a certain contractual relationship. This relationship in turn had a soul or essence by which questions of interpretation or enforcement could be judged.[34] This came to be an area of common ground between different theorists on different sides of the subjective-objective divide. "Both will theorists and moderate objectivists came to this position in the end."[35] This may be seen as the beginning of the demise of the promise and bargain principles of contract. Subjectivists would argue that the will as represented by promise was still the controlling force of contract; instead of a specific will as to a particular term. The term may still be implied within the confines of the will theory. The implication would be in conformity with the general will of the parties as represented by the type and the essence of the contract. In the 1889 case *The Moorcock* Lord Justice Bowen made the case for the will theory of implied terms. It is "the law raising an implication from the *presumed intention of the parties* with the object of giving to the transaction such efficacy as both parties must have intended."[36]

The counterargument is the implication of terms through the reasonable person. This can be seen primarily as the imposition of community standards and not necessarily a reflection of the general will of the contracting parties. Lord Denning recants the potential conflict between the implication of intent and the implication of the reasonable person standard. "Is it right only to imply a term when it is necessary to effectuate the intent of the parties or is it permissible to imply it when it is reasonable to do so in order to do what is fair and just between the parties?"[37] An attempt to rectify this conflict is what Lord Denning refers to as the doctrine of presumed intent. This doctrine presumes that the parties would have intended the implication of the term provided by the reasonable person.

The congruency between the implied intent of the parties and the reasonable person's intent is likely to increase proportionally with the parties' familiarity with community or trade standards. Assuming such knowledge, one may imply that the parties willed these standards into their contract. If these standards were unacceptable, then the parties would have opted out by fashioning specific contractual language to the contrary. The true test is when this objective will comes into conflict with the subjective will. The imposition of a term by the court inconsistent with the subjective will of the parties is a clear acknowledgment of the defeat of the will theory and the promise principle. The contract has moved from that of purely private law to a quasi-public domain. The contract comes to at least partially reflect what society believes is fair. There is a reading into the contract of terms that were not consciously willed by the parties. In fact, such terms may be inconsistent with their subjective wills.

One may complete the circular nature of the dialectic by completing the philosophical circle. First, we can begin with the doctrine of subjectivism in its purest form. Contracts were formed when there was a meeting of the minds. They were enforced purely in conformity to the subjective wills of the parties. As contracts began to grow in complexity and the role of the courts in contractual enforcement expanded, the evidentiary shortcomings of the subjective theory became more pronounced. At first the subjectivists were able to conform their will theory to the imposition of contractual terms through the bifurcation of will into specific and general wills. The specific will is reflected in the dickered, precise terms of the contract. The general will is reflected in the contractual type selected by the parties. Each contract type possesses an essence which is a metaphysical expression of the general will. The implication of terms is filling in the gaps of the contract in conformity with this general will. The philosophy of essence can be seen at work in the 1936 English case of *Tate & Lyle Ltd. v. Hain Steamship Co. Ltd.*[38] The case involved the contracting for a charterparty. The issue was whether a route deviation by the shipping company amounted to a material breach. Lord Atkin held that "any departure from the voyage contracted . . . is of such a serious character that the other party to the contract is entitled to treat it as going to the *root of the contract.*"[39] For the subjectivist, it is not a reflection of what the reasonable person would imply but is merely a further extension of the subjective will of the parties as interpreted through the essence of the contract.

The difficulty of determining the general will of the parties and the essence of the contract opened the door to the objective theory of contracts. The implication of will for terms never contemplated by the parties began to be discarded. External standards of fairness and reasonableness were substituted for the implied will of the parties. The movement toward the intent of the reasonable person represented a shift from the *is* of contract to the *ought*. The role of the court was no longer the discovery of the mystical will, it was the creation of a fair and reasonable contract. It was a movement from the covert to the overt, from passiveness to interventionism, and from implication to imposition.

The subjectivists were not without retort. For them the essence of contract was still will and promise. The reasonable person's authority to imply terms continued to derive from the will of the parties. The parties' general will controlled the court's interpretation and implication of nondickered terms. Due to the high transaction costs of quantifying all issues of negotiation, it can be implied that the parties intended that the reasonable person would salvage the essence of the contract through the imposition of unspecified terms. However, the divergence of intent and implication is limited by the fact that the general will of the parties as expressed by their selection of a specific normative relationship[40] is generally consistent with the default rules of contract as imposed through the reasonable person. This is the essence of the dialectic as used by many a practitioner of law and by philosophers from Socrates to Sir Thomas More.[41] Both the subjective and objective are required halves of any definitional undertaking.[42]

Another philosophical-based analysis revolves around theories of interpretation. Professor Greenawalt distinguishes between descriptive and normative theories of interpretation. He groups theological and legal interpretation together as essentially normative. One may take Greenawalt's analysis out of context and apply it, by analogy, to the objective theory of contracts. Since the objective theory is mainly descriptive in application, it focuses on what people actually do. The devices of custom and usage provide a descriptive base for contractual interpretation. These devices, along with the fabrication of the reasonable person, are applied through the mind of the judicial interpreter. "The interpreter typically will engage in some normative evaluation when aiming to provide a descriptive account"[43] of the contractual event. Thus, the reasonable person standard is both descriptive and normative in its affixation of meaning to the actions and statements of the two contracting parties. Its application to specific parties is both a confirmation of what they in fact intended to do and what society believes they should have done. In philosophical terms custom and trade usage can be connected to the notion of behaviorism. Behaviorism holds that "thoughts are tendencies to behave in certain ways, or dispositions to behave."[44] Businesspersons possess a tendency to behave in acceptable, uniform ways. These *ways* have been codified in a behavioral code, the customs and usages of their specific business or trade.

Durkheim's Objectivity and the Just Contract

Sociologist Émile Durkheim saw contractual obligation as historically embedded in external formality. He traced the development of consensual contract from its roots in Roman ceremonial formalism and the ritual contract of the Middle Ages. He asserts that the modern consensual contract is the culmination of an evolutionary process. Contract became increasingly a reflection of a dual objectivity, the objectivity of external consent and the objectivity of just exchange. "Just as the consensual emerged from the ritual contract, so a new form succeeded to the consensual. This is the contract of equity, that is, *objectively* equitable."[45] A contract that is consensual should be rendered unenforceable if it does not meet the dictates of equity as objectively determined.

The notion of just contract is consequentialist-based. There is an acknowledgment that the will of the parties as objectively formed is the starting point of contract. There is, however, a second analysis that has an impact on enforceability. This analysis stems from the influence of human sympathy[46] and the inability of humans to detach their sympathetic leanings from contractual obligation. "A just contract is not simply any contract that is freely consented to . . . it is a contract by which things and services are exchanged at the true and normal value, in short, at the just value."[47] If the values in the exchange are abhorrently divergent, then the sympathy factor would favor unenforcement in order to avoid unjust consequences. Durkheim's dual objectivity of mutual assent and objective justice can be placed within a school of thought that includes the *equality of exchange*[48] of nineteenth-century contract law and Professor Atiyah's *fairness of exchange*.[49] The dialectic's notion of just contract as being objectively based provides an interesting counterpoise to the general idea that sympathy is subjectively grounded. Durkheim asserts that there is an objective *scale of values* that can be used as a "touchstone by which the equity of exchanges is to be judged."[50] The judicial decision is to be premised on the notion of an objective scale of values. It is difficult, however, to see how the sympathetic urge is not subjectively influenced. It may be sufficient to acknowledge that contract enforcement is inherently influenced by the constructs of sympathy and justice. It is also important to acknowledge that the objectification of subjective impulses is unlikely to expunge the imprimatur of subjectivity from the contractual landscape. Instead, we should acknowledge that the law of contracts responds to behavior and conduct through its objective approach and that it responds to subjective elements through the human capacity to sympathize.[51]

PHILOSOPHY AND THE REASONABLE PERSON

In *The Problems of Philosophy* Bertrand Russell posed a pertinent question. "Is there any knowledge in the world which is so certain that no reasonable man could doubt it?" That is the pivotal tension between the objective and subjective poles of the dialectic. The objective theory is premised on the objectification of knowledge. There is an inverse relationship between the ability to objectify knowledge and the importance of subjectivity in contract law. Objectivity in contract is partially a subcomponent of the human search for certainty. Simplistic objective certainty is only an illusion; the search for truth is most often beset by complexity.[52] The objective and subjective approaches are to be viewed as checks upon one another to be used to unravel the complexities of human interaction. Like a good murder mystery, the apparent facts often do not add up to the correct conclusion. The subjective elements should be factored in with the objective in the search for the truth. Russell refers to this as the philosophical problem of distinguishing between appearance and reality. He illustrates this distinction by questioning our ability to determine the color of a table. We view the table and assume that it is uniformly the same color all over, a color upon which all reasonable persons would agree. The color perceived, however, is a function of both color and light. "It follows that if several people are looking at the table at the same moment, no two of them will see exactly the same distribution of colors, because no two can see it from exactly the same point of view."[53]

The dialectic is seen at work in the writings of Western philosophers. John Locke can be seen as a representative of the objective pole. As an empiricist, "Locke sought data outside of himself . . . he relied on experience instead of innate ideas, on induction more than on deduction."[54] Immanuel Kant had a subjectivist view when he perceived the reasonable person as embodied within the rational person existing in all of us. "He based his solutions on inner experience, on the subjective consciousness of duty or obligation."[55] To limit law and its application to one or the other of these poles is to limit the fulfillment of the law's goal, the discovery of truth. A purely objective reasonable person is still a diminishment of the complete human. The abstracting of a reasonable person from the manifestations of reality remains a facsimile of that reality. Detached objectivity provides insight into the truth, but should not be mistaken for the actual acquisition of truth. It is in the accommodation of subjectivity with the reasonable person standard that the gap between the apparent and the actual may most closely be bridged.[56]

The reasonable person can be seen as a creation of the general will. As such we can borrow from Hobbes's and Rousseau's notion of the social contract. As citizens of a society we have agreed to conform to its conventions. "Each one of us puts into the community his person, and his powers are put under the supreme direction of a general will."[57] The reasonable person is a convention that reflects the general will. Immanuel Kant provides another incarnation of the reasonable person, the impartial Spectator. The Spectator acts above the personal and emotional concerns of the populace. Like the reasonable person "he is a disinterested judge whose aim is to produce harmony among men."[58] To the degree that a contracting person conforms her conduct to the expression of the general will as reflected in the reasonable person, the greater is the likelihood that her conduct is morally correct.[59] Finally, we can look to John Rawls's veil of ignorance as a further philosophical foundation for the use of an impartial, reasonable person in the law.[60]

The reasonable person hides behind a cloak of anonymity applying community standards to prince and pauper alike.

Another faction of modern philosophy holds that objectivity is a myth. The subjectiveness of human perception cannot be divorced from the interpretation of objective facts. Professor Frug calls into question the philosophical soundness of a purely objective theory of contracts. Such a theory requires the treatment of facts "as something objective—as something available for a dispassionate, empirical discovery by a *factfinder*."[61] This is in contrast to the view that "one can never discover *facts* without simultaneously engaging in an act of interpretation."[62] The notion of objectiveness remains the paramount goal of contract law. The search for objectivity in contract is limited, however, by the infusion of the viewer's perspective.

The Psychological Dimension

Psychology informs us that the attachment of meaning to real-life events is a function of intent.[63] Importing meaning to a contract is an example of this intentional enterprise. The parties at the formation stage intend to negotiate a meaningful contractual relationship. The process of contractual interpretation is guided by the court's intent to give meaning to a transaction or relationship that is facially ambiguous. Because of the limits of human perception, the process of contractual interpretation is necessarily selective. The intent of the interpreter will determine the variables to which she turns her perception. "An intention is a turning of one's attention toward something. The selective . . . character of perception is one aspect of intentionality. We cannot see one thing without refusing to look at another."[64] The objectivity of contract is thus coupled with the subjectivity of interpretation. There is a binary relationship between the objective facts of a contract and how those facts are seen and interpreted by the parties and the courts. There is a "continuous reciprocal relationship between subject and object. Such is the amazing intimate interrelation of subjective experience and the objective world."[65] Our conception of contract will determine how we perceive specific contractual events or fact patterns.[66]

The importance of psychology to law's subjectivity and its objective manifestations was described by Pierre De Tourtoulan in his study of the *characteristics of juridical psychology*. "Law is a psychological product. If we abandon the attempt to study it through psychology, we abandon the attempt to understand its true nature in order to content ourselves with observing its various manifestations."[67] He elaborates on two important premises involving the interrelationship of law and psychology: the increased importance of psychological elements in the evolution of law; and the existence of multiple dimensions of psychological influences at the individual and collective levels.

There are similarities between the objective theory of contracts and its ancestral predecessors in religion, magic, and ritual. For instance, they all place a premium on objective manifestations. However, the ultraformalism of ancient ritual and dogma renders it a quite different form of objectivity. Its objectivity was one of simple application and not of substance. In contrast, the objective theory of contracts views external manifestation as a vehicle to interpreting underlying intent. The objective theory has not been immune to the influences of the sentiments of fairness and justice in the particular case. De Tourtoulan asserts that the secularization of religious ritual and the law has made the law more susceptible to subjective influences. "Legal systems influenced by dogma and ritualism are formalistic; on the other hand, those in which sentiment predominates are psychological and subjective."[68]

De Tourtoulan's second premise is that psychological influences upon the law work at both the individual and the collective levels. The notion of mutual assent is itself a collective concept. It is a melting of two separate belief systems. The court's goal is the uncovering of this collective consciousness. Its interpretive tools of prior dealings, usage, language, and custom are products of an even larger group consciousness. The wills of the contracting parties are thus transplanted by the will of the collective.[69] Contract law as represented by its rules, its institutions, and its lawmakers is a product of a process of socialization. Psychologist Henry Murray speaks of the complexity of individuality in terms of *personology*. It can be ventured that lawyers and judges are generally successful, well-socialized individuals. Part and parcel to this well-socialized personology is the need for *roleship*. The mind-set of those who create contract law causes them to see themselves as fulfilling well-defined, accepted roles such as lawyer *qua* lawyer, judge *qua* judge. It is in these preconceived roles that the judge or lawyer conforms to the decrees of society and feels a belonging to a functioning group.[70]

Many of the terms found in the psychological field pertaining to perception and representation are applicable by analogy to contractual practice. Terms such as iconic memory, masking, imagery, symbolization, coding, and representation are applicable to the transformation of doctrine into practice. Many of the thematic symbols of contract can be seen as iconic images. Once learned, these icons of contract continue to render a strong *afterimage* in the judicial mind. Freedom of contract, *consensus ad idem*, infant incapacity, bad faith, and unconscionability are but a few of the iconic images of contracts. Once brought to the conscious mind they trigger preconceived bundles of beliefs and rationales that are brought to bear upon the impending legal issue. Masking is the process in which "perceptions continue although external stimulation has ceased."[71] A type of legal masking exists in the learning and application of contract law. The complexity and expansiveness of contracts require the legal mind to order the acquisition of doctrinal knowledge and application along channels already existing in its thought processes.[72]

Imagery is the fuel of the judicial hunch. Legal imagery is acquired through the lawyers' indoctrination into the law beginning in law school and continuing into practice. The size and growth of law prohibits the practitioner from ever knowing the law. The tools of imagery, analogue, coding, and symbolization are used subconsciously to bring coherence to the large body of subject matter. The law becomes a system of symbols which are used as organizational tools. These symbols include the rationales of autonomy, justice, compensation, security, and certainty. The doctrines of contract law can be viewed as facades or symbols for large bodies of knowledge and experience. Through the technique of symbolization the practitioner and the judge structure its content into a functional form.

On the psychological level at which the dialectic is played out one finds the internal perception of what the law is and the ability to communicate that perception. "The objects perceived are external to the observer and so are consensually reportable; their perception is internal and private. The problem is to find a way of correlating these symbols in personal experience with the objects attributed to the world external to the perceiver."[73] The dialectic can be seen as a coding system for ordering the external world of contracts. If the law is viewed as *object*, then the benefits of psychological research can be utilized to better understand the mechanics of the dialectic.[74]

The relationship of group psychology and the law is evident in the common law doctrine of stare decisis. The individual judge feels the pull of two groups in his or her implementation of a rule of precedent. First, fellow judges will criticize a departure from precedent without proper justification. Second, litigants enter the legal arena with the expectation that the law will maintain a certain degree of certainty, stability, and predictability. Judges have a "psychological need to satisfy reasonable expectations."[75] The legal definition of stare decisis is a static one. The decision of a court is binding precedent in courts of equal or lower rank.[76] In practice the following of precedent is more technique than reality. It is less a straight-forward application of existing rules than the innovative use of various rules of precedential value to justify a decision. Courts are compelled to recognize past decisions and to justify departures from them, but the constraint of precedent is more elastic than its legal definition would indicate. The subjectivity of stare decisis in practice belies the objectivity of its definition.[77]

Despite the relevancy of psychological insight, the relationship between psychology and law has been demonstratively hostile. The basis of this conflict is the perceived divergence of the two disciplines' philosophical underpinnings.

Psychology and law are often in conflict. Law is deductive, psychology is inductive; law is doctrinal, psychology is empirical. Common law prefers decisions easily justified to a public that sees courts as having a limited role in making policy. Judges, therefore, show decided preference for custom and history. Psychological science tends to pay much less attention to historical precedents; its acceptability to courts, for these and other reasons, is somewhat tentative.[78]

For the psychologist, the law's characterization of itself as objective in theory and in application is more fiction than fact. In turn it can be argued that the ad hoc objectiveness of the psychological sciences poses a threat to the law's adherence to precedent on one hand and to its flexibility in rendering justice in a particular case.[79] The heightened objectiveness represented by the use of psychology in the law further limits the discretionary aspects of the legal system. Nonetheless, if the law is to be true to its self-proclaimed creed of objectivity, it will have to continue to incorporate the *work products* of applied psychology and the other social sciences.

THE JUDICIAL MIND AND THE REASONABLE PERSON

The reasonable person is intimately connected with the judicial mind. For it is in that mind that the reasonable person is concocted. The parameters of reasonableness are formed within the judge's mind. These parameters play the predominant role in the eventual resolution of a case. It is the discretionary venue of what Professor Gilmore labeled "the arrogance of unlimited power by the judges."[80] In *Swift v. Tyson*[81] Judge Story laid the basis for objectiveness in relationship with the subjectiveness of *judge as legislator*. Judge as legislator can be seen as the not-so-conscious interconnection of private law with public law. It is what has been referred to as the policy-oriented approach[82] to commercial law stemming from Story's unhatching of the doctrine of a general commercial law.[83] This federal commercial law in Story's eyes would look outside of the case at bar to its greater repercussions. To borrow from German jurisprudence, the courts' decisions would be consequential-based. "It should take into account the social and economic consequences of its decisions."[84] It is an expanded utilitarian analysis with the teleological lens expanded beyond party-specific consequences. This policy-oriented mind-set mandates greater judicial discretion. This greater discretion is a strong ally of subjectivity as constituted in the judicial mind.

This expanded role of private law can be seen in the jurisprudence of Justice Holmes.[85] There is, however, a reversal of the causal flow. In the policy-oriented approach the subjective assessment of a decision's impact on society exists as an input into the decision. In Holmes's *community-dictated* approach the assessment is objectively based. The role of judge and of the law is to objectively determine the dictates of the community and to apply them to the case. It is the rule of the majority as determined by the majority. In the event that the rule served an injustice upon the minority, it was for the majority, not the courts, to rectify its demands. This approach places the role of the judge into a cold, objective world. The progress of the law is measured by its ability to reach a set of legal rules "in which liability . . . will be governed by formal, external, and objective standards."[86] Justice Holmes can be seen as the patron saint of the dialectic's objective pole.

It can be argued that the law as a man-made invention is inherently subjective. The law is simply what a particular judge interprets it to be at any moment in time. This is both correct and incorrect.[87] Law can be viewed as having a subjective core encased within the parameters of objectivity. Professor Frug differentiates two aspects of our legal system—the inherited and the constructed. "Legal decision-makers operate within a legal system that they both inherit and construct. The fact that they inherit it means that their decisions cannot adequately be understood as subjective, and the fact that they construct it means that their decisions cannot adequately be understood as objective."[88] The inherited and constructed aspects of our legal system ensure that objectivity and subjectivity will continue to characterize the relationship between the lawgivers and the legal system.

Owen Fiss defines the art of interpretation as the "proper recognition of both the objective and subjective dimensions of human experience."[89] The judicial mind is in a constant state of interpretation and the adjudicative process is itself a form of interpretation.[90] It is within the judicial mind as interpretive agent for the adjudicative process that both the subjective and objective elements of contract are to be understood. Fiss's major contribution is the idea that judges are part of an interpretive community[91] that influences each judge's interpretive processes. Each judge's subjective nature is constrained by institutional rules found within the judicial community and within the institution of law. Fiss recognizes that there are both objective and subjective influences on judicial interpretation. The subjective element is represented by the personal role played by the judicial interpreter. The objective element or constraint is grounded in an intersubjective meaning provided by the interpretive community.[92] Fiss' model of judicial interpretation is one of *bounded objectivity* in which the constraints of institutional rules (rules of contract interpretation) and of the community of judges act to "transform the interpretive process from a subjective to an objective one."[93] Pierre De Tourtoulan, some seventy years ago, asserted that the making of law was a phenomenon of both individual and collective psychology. Lawmakers are undoubtedly influenced by a collective consciousness involving the community of law and society in general.[94]

6

LAW OF SATISFACTION

The question is how one can include in the objective world a mental substance having subjective properties?[1]

This book has focused on objectification of contract law and how it has been applied
to contractual ambiguity. The implication of mutual assent has been examined in a
number of common scenarios. The classical element of contractual intent to be legally
bound is implied through the parties' manifestations of intent.[2] The reasonable person is
also used to imply terms in order to salvage the efficacy of a contract.[3] This is the situation where the parties exhibit manifestations of a general intent to be bound but fail to
communicate an essential term into the contract. The reasonable person through both its
common law[4] and codified forms is used to supply a reasonable or customary term.[5]

The objectification of contracts has reached beyond the clarification or interpretation
of ambiguity or the filling of gaps. For instance, what course will a court take when
relief is sought from an express clause that is at odds with what would be provided by
the reasonable person? A common example is when two parties expressly agree that the
one's performance will be judged solely upon the subjective satisfaction of the other
party. The reciprocal consideration is not triggered unless that satisfaction is obtained.
Will the courts uphold such satisfaction clauses in face of the hardship that may result
from their enforcement? Or will the court impose an interpretation contrary to the
expressed intent of the parties? A review of the law of satisfaction will provide some
insight into these questions.

THE "LAW OF SATISFACTION" AND THE OBJECTIVE THEORY OF CONTRACTS

Express subjective satisfaction clauses pose a quagmire for the realm of objectivity. To
uphold such a clause is an affront to the reasonable person and to community standards

of reasonableness. Satisfactory performance is a norm of contract that applies to all contractual obligations.[6] The issue becomes to whose satisfaction should the performance be judged? The law's preferred response is that good faith, reasonable performance requires reciprocal performance. Satisfaction should be what a reasonable person would accept as satisfactory. This notion of satisfaction pervades our common law. It can be seen in the rise of the doctrine of substantial performance[7] and in the notion of reasonable commercial standards.[8]

The quagmire is that the courts are technically prevented from applying such objectivity in the face of an express contractual term sanctioning the subjective. The objective theory of contracts holds that the court is to interpret a contract based on the manifestations of mutual assent. In the case of an express satisfaction clause this manifestation clearly indicates that performance and breach are to be determined by the subjective will of one of the parties. Theoretically, the objective theory would dictate that such a promisee could reject a good faith, reasonable performance based on her own subjective standards. In practice, however, one cannot be certain of the judicial enforcement of a negotiated satisfaction clause. English law places an obligation to not only accept a good faith performance but also to accept a good faith attempt at the mitigation of a breach of performance. "Good faith requires that a genuine and reasonable offer to mitigate the breach should be accepted."[9] The reasonableness of the offer to mitigate is to be objectively determined.[10] In determining good faith conduct the objectivity of custom and usage is to be considered.[11] Satisfaction in the sale of goods is generally regarded as being responsive to objective quantification.

Satisfaction clauses have commonly been divided along the lines of subject matter. A satisfaction clause within a commercial contract will generally be judged on an objective standard.[12] Contracts dealing with factors of "fancy, taste, or judgment"[13] are generally held to "a *subjective* test of honest satisfaction."[14] The *Second Restatement* gives an illustration of a court being required to accept a subjective test. An artist is commissioned to paint a portrait to the personal satisfaction of a party. The party rejects the portrait for no apparent reason and "according to experts the portrait is an admirable work of art."[15] The *Second Restatement* concludes that the artist would have no legal recourse since "it is not practicable to apply an objective test."[16]

The following examples make it clear that the line between the use of the subjective or the objective standard is often blurred. In the seminal case of *Mattei v. Hopper*,[17] which invited the use of the objective approach, the court's decision rested upon the use of a subjective standard. A contract was premised on the evaluation of commercial leases by the prospective purchaser. The ability to procure commercial leases and the sufficiency of such leases would seem to be conducive to a purely objective analysis. The availability of readily available leasing information, expertise, customs, practices, and guidelines would allow the court to create a reasonably prudent, sophisticated lessor. Instead the court held that the evaluation of real estate leases was unique enough to call for the allowance of a subjective determination, whether reasonable or not. The court used a person- or buyer-specific criteria in upholding the prospective purchaser's right to reject the leases based upon her sole discretion. The ability of a subjective standard to preempt the law's preference for reasonableness[18] was clearly stated in *Beasley v. St. Mary's Hosp. of Centralia*.[19] "Where . . . a contract incorporates a subjective satisfaction standard, the objective reasonableness of the obligee's performance is *not* dispositive."[20] *Forman v. Benson* clearly broached the line between the purely subjective[21] and satisfaction that is capable of objective evaluation.[22] "It is clear that the parties may agree to a reservation in one party of the absolute and unqualified freedom of choice on a matter *not* involving fancy, taste, or whim."[23] Professor Wiesner poses a similar question in analyzing judicial interpretations of technical and performance specifications expressed in contracts. "Does the law enforce the seller's candid and explicit promise that the entire risk of satisfying the buyer's objectives regarding the use of the contracted for product rest with the seller?"[24] His analysis of the law leads to an interesting conclusion. "At first one may point to the freedom of contract doctrine and say yes. But this would be incorrect."[25] The subjectiveness of satisfaction clauses continues to be a stage for the acting out of the subjective-objective dialectic.

FREEDOM OF CONTRACT AND THE PRESUMPTION OF REASONABLENESS

Homage is often paid to freedom of contract before it is disregarded in the process of reforming a contract. In *Morin Bldg. Products Co. v. Baystone Const.*,[26] the seventh circuit court visits the altar of freedom of contract. "Lest this conclusion be thought to strike at the foundations of freedom of contract . . . if it appeared . . . that the parties really intended one to have the right to reject . . . for failure to satisfy her private aesthetic taste, the rejection would have been proper even if unreasonable."[27] The court then rejects the clear and plain meaning of the satisfaction clause at issue in favor of a presumption of reasonableness. "The presumption is that the performing party would not have wanted to put himself at the mercy of the paying party's whim."[28] This judicial reformation or interpretation of intent is another example of *ex fictione juris*.[29] In essence, the court weaves a fiction that what the contracting parties clearly *presentiated* is not what they intended.

In *Misano di Navigazione SpA. v. U.S.*[30] the court fabricates a creative slant by overlaying a modified objective intent upon a clearly manifested subjective intent. The reasoning used by the court was that the promisor possessed two subjective intents, one manifested in the acceptance of the satisfaction clause and the real one regarding the future interpretation of that clause. Although the promisor understands the meaning of the clause, she projects a different meaning into the future. The promisor is presumed to have believed that a subject to satisfaction clause would be enforced only by a court after a determination of the reasonableness of the promisee's rejection. The belief is that if a performance is one for commercial or consumer goods or services, then satisfaction will be determined by customary or community standards of reasonableness.[31]

The rue that the objective theory is an attempt to give life and meaning to the external manifestations of the contracting parties is exposed when one studies the law of satisfaction. Such a study reveals a duality within the objective theory of contracts. The dual formulations are the viewing of manifestations to discern intent and the communal objectivity of what is fair and just given the circumstances of the case. These different views of objectivity are at times at odds. This conflict is most apparent in the area of subjective satisfaction clauses. The temptation to disregard clear contractual intent (contractual objectivity) in favor of *ex post* reformation in order to render a fair result (communal objectivity) is great.[32] This inherent conflict between freedom of contract mandates and judicial interventionism in the name of contractual fairness is often cloaked in the ancient device of the judicial or legal fiction. Judge Jerome Frank states that "anyone can see who reads the large number of cases . . . the numerous intricate methods of getting around the objective theory."[33] One such method is the outward acceptance of subjective satisfaction clauses while at the same time evaluating their applications objectively.

Subjective Satisfaction and Objective Dissatisfaction

A number of courts have recognized the power of parties to agree to a subjective standard while at the same time judging the rejecting party's dissatisfaction through an objective gaze. This objective safeguard upon the application of subjective satisfaction is often framed in terms of good faith or honest dissatisfaction. Some courts have applied the safeguard without acknowledging its objectivity. "Under the law of satisfaction contracts, the party to whom performance is rendered may reject if his dissatisfaction is *genuine*. There is no objective standard. The relevant inquiry is not whether he ought to have been satisfied, but whether he was satisfied."[34]

How does a court determine if the dissatisfaction was in fact one of good faith? It generally will determine good or bad faith based on objective or community standards. Comment *a* of section 205 of the *Second Restatement* defines good faith performance as excluding "a variety of types of conduct characterized as involving *bad faith* because they violate *community standards* of decency, fairness or reasonableness."[35] *The Uniform Commercial Code* defines good faith as "honesty in fact and the observance of *reasonable commercial standards* of fair dealing."[36] Courts have worked under an illusion or fiction in believing that the subjective sanctity of satisfaction clauses may be maintained while at the same time filtering its judgment through the objective lens of good faith.

In *Larwin-Southern Cal., Inc. v. JGB Inv.*[37] the court also faced the dilemma of validating the clear intent of the contract while attempting to prevent capriciousness on the part of the dissatisfied party. The case involved a typical development land purchase contract that provided contingencies based on the results of the purchaser's engineering and feasibility studies. The contract provided that the studies' conclusions were to be judged upon the purchaser's subjective satisfaction. "Buyer's approvals provided for in this contract may be given or withheld in its *sole judgment and discretion.*"[38] A clearer statement of contractual intent would be difficult to find.[39] Nonetheless, the court tempered the clear intent with "an implied duty of good faith."[40] The rationale given was that a party should not be able to avoid a bad bargain under the rue of dissatisfaction with an otherwise satisfactory performance. The difference between honest, subjective dissatisfaction and reasonable dissatisfaction is often missed in the enforcement decision. Given the rationale for implying "good faith" or "honest dissatisfaction," the subjective state of mind of the party exercising her right of dissatisfaction becomes the operative factor.

In reality, the courts have generally applied an objective standard of good faith. "The expression of dissatisfaction must be genuine and not arbitrary, and that an *objective criterion of good faith* controls the exercise of the right to determine satisfaction."[41] This philosophy in favor of objectivity was succinctly stated by Judge Frank some fifty years ago. "Advocacy of the 'objective' standard in contracts appears to have represented a desire for legal symmetry, legal uniformity, a desire seemingly prompted by aesthetic impulses."[42] That impulse is magnified in cases where an objective standard is readily available. This factor was not lost on the court in *Misano di Navigazione* when it noted that "a definite objective test of satisfaction is available."[43] This evidentiary rationale for the difficulty of assessing the subjective is somewhat disingenuous. Much of law is given to the task of *proving* a party's or a defendant's state of mind.[44] Borrowing a term from conflicts of law, the courts are pursuing a *renvoi.*[45] They are cloaking subjective satisfaction under the garb of objectivity in order to mask their disdain for subjective standards.[46]

The difference in approach was evident in *Ricketts v. Pennsylvania R. Co.*[47] which questioned the validity of a release signed by an injured railroad worker who had been represented by an attorney. The worker subjectively believed that he was signing a release of a claim for wages. In fact, it was a general release precluding any future claim for personal injuries. Judge Learned Hand held that the release was invalid, resorting to the law of agency for justification. "An attorney has no implied authority to compromise a claim."[48] The objective theory of contracts in its purest form would conclude otherwise.

Willistonian objectivity would conclude that "a document binds one who signs it, but who does not read it, because objectively he accepts it whatever may be its contents."[49] Professor Fried would likely argue for enforcement of the release under his formulation of the promise principle.[50] The signing of a release while being represented by an attorney is a paradigmatic use of the convention of promise warranting a legal and moral obligation to be bound.

> There exists a convention that defines the practice of promising and its entailments. This convention provides a way that a person may create expectations in others. By virtue of the basic Kantian principles of trust and respect, it is wrong to invoke that convention in order to make a promise, and then to break it.[51]

Jerome Frank offers one way to reconcile the objective theory's mandate and the injustice that would result in upholding that mandate by enforcing the release agreement. He explains how Williston, the patron saint of the objectivist, reconciled the contrary leanings of objectivity and fairness in a given case. "Williston takes a position . . . which seems highly casuistical . . . since equity departs from the objective appearance, the objective theory . . . cannot be said to be consistently applied in our legal system. It is far more helpful to acknowledge frankly that there exist important exceptions to that theory."[52] This is the type of application of the general rule of law against which Kant warned.

KANT'S CONCEPTION OF LAW

Kant believed that the inclination to ensure fairness or to prevent injustice by creating an exception to a general rule should be avoided.[53] He argued against the illusion of doing justice in a given case in his *Foundations of the Metaphysics of Morals*.

> A natural *dialectic* which arises, i.e., a propensity to argue against the stern laws of duty and their validity, or at least to place their purity and strictness in doubt and, where possible, to make them more accordant with our wishes and inclinations. This is equivalent to corrupting them in their very foundations and destroying their dignity—a thing which even common practical reason cannot ultimately call good.[54]

One can understand Fried's discovery of a Kantian basis for the convention of promise as the basis for contractual obligation. A rational being should be held accountable for her promissory actions. This is based on a unifying conception of the law that obedience to law is itself an ultimate good. "The only object of respect is law, and indeed only the law which we impose on ourselves and yet recognize as necessary in itself."[55] Exceptions to the enforceability of one's obligatory duties are anathema to this conception of law. The perceived negative effects of applying a rule in a given situation are considered a necessary evil in the quest for systemic and societal justice. Kant explains the conflict between individual justice and systemic justice by way of a dichotomy in which there are two worlds—the world of the sense and the rational world. The rational world forsakes the consequences of an action in order to preserve the categorical nature of duty. The world of the sense is tempted to ignore the greater duty in order to prevent the personal hardship at hand. This world of the sense is anathema to Kantian ethics. Kant displays a firm belief in the objective world.

> I recognize myself qua intelligence as subject to the law of the world of understanding and to the autonomy of the will . . . I recognize myself as subject to the law of reason which contains in the idea of freedom of the law of the intelligible world, while at the same time I must acknowledge that I am a being which belongs to the world of the sense. Therefore, I must regard the laws of the intelligible world as imperatives for me, and actions in accord with this principle as duties. . . . Thus categorical imperatives are possible because the idea of freedom makes me a member of an intelligible world.[56]

I would argue that this dichotomy is analogous to the dialectic. Replacing the word subjective for the word sense and the word objective for intelligible provides a sensible statement of the dialectic and of the objective theory of contracts. A rational being is one who acts and decides based on an absolute conception of law. The rationalism of the objective theory of contracts can find much grounding in this moral philosophy. The ad hoc inquiry required for an analysis of the subjective intentions of each party finds little support in Kant's conception of law as absolute in obedience and in application. This conception of law is objectivity magnified. For Kant compliance with the law was the ultimate object. "Act according to maxims which can at the same time have themselves as universal laws of nature as their object."[57] Objective compliance with the law is the ultimate guide to legal and moral obligation. Justice Cardozo echoes Kantian objectivism. "If we were to consider only the individual instance, we might be ready to release the promisor. We look beyond the particular to the universal, and shape our judgment in obedience to the fundamental interest of society that contracts shall be fulfilled."[58] This somewhat begs the question of the dialectic. Cardozo is operating under the assumption that a contract is in hand. The dialectic focuses primarily on the issue of whether a contract is in existence, but, the dialectic need not be construed so narrowly. It plays an important role in the interpretation and the construction of the terms of a contract.

97

In reality, judges have not been willing to abandon justice in a particular case or to ignore the subjective elements of a case. In the landmark case of *Ricketts v. Pennsylvania R. Co.* Judge Frank declared that "courts not infrequently have departed from the objective theory when necessary to avoid what they have considered an unfair decision."[59] He takes both objectivists and subjectivists to task for extremism. Judge Frank argues that both approaches in their purest forms were based on judicially and scholarly created fictions. The objectivists believed that subjectivity "would destroy that legal certainty and stability which a modern commercial society demands."[60] They then attempted to apply the abstraction of the reasonable person to "virtually all the varieties of contractual arrangements in the same way."[61] The subjectivist, on the other hand, irrationally attempted to apply the subjective meeting of the minds principle to all contractual disputes. "The *actual intent* theory induced much fictional discourse which imputed to the parties intentions they plainly did not have."[62] Between the extremes of pure objectivity and pure subjectivity we find the dialectic. The doctrine of substantial performance is an example of judicial modification of the objective theory. Equity has been superimposed over objective legality in order that justice, as subjectively determined by the courts, may be done.

THE DOCTRINE OF SUBSTANTIAL PERFORMANCE

Under a strictly objective approach to law, a reciprocal performance would be discharged in the event that the first performing party does not render a complete performance. This straight-forward, strict approach was adopted in principle by the *Uniform Commercial Code*. Often referred to as the perfect tender rule it allows for a rejection of goods delivered "if the goods or the tender of delivery fail *in any respect* to conform to the contract."[63] This definition of nonperformance is administered easily under the objective theory. Akin to the strict compliance principle in the area of negotiable instruments, one need only compare, coldly and objectively, the terms of the contract to the performance rendered. Any discrepancy, no matter how small, dictates a verdict of nonperformance. Good faith and materiality become nonfactors in this regime of pure objectivity. This harsh rule can be traced to the English courts of the nineteenth century. Their rationale for the rule was simple: all terms in merchant contracts are considered to be material. The English courts took the view that "merchants attached value and importance to every item in the contract."[64]

The roots of the doctrine of substantial performance may be found in the development of the notion of good faith in canon law and in the equity courts. "The canon law development of good faith and conscience enabled the royal justices to give practical effect to vague equitable ideas which existed from the beginning of the common law."[65]

The strictness of *pacta sunt servanda* eventually became tempered by the doctrines of good faith and substantial performance. The common law came to the view that it was "unfair to deprive the other party of his entire entitlement because of some minor defects in his performance."[66] The objectivity of good faith and substantial performance replaced the objectivity of absolute obligation.

The doctrine of substantial performance has held a strong foothold in the area of nonsale contracts. It requires a more in-depth, discretionary inquiry by the court. The court must determine whether the breaching party had rendered substantial performance. There first has to be an objective determination regarding the type of performance intended by the parties and their contract. If such intent is unclear, then an analysis of substantiality is precluded. Substantial performance can be measured only if there is a determination of expected performance to judge it against.[67] If such intent is manifested, then an objective inquiry of substantiality is to be undertaken. Justice Cardozo states that "the line to be drawn between the important and the trivial cannot be settled by a formula."[68] The *Second Restatement* frames the inquiry in terms of the notion of materiality. It does not distinguish, per se, substantial performance as a separate category within the performance-nonperformance spectrum.[69] Instead, the consequences of breach are determined by a factual analysis of materiality.

The doctrine of substantial performance as well as the determination of materiality can be seen as equitable moves away from the pure objectivity of perfect tender. Both substantiality and materiality possess ingredients of objectivity and subjectivity. The *Restatement* lists a number of circumstances that are significant in determining whether a failure is material.[70] It is generally framed as a reasonable person analysis. The circumstances are stamped with the sign of reasonableness. The court is to look at the extent to which the nonbreaching party is "deprived of the benefit which he *reasonably* expected, to the extent that he can be *adequately* compensated," and the likelihood of full performance "including any *reasonable* assurances."[71] Materiality is not simply a mathematical notion of the attainment of a certain portion of performance. Proportionality of performance is to be measured against the backdrop of the intent and purpose of the contract.[72]

The subjective element is introduced by way of factoring in the breaching party's state of mind. The state of mind component converts the materiality analysis into a two-step process. First, the court focuses on the performance itself in deliberating upon materiality. Second, the focus shifts to the state of mind of the breaching party to determine if her behavior comports to standards of good faith and fair dealing.[73] This provision was a conscious attempt by the *Restatement* writers to distance themselves from the subjectively based concept of willfulness found in the *First Restatement*. The focus shifted from the person's subjective state of mind to the objective good faith of her behavior. The innocence of the breacher's state of mind was converted to a mere factor in the determination of materiality. The *Second Restatement* fails to adequately explain just what impact the willfulness of the breaching party's behavior has on materiality. I submit that the subjective state of mind of the breaching party remains a potentially independent obstacle to the defense of substantial performance. Independent of materiality, the notion of willfulness continues to play a role in the common law's substantial performance doctrine. "Substantial performance will be found where there is an *honest* and good faith performance and no *willful* departure from or omission of the essential parts of the contract."[74]

In the 1888 case of *Gillespie Tool Co. v. Wilson* the court placed the onus upon the breaching party to prove nonwillfulness. "It is incumbent on him who invokes the protection of substantial performance to present a case in which there has been no willful departure from the terms of the contract."[75] In short, a person substantially performing cannot benefit from the doctrine if the minor breach was willful. The sharpness of this rule of subjective innocence has been somewhat dulled over the years. Nonetheless, equity's concern for purity of mind and intent prevents the complete extinguishment of the subjective element in the substantial performance doctrine. A corollary dialectic stemming from the historical duality of law and equity has long been recognized. The rationale for the stern use of the rule of law was the advancement of the norms of certainty, generality, and predictability. Equitable doctrines such as substantial performance have been employed to advance the norms of fairness and justice on an ad hoc basis. The harshness of rules has provided the organic material that the courts have used to fashion countervailing or limiting principles to mitigate the effects of law's generality. The objectivity of law has been intertwined with the subjectivity of equity since the days of the dual English court systems of law and chancery.

7

THE REALITY OF INTENT

Everything that is thought and expressed in words is one-sided, only half the truth; it all lacks totality, completeness, unity.[1]

A number of per se rules have truncated the legal reasoning process pertaining to certain classes of individuals. Intent, whether subjectively or objectively determined, is disregarded because of the historical evolution of common law rules removing the importance of the subjective-objective dialectic. Common law doctrine provides a predetermined edict for the issue of contractual consent. Certain select groups are conclusively presumed to lack the capacity to create contractual obligations. Proof of subjective intent to create legal obligations is regarded as irrelevant. The intent of an infant or a lunatic is considered to be misinformed and ill-conceived. The party is considered to lack the capacity to fully comprehend the gravity and meaning of the proposed contractual obligations. This *non compos mentis*[2] argument has lost its vitality over time. The categories listed within the law of incapacity have been significantly narrowed. The notion that these parties possess "disabilities" that render them incapable of forming consensual intent has increasingly been banished as a common law relic. For example, the law of incapacity once included married women[3] and prisoners.[4] The doctrine of capacity rendered these large segments of the population *civiliter mortuus*.[5] These categories have been returned to the mainstream of common law capacity, such parties are presumed to have the capacity to contract. This presumption is rebuttable by objective proof of incapacity.

Two areas of incapacity will be addressed to determine if they can be aligned with the objective-subjective dialectic. The infancy law doctrine remains a common law affront to the reasonable person standard. The soundness of its theoretical basis along with its practical import needs to be re-examined. The doctrine of economic duress is of more recent vintage.[6] Its practical import seems to be on the rise. More important, its theoretical underpinnings are aligned with the mainstream workings of the dialectic.

101

THE INFANCY LAW DOCTRINE

The infancy law doctrine holds that minors do not possess the required contractual capacity to be bound under the law of contracts.[7] The law of capacity mandates that certain contracts are to be rendered void or voidable. Infancy, insanity, and intoxication have all been given as grounds to rebut the general presumption in favor of capacity. Capacity is often regarded as a separate element in classical contracts' litany of requirements. One may argue that it is a component or factor in the determining of contractual intent. If one of the parties lacked the mental capacity to formulate the required intent, then there can be no mutual assent to create a legally binding contract. The general rule of law is that "an infant has not the capacity to bind herself . . . since any contract made by her during infancy may be avoided."[8] Objective reasoning aside, the "common law's view has traditionally been that children are naive and unsophisticated, especially in the marketplace."[9] The likelihood of the doctrine to work injustice, along with its affront to the objective theory of contract, has increasingly been noted. Professor Mehler summarizes the criticism of the doctrine:

> The minor has long remained a special charge of the law. But in our fast-moving and rapidly changing society, the ancient timeworn cloak of protection thrown over him has long since lost its real need or useful purpose. The technologically oriented and knowledgeably mature youth of our hectic age is not at all comparable to the minor of even five or six decades ago who needed the solicitous attention and protection the law so thoughtfully afforded him.[10]

This artificial preclusion of the finding of contractual intent is antithetical to the public policy rationales represented by the notion of freedom of contract. In his commentary on the *Second Restatement* Professor Braucher noted the growing importance of freedom of contract. "[T]he most noticeable shift . . . is the increased respect accorded to freedom of contract—to the power of the contracting parties to control the rights and duties they create."[11] This divergence between law as taught and law in practice is further illustrated by the infancy law doctrine. The right of disaffirmance[12] as taught in our law schools has increasingly had little practical import in the billion dollar juvenile marketplace. Roscoe Pound foresaw this type of divergence: "A jurisprudence of conceptions . . . grew up as a result of which the law in its application was out of accord with life and a gulf arose . . . between teaching and practice."[13] This divergence between the "real world" of contractual capacity and its theoretical jurisprudence provides a framework for studying the subjective-objective dialectic.

How can per se exceptions to the capacity to consent be justified under the objective theory of contracts? How has the infancy law doctrine been doctrinally aligned in the face of our jurisprudence of enforceability? Contract theory has uniformly sanctioned the enforcement of obligations incurred through the contractual process of mutual assent. The classical theory of contract as embodied in the bargain or will theory holds that an agreement involving the mutual assent of two parties is the type "for the breach of which the law gives a remedy."[14] An exception to this formula is where one of the parties is not in possession of legal capacity. Willistonian formalism reasons that since a minor lacks such capacity, then, by definition, there can be no contract.[15] *Forma non observata, infertur admullatio actus.*[16] Since the classical formula is unsatisfied, judicial reasoning and an analysis into the "equities" of the transaction would be misplaced. An analysis of the equities would likely entail the fabrication of the reasonable minor possessing the qualities of the minor seeking to disaffirm her contract. This objective analysis would be consistent with our current jurisprudence.

The Objectification of the Infancy Law Doctrine

The formalism of the infancy law doctrine began to weaken in the face of an objective onslaught. The inherent injustice and unfairness of such formalized generalization began to be questioned as too high a price for the doctrine's protective shield. "Shall its sanctity be preserved when justice obviously requires a remedy for the victims?"[17] The divergence between doctrine as taught and as practiced is fully revealed in the law of infant incapacity. It has been preserved in the cloistered domain of black letter law. In reality it has been dismantled piece by piece by twin adversaries: the courthouse and the statehouse. The right of disaffirmance has been judicially limited by the creation of an assortment of subdoctrines intended to mollify the harsh effects of the per se rule. The proliferation of statutory preemption of the doctrine has been even more profound.

The Judicial Assault

Lord Mansfield opened the floodgates with the enunciation of the "necessities doctrine." He held that infants were liable on their contracts for "life-supporting goods on the grounds of necessity."[18] In *Porter v. Wilson*[19] the court called for the liberalization of the necessities doctrine. "If the benefit is the foundation of the right, why should it be limited to necessities?"[20] This has evolved into the "benefit rule" which holds that an infant is liable in restitution for the benefit he received from a disaffirmed contract.[21] A corollary principle limits the restitution to the value based on the benefit received by the particular minor. "This would be the benefits received, not necessarily the market value ... of the goods or services."[22] In essence, the objective approach to the calculation is disregarded in favor of the subjective.

The courts have used freedom of contract rationales in limiting the repercussions of the exercise of the right of disaffirmance. However, this is not the freedom of contract banner that waved atop the citadel of contract in the nineteenth century. Rather, it is the freedom to contract grounded in the objective reality of the late twentieth century. It is the reality in which "minors . . . transact a great deal of business . . . long before they have reached the age of legal majority."[23] It is a reality in which adults innocently and justifiably rely on the representations of minors. "It would be intolerably burdensome for every one concerned if merchants could not deal with minors safely."[24] Such reliance is justified under the principal rationale of the objective theory of contract, which holds that the efficient functioning of business and commerce requires the greatest amount of certainty in the enforcement of contractual obligations.

The reasonable person standard can be used to illustrate the logical flaw in the ratio-nale for the infancy law doctrine, the protection of minors.[25] The fallacy of placing all minors outside the grasp of the reasonable person analysis was recognized early on by Professor Williston.

> In view of the general education and early sophistication of youth, when minors commonly transact a considerable volume of business on their own behalf, the . . . view which rests upon the equitable basis that, if the contract is fair and *reasonable*, then the minor should not be permitted to overreach any more than the adult seems clearly the better [view].[26]

Some courts have recognized that the age of majority is simply an arbitrary dividing line. In *LaRosa v. Nichols*[27] the court noted the growing inconsistency between the law of contracts and criminal and tort law. "It seems anomalous . . . that youths of sufficient age and capacity . . . may be convicted of crime, and be held liable for their torts, and yet not be liable on their contracts when apparently of sufficient capacity to make them."[28] This infancy dividing line has increasingly become a weaker approximation of objective reality. It is more a product of historical whim than founded upon any mean-ingful distinction.[29]

The rule and the common law's continuing embrace of it was noted in *Boyce v. Doyle.*[30] "The soundness of this rule has come under increasing attack."[31] Our jurispru-dence has yielded a premonition as to the likely de-evolution of such common law rules. Those rules that do not incorporate some notion of the subjective-objective dialectic will increasingly be untenable. The history of the infancy law doctrine is an example of this deconstruction in the face of the subjective-objective onslaught. Nonetheless, its continued persistence into the modern age remains a puzzlement. Its affront to objectivity was acknowledged more than sixty years ago in *Sternlieb v. Normandie National Securities Corp.*[32] "With respect to [minors] having the semblance and appearance of adults . . . how are the persons dealing with them to be protected if the infant's word cannot be taken or recognized at law?"[33] The power of authority as revealed in the doctrine of stare decisis imposed an unattractive answer: "well the law is as it is!"[34]

The courts have refused to overtly overturn the infancy law doctrine and replace it with a case-by-case reasonable person standard. With adoption of the misrepresentation of age principle, however, the courts have covertly allowed the reasonable person to enter through the back door. The entry has been limited to a narrow application of the analysis. In *Haydocy Pontiac, Inc. v. Lee* [35] the court restricted the entry based on whether the reliance on the misrepresentation was reasonable. A two-pronged test needed to be satisfied before the adult would be given relief from the sweep of the infancy doctrine's protective net. First, there had to be a misrepresentation of age by the disaffirming minor. Second, the minor had to possess the "appearance of adulthood" so that a reasonably prudent person would have believed the minor to have been an adult. A number of factors can be used in an objective reasonable person analysis including "personal appearance, family surroundings, and business activities."[36] The misrepresentation of age principle brings the minor within the general law of capacity by fashioning a presumption in favor of the adult party. "When we see [minors] engaged in business and acting in almost all other respects as an adult, it seems timely to re-examine the case law pertaining to contractual rights and responsibilities of infants."[37]

Another factor in a reasonable person analysis is emancipation.[38] Traditionally, common law has viewed the factor of emancipation as important. However, it has been used primarily to expand the scope of the necessities doctrine. When "emancipation [is combined] with necessity there is often an enlarged and more extended necessity."[39] The proliferation of these limiting rules is evidence of a slow but clear evolutionary process of deconstructing the protections provided under the traditional infancy law doctrine. In their place is an expanding regime of responsibility and accountability in accordance with the type of analysis found in the subjective-objective dialectic. Under this regime the intent of the minor, whether objectively or subjectively revealed, becomes the central focus of the enforceability determination, and age is but one factor to be weighed by the courts. Professor Williston foresaw this change when he perceptively critiqued the development of the doctrines of misrepresentation of age and emancipation as "merely incidental step[s] toward the recognition of the broader underlying principle."[40] In such a setting, what the minor subjectively believed she was doing and what a reasonably prudent adult could rely on are to be weighed heavily in the liability equation of contracts.

The Legislative Assault

Both the growing incongruency of the infancy doctrine with the real world and the slowness of the courts to react accordingly have paved the way for legislators to take up the banner of accountability. Scores of statutory limitations have been placed on the use of the infancy law doctrine. The statutory potpourri includes the lowering of the age of majority from twenty-one to eighteen, the passage of "doing business" statutes providing for judicial approval of infant contracts,[41] and the removal of the right of disaffirmance from specific types of contracts.[42] The growth of the infant consumer industry and the increased buying power of those under the age of eighteen have been the fodder for the public policy apparatus. "The magical age limit . . . as an indication of contractual maturity no longer has a basis in *fact or public policy*."[43] The most sweeping assault on the infancy law doctrine has been proposed in a model contract code prepared on behalf of the English Law Commission. It eliminates the per se rule that a contract with a minor lacks the necessary reality of assent. Instead it holds that a contract with a minor is unenforceable "if it can be shown that enforcement would be unfair or unreasonable."[44] It then adopts a punch list of criteria for making the reasonableness determination. The criteria include the nature and value of the contract to the minor, the burden the contract places on the minor, the actual and apparent ability of the minor to perform, whether there was parental consent, and whether any misrepresentations were made by the minor.[45] One can argue that these same factors would be considered under the general reasonable person analysis. The code's presumption of enforceability, coupled with the reasonable minor analysis, effectively eliminates the infancy law doctrine.

The search for statutory justifications for preempting the doctrine yields a bountiful harvest. One of the philosophical underpinnings of contracts is the belief that persons in a civilized society "ought" to keep their promises or suffer the consequences. Professor·Macneil notes that the social purpose of contract law "may very well be as nonlegal and diffuse as simple internalizations by the parties of *ought*."[46] This rationale has been used to bolster the sanctity of promise. It can also be used to justify the removal of infancy law paternalism. John Finnis speaks of the notion of "practical reasonableness." It is simply the *oportet facere* of the law. The acknowledgment that "there is a basic good to bring one's own intelligence to bear effectively . . . on the problems of choosing one's actions and shaping one's own character."[47] What better time than the "formative years" for one to take command in shaping "one's own character?" This is the "policy" justification for the elimination of the doctrine.

The "fact" justification is that the doctrine is insupportable due to the change in the socioeconomic conditions of infancy. The idea that all people under the age of eighteen should categorically be excluded from the domain of contracts is quite simply draconian. It has prevented a more thorough analysis that would be provided by the subjective-objective dialectic. The protection of youth, the stated rationale for the doctrine, could be achieved more rationally through the dialectic. An overreaching adult would be precluded from the fruits of her overreaching under the dialectical analysis that has policed most of the rest of contracts' domain. A transaction imbued with "good faith" from both parties is likely to be judged as fair and reasonable. An overreaching adult is likely to foster a contract that would not pass such scrutiny. "Overreaching" and "good faith" are part of the nomenclature of the objective theory of contracts. The fundamental premise of the theory is the liberation of free will. The free enterprise system proffers that such liberation will encourage the full and efficient use of resources. From this perspective, "the interests of infants . . . would best be served by granting them full freedom of contract"[48] and the accordant accountability as judged by the subjective-objective dialectic.

LAW AS EVOLUTION

The evolutionary process of the common law was poetically stated by the court in *Dunn v. Palermo*.

> The common law of America is an evolutionary process; it is not static and immutable. It is in constant growth, going through mutations in adapting itself to changing conditions and in improving and refining doctrine. . . . The common law does not have the force of Holy Writ; it is not a last will and testament, nor a cadaver embalmed in perpetuity.[49]

Such a statement would have pleased Henry Sumner Maine,[50] but in the case of the infancy law doctrine this evolutionary process has been unexplainably slow. It remains the letter of the law despite the fact that the spirit of the common law rationale existing at the time of its genesis has mostly dissipated. The protection rationale gradually lost its force as society was transformed from its agrarian roots to a modern industrial, technological giant. The law of capacity is out of sync with this new age of competency.

The disabilities that the law of capacity have attended to can be addressed through the application of the common law's subjective-objective dialectic. The infancy exception to the common law's case by case factual determinations should be eliminated. In its place the court should follow its mainstream mandate of objectivity. Did one party knowingly take unfair advantage of the other? Would a reasonable person have realized that the other party was incapacitated? It is this analysis of fact and reason that energizes the Anglo-American legal process. "Reasoning is a process of thought aimed at reaching or justifying a conclusion. The process includes a consideration of facts and impressions, experiences and principles, objectives and ideas."[51] The facts bear out that minors are not the incompetent lost souls of years past.

The subjective-objective dialectic would affix contractual liability by a determination not of the "age of majority" but by the "age of maturity." The former is a simple chronological calculation void of any reasoned analysis. The latter would entail a case-by-case subjective-objective analysis. Such analysis is performed in the mentally ill and "under the influence" categories of incapacity. Jurisprudentially, it would bring the law of incapacity into congruency with the rest of contracts. Doctrinally, we would no longer speak of the law of incapacity, but would operate under the presumption of capacity.

The objectification of contracts has coincided with a more general metamorphosis in twentieth-century contract law. The rigidity of the formalities of classical contract theory has given way to more case-by-case factual analysis. Ironically, it is these rigid rules that have been associated most closely with the objective theory of contracts. But in reality they work to truncate the objective analysis. "Courts found that rigid rules applied in an objective manner required a lot less inquiry and thought than attempting to inject equity and fairness into a consensual transaction."[52] In fact the decline of contractual formality has allowed the courts to expand their objective viewfinder beyond the Willistonian "snapshot" of the contract's formation. Instead the courts are free to analyze all the objective and subjective facts pertaining to the issues of competency and consent.

This expanded analysis can also be reconciled with the classical view of contracts. The classical view requires that both parties be of competent minds. If new "evidence" proves that minors are of competent minds, then the infancy law doctrine may be justifiably reformed within the classical theory. By analogy, in the area of standard forms, the courts have looked outside the four corners of the document to pierce the illusion of assent. The English case of *Thornton v. Shoe Lane Parking*[53] involved the enforceability of an exculpatory clause in a parking garage admission ticket. The procedural and substantive reasonableness of the clause was scrutinized. If the clause is a type not normally found in such forms, then actual notice must be given in order for the clause to be legally operational. The intention to include standard-type conditions is all that is required unless such conditions have been ruled to be against public policy. In the Thornton case the clause was considered to be a type in which the issuer "must show that his intention to attach [a clause] of that particular nature was fairly brought to the notice of the other party."[54] The court held that the plaintiff was not given proper notice of the existence of the exculpatory clause. Llewellyn's notion of "specific assent" had not been achieved.[55]

An example of this expanded analysis is the adoption of the concepts of "good faith" and "unconscionability" as implied terms of every contract. The *Second Restatement* mandates that "every contract imposes upon each party a duty of good faith and fair dealing."[56] This imposition questions the continued usefulness of the artificial protection offered by the infancy law doctrine. Professor Knapp concludes that the objective good faith requirement is "capable of application to an infinite variety of factual situations."[57] Others see it as a move from formalism to substantive reasoning. "Where reasons of substance ought to be considered by the decision-maker, and he refuses to consider them, any formal reasons he gives will be . . . unjustifiable, and formalistic."[58] The movement toward the dialectic transforms the litmus test from that of age determination to that of competency determination. The objective factors to be analyzed in a competency inquiry include the intelligence, experience, knowledge, and sophistication of the relative parties. The objective fairness of the contract would be evidence of overreaching by the adult. Finally, the intersubjective reality of the particular contractual relationship should be brought to bear. What did the parties intend to achieve and were they competent to do so?

The illusion of pure objectivity of law can be seen at work in the infancy law doctrine. The positive law clearly states that the age of majority is the conclusive factor in the judicial decision-making process. The right of disaffirmance is a simple chronological calculation. Pure objectivity of this sort leaves little room for judicial discretion or legal evolution. If there was indeed such an ironclad rule objectively applied, then infancy law would be forever fixed. Georgio Del Vecchio sees such pure objectivity as possible only if there is a "perfect correspondence between the juridical aspirations of consciousness and the *positive law*."[59] As we have seen, the law of infancy has not shown such a correspondence. Despite the simplicity of the age of majority criteria, the law of infancy has been volatile. The harshness of its application has led many a court away from the abyss of pure objectivity. The notion of pure objectivity or of Del Vecchio's *perfect correspondence* is antithetical to law as evolutionary in nature. A regime of pure objectivity would place law in "a stasis which would be in opposition . . . to that of the *evolution* of law."[60] In the area of infancy law the courts have shunned pure objectivity. They elected, instead, to tinker with established doctrine in order to attempt to conform it to the reality of modern society.

THE CASE OF ECONOMIC DURESS

Another case in which the subjective and objective intent of a party may be proved and yet be disregarded by a court is in the area of economic duress.[61] The doctrine of economic duress involves the submission of an adverse party to a "coercive act" of another party. Karl Llewellyn stated that the "problem of *reality of consent* is essentially one of determining what types of pressure are sufficiently out of line with our general presuppositions of dealing to open the expression of agreement to attack."[62] For example, two parties enter into an agreement that provides that one party is to provide services to the other in return for a monetary payment. Upon a satisfactory performance the performing party demands payment but is refused. The nonpaying party is privy to information that the performing party is in dire financial need. With this knowledge, the nonperforming party "negotiates" a settlement and release agreement for payment of a "disputed" amount below the contract price. From the objective standard, the settlement contract is clearly worded and not in need of interpretation. From the subjective standard, although a reluctant signer, the performing party understood and agreed to accept the lower amount in order to obtain payment. In *Rich & Whillock, Inc. v. Ashton Development, Inc.* the court was faced with such a fact pattern.[63] Two conflicting public policy concerns were discussed in the court's analysis. First, the "reluctance to set aside agreements because of the notion of freedom of contract and . . . the desirability of having private dispute resolutions be final."[64] Second, the "recognition of the law's role in correcting inequitable . . . exchanges between parties of disproportionate bargaining power and . . . not to enforce agreements which were entered into under coercive circumstances."[65]

This case can also be analyzed in terms of the objective-subjective dialectic. The first policy concern of "freedom of contract"[66] can be attributed to the reasonable person standard: that a settlement agreement objectively clear and fair on its surface should be enforced in order to forward the enunciated policy goals of freedom of contract and dispute settlement. The second group of policy objectives can be understood more easily under the subjective pole. Despite the agreement's objective clarity, an analysis of the *totality of the circumstances* yields evidence of a lack of subjective free will. In the words of the court, the reluctant signer had "no reasonable alternative but to succumb when the only other alternative [was] bankruptcy or financial ruin."[67] In deciding that the reluctant party's consent was illusory the court applied the "reasonably prudent person standard." The issue was phrased as whether the withholding of payment constituted a "sufficiently coercive" act to cause a reasonably prudent party to "succumb to the perpetrator's pressure?"[68] The malleability of the objective reasonable person standard is never more evident. The reasonable person as embodied by the policy rationale of freedom of contract is one of detached objectivity. The third-party arbiter reviews the written memorial of the parties' agreement to find clear objective intent, but the reasonable person standard as embodied in the economic duress doctrine is party-specific. The subjective intent of the reluctant party is measured objectively through the wider lens of the "totality of the circumstances." In this case the latter incarnation of the reasonable person proves to be stronger. In practice, "the courts generally refuse to lend themselves to the enforcement of a *bargain* in which one party has unjustly taken advantage of the economic necessities of the other."[69]

The issue was broached again in the case of *D. & C. Builders Ltd. v. Rees* which involved an accord and satisfaction of a debt owing under a construction contract. Lord Denning recognized the general rule that a lesser sum cannot be paid to discharge a larger debt, the discharge or accord being without the required consideration. He then outlined a prestigious lineage of dissent ranging from Sir George Jessel to Lord Blackburn. The reasoning was that such a settlement should be encouraged as long as the accord is entered into *voluntarily* by the creditor. Denning held that such was not the situation in the case at bar. The creditor's dire financial position, the debtor's knowledge of that financial position, and the debtor's threat to breach the contract cumulatively resulted in the creditor being placed under undue pressure to accept a lesser amount. "In these circumstances there was no true accord . . . no person can insist on the settlement procured by intimidation."[70] Thus, the objective clarity of the accord and satisfaction were preempted by the *subjective reality* of its negotiation.

THE UNDUE INFLUENCE DUALITY

The dialectic can be seen at work in the law of undue influence. What should the law focus upon: the pressure brought to bear by the dominant party or the susceptibility of the weaker party? Ought the law negate a contract in which only one of the components of the pressure-susceptibility duality is readily apparent? The susceptibility of the weaker party to pressure would be the likely focus under the classical theory of contract. If the party lacked the necessary free will to avoid the contract, then the entrance into the contract was not founded on "true" mutual consent and is thus rendered a nullity. Professor Atiyah explains the practical importance of the duality.

> If the law were truly concerned with the degree to which a choice was an exercise of free will, the question before the court would presumably be of a psychological question . . . has the will been over-borne? If the true question concerns the legitimacy of the pressure, the question must be one of law, which has nothing to do with the psychological state of mind of the party in question.[71]

The objective-subjective dialectic can be seen at work in this susceptibility-pressure duality. The focus of the susceptibility component is on the subjective state of mind of the vulnerable party. The pressure component focuses upon the knowledge or culpability of the stronger party. The legitimacy of the pressure is a "matter of law." As such, the reasonableness of the pressure is the key factor in determining the "legitimacy" issue.[72] Atiyah downplays the importance of the lack of free consent rationale given the fact that most contractual relationships are bound together by pressures. Harkening back to Aristotle, the fact that one's alternatives are not very appealing does not render a choice involuntary or lacking of free will.[73] Nonetheless, the interactive nature of contracts makes it difficult to avoid the communal nature of economic distress. This is implicitly recognized by Atiyah in characterizing the negotiation of a contract modification as a "bilateral monopoly."[74] The restraints of time, availability of substituted performance, and financial concerns may severely limit the "free will" of the parties in such a bilateral relationship.[75] Thus, the objectivity of the pressure can never be truly divorced from the subjectivity of susceptibility to that pressure.

A case that provides analogous insight is that of mistake induced by fraud. In *Ingram v. Little* the purchaser of an automobile impersonated a reputable businessperson. Based on certain assurances, the sellers accepted his personal check, which was subsequently dishonored. The sellers brought suit for a return of the car. The issue is whether the contract was in fact induced by fraudulent mistake. If so, did the mistake as to the identity of the purchaser prevent the formation of a contract or does the claim lay in breach of contract? Were the sellers intending to deal with the person physically present or were they intending to deal with the fraudulently endowed identity? The court discussed the respective results of the application of both the subjective and objective approaches and concluded that "the objective and subjective tests produce the same result."[76] The sellers' subjective state of mind intended to deal only with the fabricated persona and not the actual "rogue." The negotiation of an apparent contract had objectively unraveled when the purchaser attempted to convert the purchase to a credit transaction by demanding to pay by check. The acceptance of the check was factual premised on the mistaken creditworthiness and identity of the purchaser. The court held that there was no objectively or subjectively created contract.

THE EXTERNALITIES OF CONTRACTS

The pillar of contractual intent can best be founded upon the rationale of freedom of contract. In a competitive environment premised on the open flow of information, the parties are to be left to their own devices in the hard bargaining of contracts. Freedom of contract principles argue that such capitalistic free-for-all is best for the attainment of *pareto optimality*. Lowering the transaction costs of contracting can be seen as helping to remove externalities that inhibit the workings of the free market system. Professor Coase offers a definition of transaction costs that places contract law at its center. "In order to carry out a market transaction it is necessary . . . to conduct negotiations leading up to a bargain, to draw up the contract . . . [and] to make sure that the terms of the contract are being observed."[77] Interventionist rules such as the infancy law doctrine can be seen as placing external constraints upon this freedom of contract resulting in

112

increased transactional costs and greater inefficiency in the sale and marketing of goods and services.

An argument can be made that such an analysis is flawed. The mandatory or immutable rules of contracts cannot be seen as externalities due to the foundational shortcomings that prevent *pareto optimality* and dictate the need for the rules of contract. The attack on interventionist doctrine such as unconscionability is justifiable only if the system of freedom of contract is free of structural deficiencies. The notion that freedom of contract requires the absence of protectionist rules is justified if the underlying system is one of pure competition, equal access to information, and hard bargaining. Rules such as the infancy law and economic duress doctrines are examples of "government intervention [in order] to correct the failure of market forces."[78] If the system of exchange possesses characteristics of concentrated market power, inside information, and contracts of adhesion, then judicially and statutorily created rules are needed to help level the contractual playing field. Another conceptual method reconciling interventionist rules with freedom of contract has been to remove the rules from the realm of contracts. In the area of bad faith negotiation or bad faith breach, a remedy may be fashioned in either contract or tort. In fact, reliance recovery in general can be premised on tort negligence theory. "Damage for a loss suffered by a promisee in reliance on a promisor to carry out a promise may be recoverable on a tort negligence theory."[79] An example of this "tortification" of contract is an insurance company breaching its promise of prompt settlement of insurance claims. It has been held by numerous courts that insurance companies may be susceptible to suit for bad faith breach.[80]

In contrast to the preemption of freedom of contract by the imposition of mandatory rules, the background or default rules of contract can be seen as an attempt to decrease transaction costs. "Institutions such as the law of contracts fulfill an economic function by reducing transaction costs."[81] The common language of a trade and of business help to facilitate the memorialization of contractual intent. The default rules of contract provide the framework for the efficient formulations of contractual exchanges. The use of trade usage as a device to imbue a contract with meaning can be seen as such a default rule. Parties are charged with the knowledge of the usages of their particular trade or profession. This helps to build a common language of exchange that increases the likelihood of meaningful assent to contract. The greater the use and acceptance of trade usage, the more likely the convergence of objective and subjective meanings. "When a court charges those in the trade with constructive knowledge of trade usage . . . there is a high likelihood that the party does have . . . actual knowledge."[82]

The use of custom and trade usage as devices to foster efficient exchange and to uncover the intentions of the parties has a long history. In the 1867 case of *J. B. Lyon & Co. v. Culbertson, Blair & Co.* the court acknowledged these two benefits. "[C]ommercial business is transacted by men pressed by their affairs, and who are not in the habit . . . of reducing their agreements to writing, beyond a mere memorandum, the courts are compelled to look to usages of trade or business to learn the real intention of the parties."[83] The purpose of such usages are to reduce the transaction costs of exchange and minimize externalities related to the negotiation and enforcement of contracts.[84] Devices such as trade usage, customs, practices, and legal default rules provide the background for rectifying the ambiguities of contractual intent.

8

ANALOGUES

The dialectic is a general phenomenon not unique to the law of contracts.[1] A look at various counterparts to the dialectic in other areas is useful in analyzing the parameters for its use within the law of contracts. The central importance of the mens rea requirement in criminal law provides insight into the place of subjective intent in contract law.[2] The law of agency provides a closer analogue in its dichotomy of apparent and actual authority. Notions of objective-subjective morality provide an overarching view applicable to the different uses of the dialectic. Comparatively, how do other legal systems deal with the dialectic in their determination of contractual intent? Specifically, what approach does the United Nations Convention on Contracts for the International Sale of Goods adopt? This expanded view offers insight into the key issues at the center of the dialectic. What does intent or consent mean in contract law? How do parties to a contract perceive those intentions? How does a court reconcile intention, the communication of that intent, and the perception of that intent by both the sending and receiving parties? The areas of criminal law, agency law, ethics and international law provide insight into these issues.

CRIMINAL LAW: MENS REA

Professor Wigmore asserts that the "underlying object of criminal administration must be to make men choose to conform."[3] In order for the sanctions of the criminal law to serve this goal of conformity, or what is more popularly referred to as deterrence, it must punish intentional acts. The conscious, knowing mind must be the instigator of the criminal act. It is the intent of the guilty mind that criminal law seeks to deter. *Salmond on Jurisprudence* defines the conditions of criminal liability as the combination of act with a guilty mind.[4] "A man is responsible, not for his acts in themselves, but for his acts coupled with the mens rea or guilty mind with which he does them."[5] The rationale for mens rea is that the purpose of the criminal law is not punishment for its own sake but to use punishment to deter future acts of misconduct. Deterrence is thought to work only upon minds that are consciously engaged in the undesirable activity. If a party can consciously intend to commit an act, then that party can be persuaded from carrying out such an intention. Criminal mens rea has been expanded, however, to include certain at least partially unconscious states of mind ranging from recklessness to negligence.[6] How can negligence and strict liability be reconciled with the deterrence rationale for mens rea?[7] It can be argued that unconsciousness can be stimulated into a state of consciousness. A party should be aware or conscious of what the reasonable person would know given the circumstances.[8] The intent or awareness of the reasonable person is conclusively transferred into the mind of the accused. *Salmond* refers to this juxtaposition as constructive intention. The guilty mind is at times replaced with a type of strict liability. One is guilty of the foreseeable consequences of her actions regardless of her mental state of mind. "A person is presumed in law to intend the natural or necessary results of her actions."[9] The use of such a presumption drastically narrows the divide between the objective and subjective approaches to mens rea.[10] Reasonable presumption often displaces subjective intent.

The reality of mens rea can be brought into question if the alleged victim consented to the act. For example, a defense to rape is that the victim consented to the act. Such consent would negate the criminal culpability of the accused. As in contract, the reality of that consent can also be negated under a number of circumstances. The criminal law's analogue to the infancy law doctrine would intervene on behalf of the consenting infant to negate that consent in the case of statutory rape.[11] In addition, just as duress can call into question the reality of assent in contract, so too can duress be used to eliminate a finding of consent in the criminal law. "Consent should be disregarded where induced by threats."[12]

The subjectivism of mens rea can be compared to the objectivity of contracts. First, an act of contracting by itself is sufficient to result in contractual liability. The manifestation of intent is all that is required to prove an obligation. In contrast, in the criminal law an act or *actus reus* cannot be detached from a finding of a culpable state of mind.[13] In recent years, however, there has been a convergence of the state of mind requirements in criminal and contract laws. One may argue that there has been an objectification of the criminal law with the acceptance of recklessness and negligence as adequate suitors to the mens rea requirement. For example, in certain areas such as careless driving or manslaughter, maliciousness or knowledge is not required. The expansion of criminal liability within the statutory and regulatory framework has given us instances of criminal culpability based on mere negligence and even strict liability.[14] This phenomenon reflects an expansion of the scienter requirement to encompass the full range

116

of the dialectic. The criminal and contract bodies of law can now be seen as occupying the same dialectical spectrum. Both possess subjective and objective elements with the criminal law skewered toward the subjective pole and contract law leaning toward the objective pole.[15]

The second benefit to the comparison of criminal mens rea with contractual intent is to dispel the notion that a subjective approach is unworkable. The mens rea requirement stands in contradistinction to the proponents of the objective theory of contract who summarily reject all forms of subjectivity as suspect.[16] A culpable state of mind, or mens rea, has long been a requirement for a finding of criminal liability. "Before the law can justly punish the act, an inquiry must be made into the mental attitude of the doer."[17] Émile Durkheim saw the notion of free will as the underlying rationale for the importance of the state of mind of the perpetrator in both contract and criminal law.

> That man is a free agent and that the consent he gives can be attributed to himself only on condition of its having been freely given. Here we find ideas similar to those we meet with concerning responsibility. If the criminal has not committed an act of his own free will, the act does not derive from him and he can therefore not be blamed for it.[18]

Criminal law not only utilizes the subjective approach to intent, it also makes a number of fine distinctions in the realm of subjectivity. It differentiates between intentional and unintentional acts. Only acts connected to the subjective will are held to be culpable.[19] For example, an act precipitated by an involuntary reflex would escape punishment. Intentionality is framed, however, by the definition of act. An unintended consequence of an intentional act does not insulate the transgressor from criminal culpability. Professor Perkins offers a definition of criminally culpable action. A criminal act is "an occurrence which is an exertion of the will manifested in the external world."[20] It is the act and not the consequences of an action that are used in the determination of the wrongdoer's will.[21] External manifestation is the basis for determining the subjective will. The criminal act is seen as giving insight into the state of mind of the accused. Manifestation, however, is only the starting point in the judicial inquiry into the finding of mens rea. In contract, however, the external manifestation has been seen as conclusive to the determination of intent.

The area of criminal negligence is the closest that criminal law comes to the objectivity of the reasonable person, albeit of the tortious variety. Perkins gives an illustration of an employer delegating a task likely to cause harm to one who is *obviously* incompetent. Another area where traditional mens rea has been discarded in favor of the reasonable person standard is that of mistake of law and mistake of fact. Actual knowledge of the illegality of an action is consistent with the notion of a guilty mind but "for reasons of policy a knowledge of the law is postulated" or presumed.[22] The defense of mistake of fact is premised upon the reasonableness of the mistake. "A mistake of fact will disprove a criminal charge if the mistaken belief is honestly entertained based upon reasonable grounds."[23] The subjective notion of honesty is combined with the objectivity of reasonable grounds. As in contract's law of satisfaction, the subjective element is qualified by an objective safeguard. If one defends himself at the peril of another, the defender must have honestly believed that his well-being was being threatened and that belief must have been reasonable. To escape culpability, the accused needs to prove that he in fact possessed that belief and that he acted in a way that a reasonable person would have acted. Both ends of the dialectic are actively and openly applied.

The goodness or badness of one's state of mind and one's actions has long been recognized in the philosophical and theological realms. St. Thomas Aquinas "distinguished the goodness of the inner act (mens rea) from the goodness of the external act (actus reus)."[24] But, just as consent was not required during the period of early Roman contract law, criminal intent or mens rea has not always been a requirement in the criminal law. In older common law, absolute liability automatically attended the occurrence of an injury. If a person was causally connected to the injury causing event, then she was guilty of a crime or a tort. The law did not differentiate between harm caused by malicious intent, accident, or mere chance. The line between criminal and civil liability was a tenuous one during the regime of absolute liability. The adoption of mens rea can be seen as an attempt to bring sanity to the criminal law because it limits its reach. Similarly, the intent requirement can be seen as a limiting device on the reach of civil liability. If the common law had chosen to remain a law of formality and absolute liability, then the dialectic would be of little consequence. Instead, it elected to connect liability to a conscious state of mind, which assured the importance of the dialectic. The difficulty in proving the subjective state of mind or intent of a party forced the courts to devise the reasonable person as a means to presume intent.[25]

Circumstantial Evidence and the State of Mind Requirement

The mens rea requirement of crime is often proven through inference. When a person has acted "we are able to infer intentions from our knowledge of *folk psychology*. Indeed, successful social intercourse depends on such accurate inference."[26] The inference of a culpable state of mind is akin to the implication of intent in contract law. Objective facts are used to build a case for the implication of the required mens rea. Unlike contract law, the causal inference revolves around the subjective element of motive. The pattern of inference includes elements of wish or motive and, by implication, intention.[27] The implication of intent as seen in the law of contracts can also be seen in the law of criminal conspiracy. The agreement to commit a crime, a la a criminal meeting of the minds, is a separate type of criminal activity. The act of agreement or of planning must be proven in order to convict someone of conspiracy. "The existence of the agreement or joint assent of the minds need not be proved directly, but may be inferred by the jury from other facts proved."[28] In case of assault, the mens rea requirement is generally proven by inference from circumstantial evidence. In *Luther v. State* the court held that "intent to injure may not be implied from a lack of ordinary care. It may be implied from intentional acts where the injury was the direct result of them done under circumstances showing a reckless disregard and a willingness to inflict the injury."[29]

The general basis for the implication of criminal intent is the premise that a person can be presumed to have intended the natural consequences of her acts. Nevertheless, there are circumstances that would negate such an inference. Such was the case in *R. v. Steane,*[30] which involved a person charged with assisting the enemy during World War II. The accused had entered the service of the German Broadcasting System as a news broadcaster. The court held that the prosecution needed to prove specific intent to assist the enemy and not just a general intent to commit the acts. Analogous to the totality of the circumstances analysis in contract law, the court speaks of a *totality of the evidence* analysis. The surrounding circumstances of the assistance need to be taken into account. Did the enemy threaten the accused and the accused's family to the extent to which he was deprived of the requisite free will to commit the crime? This type of situation does not call for the inference of general intent but requires the prosecution to prove, and not presume specific intent.[31]

Professor Marshall notes the distinction between criminal intent and civil intent. "In discussing intent we may have wishes of two different characters: one giving a basis for civil liability and another which would support criminal liability."[32] For example, the acceptance of someone's property is sufficient to imply civil intent to pay for the property taken. Criminal intent would require a felonious intent, the taking of another's property without that party's knowledge or consent. In the 1882 case of *United States v. Thompson* the court addressed a ship captain's defense to a charge of smuggling illegal aliens into the country. The defense argued that there was no evidence of a specific criminal intent.[33] The court held that there are various degrees of scienter. In the case of smuggling, actual knowledge was not required to satisfy the requirement of criminal intent. It found that all passengers boarded the ship with the "implied consent of the master."[34] Furthermore, the captain's failure to take steps to ascertain the number and status of those passengers was an act of gross negligence which is "equivalent to criminal intent."[35] The reasonableness of a defendant's conduct can thus be grounds for mens rea.

119

Another example of the dialectic at work in the field of criminal law is the right of the accused to be informed of her right to an attorney. An objective test would simply require proof that the police informed the accused of her rights. The subjective approach would require proof that the accused actually understood the disclosure. A study of New Zealand Bill of Rights cases concluded that a "test of subjective understanding ought" to be the preferred approach.[36] Outward manifestations of understanding provide a strong inference of understanding but are not conclusive. "Though the inference is a powerful one, it is none the less susceptible of rebuttal and the test retains its essentially subjective orientation."[37] The courts have dismissed fears of the abuse of subjectivity as unfounded. A subjective misunderstanding defense still must meet a rigid evidentiary threshold. The subjective approach best advances the rationale for the right to be informed. Professor Butler argues that "acceptance of a reasonable-person test is acceptance of a law-enforcement official perspective."[38] He concludes that unlike the law of contracts, "the criminal law has long had to deal with elements of subjectivity."[39]

Another issue in the realm of state of mind requirements is the notion of corporate intent. How do requirements of contractual intent and criminal mens rea mesh with artificial beings? Whose intent or guilty mind is to be analyzed in fulfilling the laws' state of mind requirements? A number of approaches may be advanced.[40] First, is the aggregation theory in which a composite state of mind combining the mens reas of the different human actors may be used to satisfy the requirements of enforceability or culpability. Second, is the American view in which the state of mind of an employee acting within the scope of her employment is projected vicariously onto her corporate employer. Third, is the English version in which a corporation is liable only for the acts of key corporate employees. This is an alter ego theory in which certain high-level managerial officers and employees make up the essence of the corporation. Only those employees possess the corporate will to expose the company to criminal liability.[41]

Professor Gobert argues for the abandonment of subjective mens rea in the area of corporate criminality. Instead, he poses the use of an objective due diligence approach. The court should inquire into "whether the company could have taken steps to identify and avoid the occurrence of harm, whether it was reasonable to do so, and whether it in fact did so."[42] A corporation would be held accountable for the consequences of its actions regardless of whether or not it possessed a blameworthy state of mind. It would be allowed a defense to avoid criminal liability if its actions were proceeded by an appropriate due diligence inquiry. This is a shifting of the dialectic from its subjective pole (intent) toward its objective one (due diligence).

The Criminal Law's Reasonable Person Standard

The inference of a criminal state of mind is made through the reasonable person as the trier of fact. Such inferences are biased by the trier of facts' own perceptions and expectations. "We perceive in large measure what we expect to perceive."[43] Professor Marshall posits that because of such shortcomings of perceptions and expectations, the most that the trier of facts is able to infer is probable reality. "What the law is saying is that the average man's expectations lead not to accurate perceptions of objective reality but to an inference of probable reality."[44] An exception to the constraints of objectiveness can be seen in the area of prosecutorial discretion. "Contemporary efforts to constrain the discretion of actors in the criminal justice system have bypassed the prosecutor."[45] Professor Reiss reasons that because of the lack of objective constraints, the subjective intent of the prosecutor is a necessary inquiry in cases of prosecutorial misconduct. "Purity of heart" is a hopeful presumption for prosecutorial action.[46] When that "purity" is questioned, the determinant of constitutionality often focuses not upon objective factors but upon intentions and motives.

The interrelationship between duress and mens rea provides a use for the reasonable person standard. The factor of duress in the mens rea determination has been debated. The fact that the accused was under duress does not go directly to whether he possessed the requisite state of mind at the time of the criminal act. Instead, duress can be seen as analogous to the doctrine of excuse in contract. In contract the doctrines of impossibility, impracticability, and frustration are used ex post facto to the formation of the contract. Likewise, the notion of duress enters the criminal law equation only after the elements of a crime have been proven. In *R. v. Paquette* the Supreme Court of Canada indicated that evidence of duress can be used to question the issue of criminal intent. "The state of mind of the accused at the time would be relevant, and should be examined in the light of the duress to which he was subject."[47] Thus, if the reasonable person would have felt *compelled* to commit the criminal act, then the accused can not be said to have possessed the necessary criminal intent.[48]

LAW OF AGENCY: IMPLIED AND APPARENT AUTHORITY

In the early part of this century, Professor Laski linked the beginnings of the notion of implied authority to the growth of the modern corporation. Vicarious liability helped satisfy the needs of society to hold those most able to pay responsible for the acts of their agents and employees.[49] Laski asserts that the attempts to juridically ground master-principal liability upon notions of implied intent or implied authority were fictitious. Instead, the evolution of *respondeat superior* and implied agency liability is teleological or consequential in its genesis. The consequences of the judicial decision have been the impetus for vicarious liability.[50] The uniqueness of this type of analysis is that the state of mind of the perpetrator is meaningless. The *consensus ad idem* of contract or mens rea of criminal law find no kinship in the law of agency. "One regrets the continual use of the fiction of *implied authority*"[51] because in reality no such authority was given. Unlike the promise breaker of contract or the villain of a crime, "in no case of vicarious liability is moral blame attached to the master."[52] The subjective state of mind or its objective manifestations do not play the role that the dialectic plays in contract. Laski explains the nature of vicarious liability as a communal application of law.[53] The individual focus of contract and criminal law is replaced by a social interpretation. Liability is visited upon the master or principal because of the collective needs of society. Vicarious liability resides in a region between moral culpability and strict liability. The consciousness of the individual is replaced with a collective consciousness. The dialectic has less relevance in a regime whose search for actual implied authority is not contractual in nature. As long as a plaintiff can bring the guilty party's mischief within the nebulous notion of scope of employment, the principal will be held responsible. The intent behind the grant of authority becomes legally superfluous.

The objective theory of law is applied most noticeably in the law of agency's determinations of implied and apparent authority. Intent is measured by the use of the reasonable person standard. The *Restatement (Second) of Agency* defines agency as "the fiduciary relation which results from the *manifestation of consent* by one person to another that the other shall act on his behalf."[54] Implied authority is the form of actual authority that is not expressly granted; it is the necessary and incidental appendage to express authority. The nature of the agency relationship makes it impossible to detail every minute aspect of the agent's authority. A number of decisions and actions are necessarily left to the agent's discretion. It is in the realm of these discretionary activities that a court must distinguish those that can be implied into the actual authority granted to the agent and those that are not authorized or beyond the scope of the delegation. The implication of authority is generally determined by a judicial review of "the relationship of the parties, by the nature and customs of the business, the circumstances surrounding the act in question, the wording of the agency contract, and the knowledge that the agent has of the facts relevant to the assignment."[55] The dialectic between objective delegation and subjective nondelegation of authority was stated in *Makousky, Inc. v. Julius Stern*. The court stated that "if the agent *reasonably* assumes the authority to engage in a transaction, it is immaterial that this action may in fact have been contrary to an *undisclosed intent* of the principal."[56] The court held that it can be implied that delegating to one co-owner the responsibility to sell jointly owned property necessarily included an implied authority to secure professional assistance. The implication of such authority is based on the objective criteria of what is the custom or practice in this *type* of business transaction.

The reasonable person apparatus in the area of agency law has also been used in the determination of apparent authority.[57] Its kinship with the objective theory of contracts has been duly noted. "Apparent authority is based upon the principle which has led to the objective theory of contracts, namely, that in contractual relations one should ordinarily be bound by what he says rather than what he intends."[58] The determination of implied authority focuses upon the principal-agent relationship. Apparent authority is a product of a principal–third party analysis. A principal can be held liable for the unauthorized, expressed or implied, actions of its agent. This occurs when the principal makes a *manifestation of authority* to a third party pertaining to the principal-agent relationship. A reasonable person standard is used by the courts in the affixing of liability. Liability of the principal depends on whether "the third person *reasonably* believes from the principal's words or from his conduct, that he has in fact consented to the agent's actions."[59] The state of mind of the third party is determinative.[60] In contrast, implied authority is premised upon actual authority. A third person's disbelief as to an agent's authority is immaterial. A binding obligation upon the principal can be created despite the third person's disbelief while no such obligation would be created in the case of apparent authority.

An analogy can be drawn between the notions of contractual essence and inherent agency power. In contract, courts often look to the essence of the contract to provide guidance regarding intent and interpretation. In the area of agency law the courts have implied inherent agency powers to a situation. The question becomes, inherent to what? The answer is that there are certain inherent powers of the agent to bind the principal that stem directly from certain relationships or situations. The *Restatement (Second) of Agency* defines inherent agency power as "the power of an agent which is not derived from authority but solely from the agency relation."[61] It is not a function of expressor implied authority.[62] This power to bind stems from the *essence* of the agency relationship. As in the defining or interpreting of contract, custom and usage can be used to define the essence or root of the agent's authority. The implication of necessary terms into a contract and the implication of inherent agency authority both stem from the essence of the particular type of contractual or agency relationship.[63]

Reasonableness and the Law of Agency

Section 10 of the *Restatement (Second) of Agency* adopts a reasonable person standard in the determination of the reasonableness of the actions and conduct of the principal and agent in respect to their relationship. "A principal or agent should know what a person of ordinary experience and intelligence would know and what he would know if, having the knowledge and intelligence which he has or which he purports to have." [64] The reasonable person standard is used in the judging of the care and performance of duties rendered within the principal-agent relationship. In the law of agency the reasonable person is not a static but a fluid fabrication. The type of businessperson and the type of business transaction are taken into account in the fabrication of the standard of reasonableness. The tools of reasonableness found in the law of contracts—that of custom, trade usage, and the totality of the circumstances—are brought to bear in the law of agency.

The interrelationship between the law of agency and contract law is expressly pronounced in the *Restatement (Second) of Agency*. Section 32 states that an agent's authority is to be interpreted by using the rules for the interpretation of contracts. It also adopts the objective theory in determining the breadth of the authority granted by the principals to the agent. "The manifestation and not the intention of the principal is important."[65] The manifestation of authority is an ongoing or ambulatory tool based on a totality of the circumstances analysis. In contracts the totality of the circumstances inquiry focuses primarily on the determination of contractual intent at the time of contract formation.[66] In the law of agency the manifestation of authority is an ongoing phenomenon that requires a constant updating of the totality of the circumstances analysis.

The totality of the circumstances analysis coupled with the interpretive tools of custom and trade usage are brought to bear on the interpretation of authority in much the same manner as in the interpretation of contractual intent. The list of interpretive rules includes conventional meanings, common usage, prior dealings, background of the agreement, purposes of the parties, nature of the subject matter, and trade and business usages. The facts and circumstances to be analyzed are open-ended, with the reasonable person as the only guide as to their materiality. The courts take into account "all matters throwing light upon what a reasonable person in the position of the agent at the time of acting would have considered." [67] The authority granted to an agent is read in light of all the customs in the community regarding the normal parameters of such grants of agency.[68]

THE DEONTOLOGICAL-TELEOLOGICAL DIALECTIC

Ethical schools of thought are generally bifurcated into duty-based or deontological theories and consequential-based or teleological theories. Deontology "makes the notion of the good relative to the *nature* of man."[69] The purity of the mens rea is the basis of this type of subjective morality. "In the field of ethics, as in the teachings of the Church, guilt depends upon the state of mind alone."[70] A person's motive or motives are the operative measurement for the rightness or wrongness of an act.[71] In contrast, the traditional teleologists look to the "objective requirements of humans as rational beings. Traditional teleologists, from Aristotle on, make use of a *prudent man* standard."[72] Utilitarians often attempt to objectively weigh the relative good and harm of an action to determine its rightness. Teleological theories such as utilitarianism can be seen as examples of objective morality.

Hume's subjectivism may be compared to Kant's rationality. For Hume moral evaluations are inherently subjective. "There are no objective moral properties to be found in persons or situations independent of their subjective states."[73] Moral judgments are not made by way of deduction from facts but by subjective reaction to facts. Professor Goldman sums up the importance of subjectivism in the judgment-making process. "On the philosophical level, only by taking account of both the objective facts and our subjective reactions can ethicists develop the proper theory of moral judgment."[74] Kant's rational person is a relative of the law's reasonable person. The reasonable person as a rational agent is able to objectively determine the rightness of an action. The universalization of contractual obligation can be seen as a construct of Kant's rational being.[75]

The Kantian notion of the categorical imperative would dictate the universalization of a rule that one has a duty not to break one's contractual promises. This is more consistent with the will theory which holds that the willful invocation of the convention of promise dictates the need to enforce such promises. The problem is that the law does not recognize all promissory commitments. The purely moral or gratuitous promise does not rise to the level of a legally binding obligation. "Thus the categorical imperative brings us back to where we were with the will theorists, no reason is given why one could not define all voluntary commitments to be binding."[76] Under Kantian ethics all promises should be equally binding.[77] The law of contracts, however, does not behave in such a way.

The circular nature of intentions and consequences can be seen in the notion of *attributives*. Both the consequential focus of teleology and the purity of duty found in deontology are couched in terms of the attributives of good and bad. It has been argued that the analysis of consequences and of intent cannot be made mutually exclusive.

> *Intentions*, considered in respect of the *consequences*, to the production of which they are directed, or at any rate in respect of the consequences which at the time of the intention, a man had, or at least *ought* to have had in view—these, together with the acts which the intentions were directed or as having a tendency to produce, will be the [types of things,] in the character of *attributives*, such as good and bad can . . . be attached.[78]

The determination of a person's so-called duty-bound intent is often performed by an examination of the objective consequences of her action.[79] In contract, the objective manifestations of a party are used to affix subjective intent at the time of formation based on what he *ought* to have had in view.[80] Subjective intent is thus constructed through the prism of consequential hindsight. Teleological objectivity is intertwined with duty-bound subjectivity. The subjectivity of contractual intent is inherently influenced by the objective consequences of that intent.

AN INTERNATIONAL COMPARATIVE: THE CISG

The United Nations Convention on Contracts for the International Sale of Goods (CISG) was completed in 1980[81] and became effective in the United States on 1 January 1988. The convention applies to the international sale of goods when two requirements are satisfied. First, both contracting parties must be citizens or have their places of business within countries that are signatories to the convention. Second, the parties have not expressly agreed that another law other than the convention or specific articles of the convention would apply. The convention has both theoretical and practical significance to a discussion of the dialectic. It provides a pedagogical tool to examine the merging of perspectives from different legal systems. The convention is the product of negotiations from representatives of the civil, common law, and socialist legal systems. From a practical perspective it has been ratified by most of the major trading countries of the world, including the United States, China, France, Germany, Russia, Italy, Mexico, and Spain.

Article 8 of the convention deals with the interpretation of the conduct of contracting parties. Conduct is considered as any act such as a statement "by which the *intent* of the respective party is to be expressed."[82] How are these acts to be interpreted? The convention expressly adopts *both* the subjective and objective approaches. Article 8(1) requires that a contract is to be interpreted according to the intent of the person making the statement or conduct. This subjective approach is then mollified by the *communication* and understanding of that intent to the other party.[83] The subjective is the preferred means of interpretation. It is, however, constrained by an *objective overlay*.[84] The objective approach is to be used only when the other party was aware or "could not have been unaware."[85]

Article 8 (2) expressly adopts the objective theory as the residual category of contractual interpretation. In the event that a party's subjective intent has not been clearly made and communicated, then the contract shall be interpreted according to the understanding that a reasonable person in the position of the receiving party would have had under the same circumstances.[86] The touchstones of the reasonable person analysis examined in chapter 4 are enumerated, including the characteristics of the parties[87] and the totality of the circumstances.[88] Article 8 (3) brings the third element of the reasonable person analysis into the equation. The circumstances include course of dealings and trade usages.[89] The importance of custom, usages, and practices is further elaborated upon in Article 9. Terms may be implied into an international sales contract under the premise that the parties knew or *ought to have known* any usage which is widely accepted in international trade and is regularly observed in that particular trade and in that particular type of contract.

The convention ultimately adopts the objective theory as the predominant means of determining contractual intent. The subjective theory, however, is openly embraced as the preemptive means of interpretation. If there is clear evidence of communicative subjective intent, then it will prevail over a reasonable person interpretation. Within the reasonable person analysis, the convention mandates that the reasonable person possess both objective and subjective elements.[90] The full range of the dialectic is openly embraced by the convention; its approach is more open and honest compared to the disjointed approach found in the common law of contracts. The full range of the dialectic exists in the common law, but most of its battles are waged covertly through a myriad of legal fictions.

9

THE INNER EXPERIENCE OF CONTRACT LAW

Most of us have no very definite intellectual temperament, we are a mixture of opposite ingredients, each one present very moderately.[1]

JURAL RUDIMENTS AND HUMAN VALUES

Georgio Del Vecchio reviewed a number of different philosophical foundations of law, including theology, utilitarianism, historical, and realism. Citing Aristotle, he discerned that there is an original power in every person to determine the just from the unjust. Because of this innate power, the basis for the foundation of law is to be found in our own human nature.[2] Despite the elaborate development of the objective approach to contracts, the fact remains that the mantle of objectivity must be viewed through the subjective gaze of judge and jury. Justice Cardozo's famous adage that the role of judge is one of *creation* underscores the subjective nature of judicial decision making. The interfacing of law and fact is as much subjective as it is objective.

Within the limits of precedent and custom thus set, within the range over which choice moves, the final selection for judges . . . is one of fitness to an end. We do not pick our rules full blossomed from the trees. Every judge consulting *his own experience* must be conscious of times when a free exercise of will . . . determined the form and tendency of a rule which at that moment took its origin in one creative act.[3]

Cardozo's creative act and Kant's notion of human inclinations[4] are both solidly within the subjective domain. Justice Holmes's prediction theory of law belies the objective slant of his jurisprudence. In *The Path of the Law*, he states that a "first principle for the study of this body of dogma is systematized prediction which we will call the law."[5] It would be difficult to deny the subjective elements involved in predicting the decisional

129

behavior of particular judges. The legal realists or rule skeptics have argued that in hard cases the law provides a menu of principles, rules, and standards that a judge may choose from in order to support her decision. At this point of choice, the objectivity of the law comes to an end.[6] John Dewey believed that the processes of thinking and inference are much influenced by a number of unseen and unconsidered causes such as past experience, received dogmas, self-interest, passion, and mental laziness.[7]

Objectivity is as much a *technique* of judicial decision making as it is a process for uncovering the truth. Quite often, objectivity comes into play not in choosing among various rules but in the rendering or writing of the opinion. Objectivity is used in weaving a decision that masks the subjectivity of judicial decision making.[8] The objectivity of judicial decision making is primarily an institutional value. Judge Newman asserts that it is one of a number of institutional values that influence the judicial decision-making process. A judge's views on the purpose of courts and other sources of law, on the process of adjudication, along with the importance of predictability and uniformity, are examples of such institutional values. The most prevalent institutional value is the judge's loyalty to the orderly and objective development of the law.[9] These institutional values are likely to have their greatest influence when a judge has the option of choosing between different rules. In the area of contractual intent, the choice may be for a rule which can best be applied to the availability of evidence in a given case. Such a match will hopefully improve the likelihood of congruence between implied intent and actual intent.[10]

The institutional value of the orderly development of law can be seen as having a natural kinship with the doctrine of stare decisis.[11] There is an overarching institutional value or expectation that a decision should be the result of a rational and deliberative process. A judge who offers no deference for stare decisis may be accused of failing to fulfill the legal community's "expectations of deliberation and uniformity."[12] Failing to give due respect to these institutional values can brand a judge as short of judicial temperament and intellect. Judges thus feel a natural compulsion to give "account for all arguably relevant rules, principles, and policies" that bear upon a case.[13]

Professor Gardner balkanized the judicial process into three intellectual stages: the scientific, the ethical, and the practical. This trichotomy can be understood within the framework of the *is* and the *ought* of law. The scientific can best be aligned with the objective theory of contracts. It is the ascertainment of what the parties did and thought.[14] This is the realm of judicial inquiry into the *is* of contractual intent. The *ought* of contract is found within the ethical stage of the judicial process. It is the determination of what ought to have been done by the parties and what they should now do.[15] This is the realm of judicial intervention in order to impose fairness onto the transaction. The practical stage is the rendering of a decision that represents the "best practicable means of bringing about a just result."[16] This notion of just result will likely reflect the human values of the judge in her determination of the *ought* of contract.

The judge's discretion, or what Llewellyn refers to as *leeways*, to advance her subjectively framed human values is not without constraints. In *Southern Pacific Co. v. Jensen* Justice Holmes poetically articulated the bounded nature of judicial discretion. "I recognize that judges do and must legislate, but they can do so only interstitially; they are confined from molar to molecular motions."[17] The constraints of precedent and of legal rules are the formal limitations on judicial discretion within the common law system. These constraints are the objective guideposts to the fabrication of decisions within a system premised upon stare decisis. The more meaningful channels for decision making, however, are carved by much more sublime influences upon the judicial mind. These influences are best described as subjective in nature and both conscious and subconscious in operation.

Pure objectivity is further diminished because the judicial mind-set is likely to be swayed by notions of collegiality and acceptance. Judges are indoctrinated by principles of precedent and professionalism in the rendering of their decisions.[18] The religious and philosophical roots of contract law have further conditioned judges to feel that their decisions must reflect the collective will. It is the belief "that the law ought to be at the time of its creation the expression of the will of all, or, at least, of the greatest number, and that this ought to be instilled into the judge."[19] A number of formulations of the inner workings of the judicial mind have been advanced to provide a framework to understand these influences. Two of the better known of these formulations are Karl Llewellyn's notion of operating technique and Stanley Fish's concept of a community of interpretation.[20] Both concepts focus on the socialization process that influences a judge and its resultant influence on judicial decision making. For Fish, the socialization process involves a judge's concerns with rendering decisions that will be in congruence with the thinking and inclinations of the professional community of judges and lawyers. There is an internal process of peer review through which a judge filters his decision-making process. It is the normative framework within which most judges consciously and subconsciously work.[21] The end result of this judicial mind-set is the creation of a subliminal community of interpretation.

Llewellyn's operating technique is more expansive in its view of judicial socialization. The socialization process involves the influences of the judicial community, judicial rules, and the judicial craft.[22] Llewellyn fashioned a number of phrases to describe these influences on the judicial mind. He references Roscoe Pound's notion of judicial intuition[23] and speaks of the sociology of doctrine,[24] of judicial operating technique,[25] and of judicial sensitivity.[26] Their influences are not uniform but vary among different types of cases. He fashions four categories of cases ranging along a spectrum from strict rule application (objectivity) to nonrule application (increased subjectivity). The *types* of decisions range from those evolving from a "judge's honest efforts to derive a conclusion from a rule," to those stemming from "a more or less malleable composite in the judge's mind of hundreds of rules," to decisions in which the more sublime influences of ethics, politics, economics, and religion become prominent.[27] The final category of decision making is one in which "judges more or less consciously behave in a policy-oriented fashion within a *leeway* bounded by rules and precedents."[28]

Communal decision making is grounded in the common law tradition of cohering individual decisions with the existing body of legal rules and thought. It is the belief that any theory of adjudication is a theory of community.[29] The centripetal force that produces coherence in adjudication is the norm of integrity. "The prudential judge is attentive to general standards of reasonableness and the need for coherence."[30] Judges feel a duty to act with integrity which translates into the obligation to render decisions that can be reconciled with the principles and standards of the community.

Llewellyn's accounting is one in which the jural and human values of the particular judge play a vital role in the decision-making process. The objectivity of rules plays a constraining role but the leeways in the rules and in their application provide room for the advancement of jural and human values. The objective theory works under the premise that rule application is fact-based. The interpretation of the facts is performed by the reasonable person who is herself a creation of fact. Llewellyn's analysis focuses on the nature of facts themselves. Facts are what the judge perceives them to be and decides.[31] For Llewellyn facts are experience-based.

Because of the indeterminacy of facts, the law often deals with *categories of facts* in which it affixes legal significance. This technique of classification ameliorates but does not eliminate the subjectivity of facts. Llewellyn devises a reciprocal relationship between facts and experience. In such a relationship neither term is static and both are susceptible to the sensitivities of the judicial mind.

> One observes a new fact situation and is sensitive to its real-life meaning, then there is a sudden and ex post facto change in the meaning of one's prior life experience in that area. . . . The *intuition* in this process lies in the judge's subconsciously using his prior experience and his sensitivity to the meaning of new fact situations. . . . A judge's intuition extends only so far as his experience and sensitivity.[32]

It is important to recognize that the judicial mind is influenced by both the objectivity of fact and the subjectivity of values. This can be seen as a positive dialectic where each acts as a check upon the other. In his influential work on *Pragmatism* William James saw the need for any system, philosophical or otherwise, to possess the influences of loyalty to facts and loyalty to human values.[33] Despite a multitude of authoritative sources, such as cases and statutes, law is an inherently complex and interpretive exercise. The line between interpretation and creation is easily broached.[34] The making or the finding of law transpires in a judicial realm in which the individual judge has a wide range of discretion available for either task.

THE SUBJECTIVITY OF JUDGMENT

The notions of objectivity and impartiality in the judicial decision-making process are viewed as the cornerstones of the judicial office. Impartiality has been defined as the "ability to bring to the task of decision a mind that can rise above all considerations of personal conviction and private feeling."[35] It is imperative that judicial decisions not be clouded by inappropriate personal considerations such as conflicts of interest. It is an illusion, however, to believe that a judge's personal beliefs and values do not enter into the fray of applying law's objective standards. The element of subjectivity is endemic to the law of contracts. The advancement of the reasonable person and the objective theory pass through the subjective filter of the human mind. It is the judge who must construct the reasonable person through her own subjective belief of reasonableness. The inherent subjectivity of the judicial process is found in judicial rule interpretation. "The judicial process is a retrospective or backward-looking process of analysis calculated to interpret general rules in terms of particular sets of facts."[36] The construction of the reasonable person is a judicially supervised enterprise. The judicial supervision is restricted only by relatively discretionary parameters. Discretion is necessary because the reasonable person needs to be reinvented on a case-by-case basis. As with human fingerprints, no two legal fact patterns are identical. Discretion in the matter of contracts manifests itself in a number of ways. Oftentimes a court may avoid injustice in a particular case through innovative interpretations of "history, custom, or social utility."[37] Through the art of distinguishing and discovery, a court may ignore the onerous result of an objective legal application. It may recognize a *new* custom and imbue it with the halo of conformity to an objective, reasonable standard. As the customary modification is placed into more persistent use, then the initial subjective act of creation will be surrounded with "the halo of conformity to precedent."[38]

Justice Cardozo aptly illustrates the role of judicial discretion and subjectivity in the application of external standards.

> The role of judge is to bring about a just determination by means of the *subjective sense* of justice inherent in the judge, guided by an effective weighing of the interest of the parties in the light of the opinions generally prevailing among the community [the *objective sense*]

regarding transactions like those in question. . . . He is to exercise a discretion [*subjective sense*] informed by tradition, methodized by analogy, disciplined by system.[39]

An objective theory of contracts needs to incorporate the *fact* that the subjective element plays a large role in the interpretation of objective reality. It is only by attempting to consciously understand the role of the subjective and its interrelationship with the objective that any objective theory can hope to serve its intended goal, the finding of objective truth.[40] The objective theory becomes a misnomer when it simply disregards the reality of the subjective element.[41]

Discretion as the Touchstone of Subjectivity

Judicial decision making can be seen as a dialectic with rules and discretion representing the interdefining poles. Discretion is defined and limited by the use and existence of legal rules and principles. "We can make sense of the idea of judicial choice and discretion only against a background of rules to which judges are subject."[42] For those who are rule skeptics, rules serve only as a legal facade. Judges roam free to ignore, avoid, and interpret legal rules in order to justify and rationalize preconceived decisions. A better view is that judicial decision making is constrained by the widely accepted legal norms of rule application and precedent. Judicial decision making is a product of the interplay between the judge's reverence for the rules of law and the discretion inherent in the art of interpretation.[43] Whether used in the mental process of arriving at a decision or as the tools of rationalizing a decision, legal rules play an important part in checking unbridled judicial discretion.

In his *Discretion and Judicial Decision* Kent Greenawalt takes issue with the belief that judges lack discretion in their decision making.[44] Under a theory of *coherence* a judge must give effect "as *objectively* as he can to the values already existing in the legal system."[45] He is bound to *cohere* his decision to existing authoritative legal standards or rules. Put simply, there is a "perceived judicial obligation to aim for a coherent interpretation of precedents."[46] Greenawalt rightfully argues, however, that the open-ended nature of many legal standards makes them vulnerable to subjective interpretation. Invariably, there will be areas in which the objectivity of authoritative standards will not render proper guidance. Legal standards of materiality, substantiality, and reasonableness, to name a few, breed the use of judicial discretion.[47] This is discretion grounded in the fact that there will inevitably be gaps or leeways in the substantive body of law. Another basis for discretion is in the demarcation of fact and law. Far from being objectively clear, a court's determination of whether an issue is one of fact or law can be used as a vehicle for creative interpretation. In *Ashville Investments Ltd. v. Elmer Contractors*

Ltd. the court held that a previous interpretation of an arbitration clause did not have precedential value. "The true meaning of the clause depended in every case on the circumstances of the particular contract."[48] An issue of law is thus converted into an issue of fact.

An associated issue is the courts' reference to community values when applying legal standards such as the reasonable person. How does a judge differentiate her personal values from so-called community values? The answer is that at least at a subconscious level personal values will enter into the mix. The objective aims of a judge in the discovery of community values will undoubtedly be tainted by her personal value system. "We are often able to find reflections of our own views in external ambiguous sources, furthermore, our capacity for self-deception increases as the level of abstraction gets higher."[49] This projection of the judge's personal values onto community values is likely when dealing with such abstract concepts as good faith, fair dealing, and unconscionability.

Societal and community values act as touchstones for the decision-making apparatus. They act as constraints upon the law and the lawmakers. A narrower value-based community, the legal community, also acts as a constraint upon judicial discretion and subjectivity. Owen Fiss speaks of *interpretive community* and Duncan Kennedy refers to the notion of *double objectivity*. Interpretive community can be seen working at different levels of consciousness. Judges have been indoctrinated in the generality, certainty, and stability of law. Their decisions are constrained by working within the narrowly confined leeways of existing law. Double objectivity can be seen as the conscious effort of a judge to conform her decisions within a range of acceptability.[50] Often her goal is to render a decision reflective of her view of objectivity and one that will be viewed as objective within the judicial and legal communities. Professor Kennedy refers to the process of rule application as a *social* one and "hence in some sense a subjective process."[51] It is in this realm of subjectivity that "the judge risks but may also gain credibility."[52] The yearning for acceptance and credibility acts to keep the judge's reign of subjectivity within acceptable limits.[53]

Judicial discretion and values can be seen lurking behind notions of judicial instinct or intuition. Beneath the confines of accepted legal doctrines and the traditional views of the legal community, the values of the individual judge are at work framing her understanding of her role within that community.

> That is not to say that any credible theorists, however sanguine about the possibility of objectivity, would describe legal interpretation as purely conscious and therefore always exposed to the disciplining light of logical deduction. Instead, the dark recesses of instinct and intuition are sometimes the site of interpretation, wherein many questionable influences reside.[54]

Judges are well aware of the need to conform decisions to the shared views of the legal community in which they work. How she arrives at that conformity may be as much a product of conforming her view of a just decision with existing legal rationales as it is objectively deriving her decision from past precedents.

DIALECTIC AS SYNTHESIS

G. W. F. Hegel was skeptical of the use of dichotomies as a vehicle of philosophical thought. Instead, "Hegel worked out a theory of logic that seeks to eliminate dichotomies or at least to unify or synthesize opposites."[55] At its best, the dialectic of contracts works as a synthesis of the subjective and the objective, of the external and the internal, of the generality of law and the sentiment of justice. The rules and principles of doctrine and their application optimally serve society when the dialectic operates to render decisions based on objective-subjective discourse. It is the recognition that behind any objectification of law there remains the subjective. Behind doctrine there are the rationales that provided its impetus. The underlying problem with a purely objective theory of contracts is that it attempts to solve "essentially subjective problems with objective tests."[56] Most of the time the utilization of objective tests is the best that the law can provide. Nonetheless, a greater recognition of the subjective element in contract formation and in the judicial interpretation of contracts should not be avoided. The generality of law must be tempered with pragmatic application. Often the concerns of pragmatism, of justice, and of subjective sentiment can be found in the courts' dictum. If these concerns find a synthesis over time, then dictum becomes rule. The subjective is converted into the objective.

The objective and subjective dichotomy can be found elsewhere in the law. Professor Frug speaks of objectivity and subjectivity in the legitimacy of governmental and organizational bureaucracy.[57] Objectivity in bureaucracy is necessary to prevent bias and the invasion of individual rights. Subjectivity is needed to ensure the values of individuality. Frug acknowledges that subjectivity and objectivity have generally been used by legal theorists as antithetical to one another. He argues that they act as *dangerous supplements* to one another. Instead of being each other's antithesis, they complement or supplement. There is an "intermixing—an assertion of subjectivity and objectivity into their antithesis as dangerous supplements."[58] This is in contradistinction to the historical demarcation of objectivity and subjectivity in contracts and in other fields of law. This demarcation is in a continual process of oscillation. In contracts the conceptual pendulum has swung from the subjective to the objective. In criminal law the subjectivity of mens rea continues its prominence. Professor Frug eloquently argues that such demarcation is illusory.

The idea of subjectivity usually refers to the sphere of the self, but we can define ourselves only through relationships with the world in which we live. To find ourselves, we seek ideas through the commonly created world of language, knowledge through interaction with others . . . The world we share in common—the objective world—is both necessary to and incompatible with our subjective identity.[59]

He then strikes to the heart, albeit in a different context, of the objective theory of contracts. The objective approach to contract is premised upon the reasonable interpretation of fact. The interpretation of fact is then used to imply the requisite state of mind or intent. Instead, Frug asserts that "the interpretation of facts suffers from the same intermixture of subjectivity and objectivity."[60] This intermixture or synthesis has always been present in some form. It is the conscious abandonment of the objective-subjective dichotomy that Frug poses. "It is important to realize that we need not understand the world in terms of *subjectivity* and *objectivity*—that this dichotomy, like many other categories through which we experience the world, is a human creation and not a reflection of what the world is really like."[61]

Professor Bronaugh analyzed objectivity in relation to the bargain theory of contract and formulated a view of objectivism that he labels "the requirement of subjective reasonableness."[62] It is an example of the mixing of the two poles of the dialectic. Subjective reasonableness approaches the issue of contractual intent with a simple question. Did the recipient of a promise given in the formation of a bilateral contract have a reasonable belief about what she was being promised? From the promisor's perspective, a similar question may be posed. Did the prospective promisor have a reasonable belief that he was or was not intending to enter into a contractual obligation? This perspective is not of the communal or detached reasonable person. It is a party-specific perspective on whether a party's subjective beliefs can be considered to be reasonable. The approach is objective but is not community-based or what Bronaugh refers to as *hard objectivism*. It is an intention-based objectivism that is more in line with the ideal of the bargain theory of contracts. The subjective beliefs of the parties are encapsulated into an objective analysis. "To test the reasonableness of someone's subjective belief is not to be indifferent to his belief; it is that *subjective* state which is the very subject of an evaluation."[63] *Hard objectivism* truncates the analytical process at the stage of manifestations of intent. The notion of subjective reasonableness allows the defending party to make her case that the manifestations did not reflect actual intent. The plaintiff's burden is satisfied by proving that the defendant's manifestations resulted in a legally binding obligation. This is proven by applying the analysis found in the traditional objective theory of contracts. A second stage analysis then becomes necessary to judge the persuasiveness and reasonableness of the party's subjective belief or intent. There is a shifting of the burden of proof from plaintiff to defendant. The defendant has the burden to prove that her beliefs were otherwise and that they were reasonably based.

The recognition of the interplay or synthesis of the subjective and objective leads to a second-order proposition. Implicit in the synthesis is the notion that the objective and subjective approaches may play greater roles individually depending upon the issue in question. Professor Eisenberg recognizes the different uses of the objective-subjective poles in his responsive model of contract law.

> The extent to which the principles that govern any issue should be . . . subjective or objective should depend on a functional analysis of the relevant issue in terms of fairness and policy. . . . Subjective principles should be employed where they serve both fairness and policy, and where they do not, it is to be expected, given the goal of facilitating the realization of individual objectives, that the principles employed will . . . typically depend on objective variables that provide a reliable surrogate for state of mind.[64]

The analysis offered by Professor Bronaugh is an example of a synthesis of objectivity and subjectivity in the affixing of contractual liability. A corollary premise was offered by Karl Llewellyn in explaining that the replacement of the subjective theory by the objective is more a matter of convergence than elimination. "Is it not clear that if in all but amazing cases manifestation did not roughly coincide with intent, we should have neither reasonable reliance in fact nor any law of contract to make an objective theory of peculiar cases necessary?"[65]

LAW'S INNER EXPERIENCE

Despite the external nature of the objective theory, law at its base or quantum level is an inner experience. In its essence it is an internal belief of what is right and wrong, of what is reasonable and unreasonable, of what is legal, and what is unenforceable. The inner experience of law is different for the different parties in the contractual enforcement process. Both parties to a dispute may firmly and in good faith believe that their view is the morally and legally correct one. Objectivity provides the tools used by the courts in the dispute settlement process. It would be naive to believe that at its core the law of contract dispute resolution is a purely objective process. This objective demeanor is most certainly colored by the inner experience of the law. It entails the processing of objective input—the facts, circumstances, and customs of each case—through the participants' subjective beliefs. The processing of factual input as presented through the framework of the adversary process has been described as more a modification of old facts than the adding of new facts. Fact analysis is necessarily colored by the inner experiences of the judicial mind. William James states that it "happens relatively seldom that a new fact is added *raw*. More usually it is embedded cooked, as one might say, or stewed down in the sauce of old."[66] Facts are rarely processed as they appear, but instead as they are perceived through the modifying lens of past experience.

The inner experience of the law is not exclusively an intrapersonal experience. It also consists of interpersonal experiences involving party to party, client to lawyer, and judge and jury to parties. An emotional bonding evolves among the participants. This emotionalism plays a part in the processing of the objective elements of contracts. Total detachment is a human impossibility. "The sentiment of pity is and always has been a constant factor in modifying usages and laws."[67] This is what Professor Sargentich refers to as the sympathetic legal structure[68] and what Professor Henderson describes as the interplay between empathy and legality.[69] Professor Sargentich studied the duality of the formal application of rules and precedents with judicial sympathy for rendering substantive justice to the parties. The judge "struggles between *empathy or emotional bonding* and legality or rational rules."[70] This tension is a side-effect of the judge's engagement with the case before her. Professor Gardner noted this phenomenon some sixty-five years ago: "The strength of English law resides in a traditional willingness to hear the parties and to decide according to the interests and habits of the parties involved."[71] This *willingness* creates a connection between the judge and the parties which has a substantial impact on the subconscious of the judicial arbiter.

The rise of objectivity in contracts has delegated the use of subjective information to the domain of nonevidence. The notion of subjectivity in the realm of contractual interpretation engenders negative connotations. Nonetheless, subjectivity continues to rise above the suppression of the current objective regime. In the area of unconscionability the subjective characteristics of the relative bargaining power and states of mind of the respective parties are directly at issue. "We use knowledge of the subjectivity of the individual and collective other when we argue that an unconscionable contract ought not be enforced, even though both parties consented to it."[72] A fuller acknowledgment of the role of subjectivity would better advance the truth seeking function of contract enforcement. The reality of consent is better served with an open embrace of an analysis of all relevant evidence, whether subjectively or objectively grounded. Professor West warns of a sort of objective blindness.

> The insistence on rational knowledge and, hence, on objects of rational knowledge, may have blinded us to the possibilities within the human spirit for arational and arationally (subjective) acquired forms of undisciplined knowledge and sight. . . . We can, do, and should use our knowledge of the subjectivity of others, sympathetically and arationally acquired.[73]

The rue of objectivity can be seen when a court attempts to conduct a fairness inquiry. The cloak of objectivity is used to disguise the court's journey into subjective fairness. Professor Eisenberg notes that the "concepts of fairness have long been smuggled into contract."[74] The rue of objectivity refers to the ability of the court to build an objective case influenced by its empathy for the parties, its sympathy for fairness and substantive justice. A skilled judiciary can combine objectivity and subjectivity within its inner experience. The facade of pure objectivity is possible because of the nature of legal reasoning.

> Adjudication routinizes both analogy and modification, each of which enables sympathy's search for common ground . . . through the vast ability of judges to distinguish cases or uncover similarities between them by shifting their *perspectives on the meaning of fact patterns* . . . analogy is, after all, imperfect. Doctrinal flexibility rests on the ability to . . . distinguish a new fact pattern without attacking the facial validity of previous holdings.[75]

The factual basis of the objective theory provides the fodder for the illusion of pure objectivity. The humanness of the parties and the lawmakers ensure that it remains a facade. The *fact* that the factual situations of case law are filtered through the human thought process ensures the role of subjectivity in the law.[76]

10

SUMMA

We . . . need stories and metaphors to understand the subjectivities of lives not our own . . . we do indeed need theories of interpretation to come to grips with the inevitable limits of our understanding.[1]

Professor Granfield speaks of a "jurisprudence of subjectivity"[2] and makes reference to Hegel's "schema on the philosophy of the spirit."[3] Hegel's three "spirits" are the subjective spirit, the objective spirit, and the absolute spirit. In his explanation of the absolute spirit we see the full force of the dialectic at work. The objective and the subjective are both vital components in the task of defining one another. "[T]he absolute spirit, resolves the opposing forces of the subjective spirit and the objective spirit, whereby the absolute spirit knows itself reflectively. The finite spirit has been transcended; subjectivity and objectivity are reconciled in a higher level of self-consciousness."[4] Granfield concludes that it is the task of jurisprudence to develop such a synthesis of "law and subjectivity."

The line between the objective and subjective is tenuous at best. It is not well defined and sharp in its division. In fact, the line of demarcation is more of a distant, shadowy hue as seen through law's Hubble telescope. "The . . . distinction between the subjective and the objective . . . is . . . evanescent, and tends to become one of words and little more."[5] Nonetheless, there surely are distinctive realms of the subjective and the objective. It is important to realize that both realms exist in our contract jurisprudence. Both realms feed off of each other, define one another, and serve together in the recognition and enforcement of contractual obligation. This is the dialectic of contracts. The poetry of Justice Cardozo illuminates the binary interrelationship of the subjective and objective. "The perception of objective right takes the color of the subjective mind. The conclusions of the subjective mind take the color of customary practices and objectified beliefs. There is constant and subtle interaction between what is without and what is within."[6]

141

Contract law is cyclical in nature, often wavering between the precepts of freedom of contract and interventionism. There is some evidence that the movement from the subjective theory to the objective theory of contract has begun to slow. The reversal of inertia begets a movement from the purely objective toward a greater recognition of the subjective. Professor Eisenberg argues this point by noting that "standardized principles are almost everywhere giving way to individualized principles, and contract theory no longer dismisses the significance of subjective elements."[7] The advance guard of objectivity may continue to limit the deference given to the role of the parties' subjective intents. It cannot overcome, however, the fact that contractual interpretation is a reflection of human decision and human discretion. "Judges and juries decide the cases. They do take *subjective factors* into account when these can be proved or inferred from the evidence."[8] Their aim is to act rationally and reasonably. Their attempt at objectivity is constrained by a bounded rationality. The number of variables involved in contractual fact patterns make pure objectivity an impossibility. "[I]n most of the situations we face we can detect only a modest number of variables or considerations that dominate."[9] We may see ourselves as acting objectively but the selectivity of our perception and the influence of personal values will continue to alter our focus. Our understanding of human relationships is internally constructed. Thinkers such as Hobbes and Rousseau "concentrated upon a self which strives to create a milieu by its own subjective will."[10] The subjective pole of the dialectic will continue to play an important role in contractual issues.

Objectivity and subjectivity in the law of contracts may simply be a realization of the dichotomy of law in theory and law in practice. The law, like science, reveres the objective and distrusts the subjective as unscientific. Thus, the dogma of contracts has increasingly been objectified with the hope of purging itself of the whims of subjectivity. In contrast, the lawgiver and the practitioner often render judgment based on hunch or intuition. It is this feel for the law that gives it the needed flexibility and compassion. This can be seen as the difference between the theoretician and the clinician. "The former strives for an impersonal formulation whereas the latter strives to formulate and work with human experience."[11] The influence of the interpretive community dictates that such subjectivism be masked in a facade of objectivity. The skill of the interpreter dictates how successful will be her attempt. The leeways of the law provide adequate fodder for the masquerade.

Contract law is laden with rules and their applications. We have seen that there is "both an internal and an external element to rule following in law."[12] It is also a practice and a process. It is an interpretive practice and it is an ever-evolving process or activity. Professor Patterson asserts that it is "an activity and not a thing. Its *being* is in the *doing* of the participants within the practice."[13] The rules of contract are constrained by the totality of the circumstances in which a case's fact pattern impacts its application. Despite objectivity's claim, the subjective elements in such fact patterns are considered in law's decisional matrix. The particular circumstances and characteristics of the parties is critical to the adjudication of their claims.

Subjectivity is often disguised under the rubric of judicial pragmatism. The 1990 English case of *Williams v. Roffey Bros.*[14] bears this out. It involved an agreement by a contractor to pay an additional sum to a subcontractor for work already under contract. The general rule of contract is that an agreement to perform what one is already under a contractual duty to perform is unenforceable due to the lack of consideration. This rule has been relaxed if it can be proved that there is at least a minimal increase or change in benefit. In *Williams* the court held that the contractor's hope of avoiding a penalty under the main contract was such an additional benefit. From the point of view of objective rule application, the decision is an absurdity. The subcontractor was under a contractual obligation to perform within the stated time, the additional benefit was a matter of circumstance, and the so-called benefit clearly did not come from the subcontractor. How can such a finding of benefit be explained? Why does the court find additional consideration to ensure performance of an existing contractual duty? The court reasoned that the contractor agreed to pay additional consideration not out of economic duress but "from a pragmatic point of view."[15] The court supported its decision by citing the twin pillars of subjectivism and pragmatism. It saw the agreement to increase the compensation as representing real assent. The agreement clearly stated the true intentions of the parties and was not compromised by any demonstration of inequality of bargaining power. The pragmatic view of the contractor was mirrored by the court. The modification of compensation was seen as a way to provide added incentive, to prevent the need to find another subcontractor, to avoid additional damages as represented by the penalty clause, and was seen as a way of "continuing the relationship" with the subcontractor. In essence, pragmatism was the true consideration for the contractual modification. The variation was enforceable because the consideration is provided by "a *pragmatic* approach to the true relationship between the parties."[16]

The illusion that law can consciously be rendered a purely objective task may be more a matter of technique than of substance. Kelsen and Summers works on the technique element of the law support this contention.[17] The law of contracts can be seen as utilizing the techniques of fostering and protecting private arrangements.[18] Professor Summers surmises that private arranging techniques, like the law of contracts, were at first purely social institutions. Because of their beneficial nature, "many societies actively utilize[d] law as an instrument to facilitate and effectuate those private arrangements."[19] The process of legalizing the private arranging technique of contracts is a three-step undertaking. There is a legal grant or recognition of the power of private persons to create contractual relationships. The codification of commercial law in the *Uniform Commercial Code* can be seen as such a grant. Such codes also provide the "rules of validation" that need to be followed if the private arrangement is to achieve legal status. Finally, contract law provides "affirmative significance" to an arrangement that fulfills the necessary validating steps.[20] The most common type of affirmation is the conferring of an element of bindingness to the arrangement. The dialectic plays its role in the allocation of affirmative significance or bindingness to a given arrangement.

The objectivity of granting affirmative significance to an activity has preoccupied jurists and scholars since the turn of the century. Can it be said with true conviction that contract law is more objective, more fair, and more efficient than it was fifty years ago? I think not. The increased objectivity of the rules of contract and their application is more a difference in perspective and in the technique of analysis. Some fifty years ago, Dean Roscoe Pound recognized the illusion of increased objectivity. The objectification of contracts was more of a simplification through the avoidance of the subjective. "Jurists have sought objectivity by elimination of the difficult problems of jurisprudence."[21]

The illusion of *consensus ad idem* was replaced by the illusion of objectivity. Institutional values, personal preferences, and the subjective posturing of the contracting parties will always play influential roles in the interpretation of contractual intent. Compared to 50 or 100 years ago, contract law is better able to channel subjectivism into the terminology of objectivism. The objective theory of contract law can be seen as a technique of judicial justification. Reasons given, "though subjectively tainted with rationalization," are made to contribute to the "rational development of the law."[22] This translation of subjective reality to objective justification ensures the continued vitality of the dialectic of contracts. It is important to view subjectivism and objectivism not in the form of a dichotomy but as a dialectic working together in the search for true contractual intent.

NOTES

PREFACE

1. Hans-Georg Gadamer, *Hegel's Dialectic*, 11 (trans. P. Christopher Smith 1976).

CHAPTER 1

1. George K. Gardner, "An Inquiry Into the Principles of the Law of Contracts," *Harvard Law Review* 46 (1932): 1.

2. Herbert A. Simon, *Reason in Human Affairs* (Stanford: Stanford University Press, 1983), 5.

3. Charles Fried, *Contract As Promise* (Cambridge: Harvard University Press, 1981).

4. Anthony T. Kronman and Richard A Posner, *The Economics of Contract Law* (Boston: Little, Brown and Co., 1979); Richard A. Posner, "Utilitarianism, Economics, and Legal Theory," *Journal of Legal Studies* 8 (1979): 103; Victor P. Goldberg, ed., *Readings in the Economics of Contract Law* (New York: Cambridge University Press, 1989).

5. See G. Richard Shell, "Contracts in the Modern Supreme Court," *California Law Review* 81 (1993): 431, 501–2.

6. Randy E. Barnett, "The Consent Theory of Contract," *Columbia Law Review* 86 (1986): 269.

7. David Charny, "Hypothetical Bargains: The Normative Structure of Contract Interpretation," *Michigan Law Review* 89 (1991): 1815, 1825.

8. Comparatively, "all legal systems worth the name must recognize juristic acts as events which actually occur in life and so require some kind of regulation." Konrad Sweigert and Hein Kotz, *An Introduction to Comparative Law*, trans. T. Weir (New York, North-Holland Publishing Co., 1977), 2. The common ingredient in all juristic acts is the element of intention. "All juristic acts necessarily contain a declaration of intention." Ibid.

9. James Oldham, "Reinterpretations of 18th-Century English Contract Theory: The View from Lord Mansfield's Trial Notes," *Georgetown Law Journal* 76 (1988): 1949.

10. Bernard F. Cataldo, Cornelius W. Gillam, Frederick G. Kempin Jr., John M. Stockton, and Charles M. Weber, *Introduction to Law and the Legal Process* (New York, John Wiley and Sons, 1965), 255.

11. Patrick S. Atiyah, "Contracts, Promises and the Law of Obligations," *Law Quarterly Review* 94 (1978): 193, 221.

12. D.W. Greig and J.L.R. Davis, *The Law of Contract* (Sydney: Law Book Co., 1987), 190.

13. David Goddard, "The Myth of Subjectivity," *Oxford Journal of Legal Studies* 7 (1987): 263, 271.

14. Roscoe Pound, *An Introduction to the Philosophy of Law*, rev. ed. (New Haven: Yale University Press, 1954), 149. Dean Pound's next sentence questions the usefulness of this "objectification." "Nowhere, . . . has the deductive method broken down so completely as in the attempt to deduce principles upon which contracts are to be enforced." Ibid.

15. 521 P.2d 937, 938–39 (Wash. 1974), as cited in David Vernon, *Contracts: Theory and Practice* (New York: M. Bender, 1980), 2–10.

16. Arthur L. Corbin, *Corbin on Contracts,* 2d. ed. (St. Paul, Minn.: West Publishing Co., 1952), 106.

17. Goddard, "The Myth of Subjectivity," 271.

18. "The actual decisions do not justify a statement that goes so far . . . the actual intent of either of the parties should not be disregarded." Corbin, *Corbin on Contracts*, 106.

19. "The standard litany of mistake and misunderstanding is an ordered mix of subjective and objective theory." Steven J. Burton, *Principles of Contract Law* (St. Paul, Minn.: West Publishing Co., 1995), 18.

20. 408 So.2d 930 (La. 1981).

21. For a discussion of this case, see David P. Dougherty, "Error Revisited: The Louisiana Revision of Error as a Vice of Consent in Contracting," *Tulane Law Review* 62 (1988): 717, 730.

22. Ibid., 724.

23. Infra, chap. 4.

24. Infra, chap. 8.

25. Timothy J. Muris, "The Costs of Freely Granting Specific Performance," *Duke Law Journal* vol. 1982 (1982): 1053.

26. Philosopher Richard Bernstein offers this definition of objectivism: "By objectivism, I mean the basic conviction that there is or must be some permanent, ahistorical matrix or framework to which we can ultimately appeal in determining the nature of rationality, knowledge, truth, reality, goodness, or rightness." Richard J. Bernstein, *Beyond Objectivism and Relativism: Science, Hermeneutics, and Praxis* (Philadelphia: University of Pennsylvania Press, 1983), 8.

27. Thomas Nagel states that the "distinction between subjective and objective is relative." Thomas Nagel, *Mortal Questions* (New York: Cambridge University Press, 1979), 206. Nagel explains that there are not just objective and subjective viewpoints. Instead, there is a "polarity . . . at one end is the point of view of a particular individual . . . from here the direction of movement [is] toward greater objectivity. . . ." Ibid.

28. Robert L. Birmingham, "Holmes on 'Peerless': *Raffles v. Wichelhaus* and the Objective Theory of Contract," *University of Pittsburgh Law Review* 47 (1985): 183, 204. The author explores the intricacies of the famous 1864 English case.

29. Ibid.

30. Melvin A. Eisenberg, "The Responsive Model of Contract Law," *Stanford Law Review* 36 (1984): 1107.

31. Infra, chap. 6.

32. Anne De Moor, "Contract and Agreement in English and French Law," *Oxford Journal of Legal Studies* 6 (1986): 275, 280.

33. Ibid., 284.

34. Infra, chaps. 2 and 3.

35. Infra, chap. 4.

36. "The invocation of the reasonable person came to play a part in extending the ambit of contractual liability." Greig and Davis, *The Law of Contract*, 187.

37. Lord Denning, *The Discipline of Law* (London: Butterworths, 1979), 36.

38. Vernon, *Contracts: Theory and Practice,* 2–10.

CHAPTER 2

1. Ian R. Macneil, *The New Social Contract* (New Haven: Yale University Press, 1980), 17 (emphasis added).

2. The "sanctity of promise" as it relates to contract had its first doctrinal hold with the development of the writ of assumpsit. See below note 3. "From the fourteenth century, a new action had begun to emerge . . . [t]his new action was assumpsit which . . . had developed by the sixteenth century into an action for breach of *promise.*" John N. Adams and Roger Brownsword, *Understanding Contract Law*, 2d ed. (London: Fontana Press, 1994), 27 (emphasis added). "Sanctity of promise" is often used in conjunction with the notions of "freedom of contract" and "sanctity of contract." The latter two are generally the philosophical underpinnings for the premise that individuals in a free market economy should be given "maximum license in setting the terms [of their contracts] and to hold parties to their freely made bargains." Ibid., 46.

3. The writ of assumpsit was itself an advancement for the legal enforceability of contract. "[In] the seventeenth and eighteenth centuries the writ of assumpsit had opened the door wider to a general remedy for the breach of an agreement and before the doctrine of consideration had been fully defined as a workable criterion for determining that agreements should be legally enforceable. . . ." David H. Parry, *The Sanctity of Contracts in English Law* (London: Stevens and Sons, 1959), 9. See generally, R. H. Helmholz, *Canon Law and the Law of England* (London: Hambledon Press, 1987), chap. 14, "Assumpsit and *Fidei Laesio.*" See also, Slade's Case, 4 Co. Rep. 92a (1604) (seminal English case for the use of the writ of assumpsit as the general remedy for breach of contract). See generally, James Barr Ames, "The History of Assumpsit," *Harvard Law Review* 2 (1888): 1. The historical reach of assumpsit is dated by the author to the year 1504. Ibid., 18. The author reviews a number of the writs used in the early royal and common law courts: assumpsit, special assumpsit (detriment), action of deceit (misrepresentation and warranty), and indebitatus assumpsit (precedent debt). The interplay between the realms of tort and contract is also illustrated. For example, initially the breach of an oral promise was considered a "deceit" and actionable under tort. "Both in equity and at law . . . a remediable breach of a parol promise was

originally conceived of as a deceit. . . . By a natural transition . . . actions upon parol promises came to be regarded as actions *ex contractu.*" Ibid., 15.

4. Ibid., 11. The duality of moral obligation and legal obligation can be traced to Roman law where some *causa* or reason was necessary in order for a promise to be enforceable. However, the expansion of contract can be understood through this ongoing moral-legal duality. Mere moral obligations are not enforceable under the "letter of the law." But the "spirit of the law" has exhibited the tendency of merging moral and legal obligations. Dean Pound in reviewing Roman law noted that there "still remained natural obligations which had not been given legal efficacy as the basis of actions. . . . Yet in reason they were morally binding and the legal and moral should coincide." Roscoe Pound, *An Introduction to the Philosophy of Law*, rev. ed. (New Haven: Yale University Press, 1954), 141. See also, James Oldham, "Reinterpretations of 18th-Century English Contract Theory: The View from Lord Mansfield's Trial Notes," *Georgetown Law Journal* 76 (1988): 1949.

5. Charles Fried, *Contract As Promise* (Cambridge: Harvard University Press, 1981), 17. See also, W. Lightsey, "A Critique of the Promise Model," *William and Mary Law Review* 26 (1984): 45.

6. Professor Speidel states that "contract law concerns the human behavior of promise-making." Richard E. Speidel, "Contract Law: Some Reflections Upon Commercial Context and the Judicial Process," *Wisconsin Law Review* vol. 1967 (1967): 822.

7. Pound, *Philosophy of Law*, 14.

8. Thus, "many agreements fall outside the scope of the law of contract, either because they concern matters of moral, rather than of legal obligation, or because the parties agree that they are not to be treated as enforceable contracts, or because they are not intended to be such." Phillip S. James, *English Law*, 9th ed. (London: Butterworths, 1976), 208.

9. John Finnis, *Natural Law and Natural Rights* (Oxford: Clarendon Press, 1989), 297.

10. Karl N. Llewellyn, "What Price Contract?—An Essay in Perspective," *Yale Law Journal* 40 (1931): 704, 712.

11. This quote is taken from David C. Cowan, *Conscience, Obligation, and the Law* (Chicago: Loyola University Press, 1966), 142, quoting, Oliver W. Holmes, *The Common Law* (Boston: Little, Brown, and Co., 1963), 38.

12. The philosophy of the civil law is one founded on "eternal and natural laws, dependent on the authority of a duly constituted state and elaborated from the central thesis that the civil law binds in conscience." Ibid., 231.

13. Society is ever faced with the problem of determining which of the many promises men make, both commercially and privately, are enforceable and which are not. The question is ancient and perennial. Conscience, honor, morality, religion, and all the conceivable personal and societal sanctions bear on the matter and furnish their respective, and sometimes varying answers.

   Bernard F. Cataldo, Cornelius W. Gillam, Frederick G. Kempin, Jr., John M. Stockton, and Charles M. Weber, *Introduction to Law and the Legal Process* (New York: John Wiley and Sons, 1965), 253.

14. Fried, *Contract As Promise*, 8 and 16. For an examination of natural law theory's view of promissory obligation see, Finnis, *Natural Law*, 298–308.

15. Steven J. Burton, *Principles of Contract Law* (St. Paul, Minn.: West Publishing Co., 1995), 1.

16. "By consenting, we entitle others to act in ways in which they could not had we not consented." Gerald Dworkin, *The Theory and Practice of Autonomy* (New York: Cambridge University Press, 1988), 86.

17. Patrick S. Atiyah, "Contracts, Promises and the Law of Obligations," *Law Quarterly Review* 94 (1978): 193, 214.

18. Ibid., 208.

19. The work of reliance theory can be seen in the adoption of the firm offer rule in the Uniform Commercial Code. It is no longer an absolute that a promise needs to be reciprocated by way of a return promise for contractual liability to ensue. An "offer made in circumstances in which reliance is known to the offeror to be likely may not be withdrawn." Charles L. Knapp, "Enforcing the Contract to Bargain," *New York University Law Review* 44 (1969): 673, 675.

20. To do so "would be nothing but a bare fiction." Cataldo et al., *Introduction to Law*, 204.

21. Atiyah, "Contracts, Promises", 205.

22. This rule of objectivity is congruent with moral norms because a person who intends something other than the reasonable meaning of his words has used language carelessly. It is congruent with policy because the security of transactions would be undermined if a person could escape contractual liability by convincing a fact finder that he had subjectively attached some special, unreasonable meaning to his expressions. It is consistent with the body of law because the law often measures conduct by a *reasonable-person standard*.

    Melvin A. Eisenberg, *The Nature of the Common Law* (Cambridge: Harvard University Press, 1988), 67 (emphasis added).

23. "It is plain that the liability is based not on some notion of voluntary assumption of obligation, but on something else. And most frequently it will be found that that something else is the element of reasonable reliance." Atiyah, "Contracts, Promises", 205.

24. Edward Yorio and Steve Thel, "The Promissory Basis of Section 90," *Yale Law Journal* 101 (1991): 111, 123. The authors argue that many of the cases involving section 90 are promise-based and not reliance-based. The enforceability of a promise is often promisor focused and not promisee focused. The liability stems from the promise and not the reliance. "Like the rest of contract law, Section 90 is about promises. What distinguishes enforceable promises . . . are the proof and quality of the promisor's commitment." Ibid., 167. The promisor's subjective state of mind takes on added importance under this point of view. In counter-distinction the objective reasonableness of the promisee's reliance can be seen to have a lesser role in the issue of enforceability.

25. *Central London Property Trust Limited v. High Trees House Limited*, 1 K.B. 130, 131 (1947).

26. Ibid., 136.

27. 6 Q.B. 597 (1871).

28. Ibid., 599.

29. Justice Hannen refers to the notion of the "rule of morality" that would dictate a different result than that which the objective theory would provide. If the seller subjectively knew of the purchaser's perception, then the purchaser would not be bound. This is true even if the reasonable person's perception was in agreement with the seller. See ibid., 610 (Justice Hannen's dissent).

149

30. Ibid., 607.

31. Under Roman law a voluntary promise or *nudum pactum* was a promise the breach of which was not actionable at law. The Romans categorized promises into formal promises such as the *stipulatio*. "It had a number of individual contracts but no general theory. An agreement, to qualify as a contract, had to be made according to certain formalities or had to fall within a certain type with a particular function. . . . The *Institutes* group contracts into four classes: real, verbal, literal, and consensual." Alan Watson, *Roman Law and Comparative Law* (Athens, Ga.: University of Georgia Press 1991), 53.

32. Albert Kiralfy, "Absolute Liability in Contract," *Journal of Legal History* 1 (1980): 89.

33. Often the terms "classical" and "traditional" contract law are used interchangeably. Classical or traditional contract law are most often associated with the work of Professor Samuel Williston. See generally, Samuel Williston, "Mutual Assent in the Formation of Informal Contracts," *Illinois Law Review* 14 (1919): 85; Samuel Williston, *Law of Contracts* (New York: Baker, Voorhis and Co., 1920). Professor Macneil differentiates between classical, neoclassical, and relational contract law. See, e.g., Ian R. Macneil, "Contracts: Adjustment of Long-Term Economic Relations Under Classical, Neoclassical, and Relational Contract Law," *Northwestern Law Review* 72 (1978): 854. "Neoclassical" contract law refers to the changes in contracts from the time of the First Restatement to the enactment of the Uniform Commercial Code and the *Second Restatement*. See generally, Arthur L. Corbin, *Corbin on Contracts* (St. Paul, Minn.: West Publishing Co., 1952); Lon Fuller and Richard Braucher, *Basic Contract Law*, 2d ed. (St. Paul, Minn.: West Publishing Co., 1964); Richard Braucher, "Interpretation and Legal Effect in the Second Restatement of Contracts," *Columbia Law Review* 81 (1981): 13; E. Allan Farnsworth, "Good Faith Performance and Commercial Reasonableness Under the Uniform Commercial Code," *University of Chicago Law Review* 30 (1963): 666. See also, Karl N. Llewellyn, *The Common Law Tradition* (Boston: Little, Brown, and Co., 1960); Zipporah B. Wiseman, "The Limits of Vision: Karl Llewellyn and the Law of Contracts," *Harvard Law Review* 100 (1987): 465.

34. The meeting of the minds or will theory held that a "man is not bound by a contractual obligation unless he willed it so." The theory under its "purest form" requires a finding of actual intent {subjective) and not the mere manifestation of intent (objective). Furthermore, there must be a communal or mutual intent *(consensus ad idem)* at agreeing to the same thing. Corbin, *Contracts*, sec. 106. The meeting of the minds in classical contract law happens at a single point in time. The Uniform Commercial Code recognizes, however, that it may be beyond the ability of the court to determine that point in time due to the nature of modern contracting. "An agreement sufficient to constitute a contract . . . may be found even though the moment of its making is undetermined." Uniform Commercial Code, sec. 2–204(2) (1990).

35. "Any assertion of a covenant necessarily required proof of the other party's assent, his will, because covenant was nothing but the combination of two individual wills in an agreement." Note, "Proving the Will of Another: The Specialty Requirement in Covenant," *Harvard Law Review* 105 (1981): 2001, 2015. The author argues that the difficulty of proving another's will was the impetus for the development of the sealed instrument or specialty as "formal" proof of consent.

36. Professor Simpson asserts that the importance of a meeting of the wills or agreement became more prominent in the nineteenth century. "[T]he nineteenth century saw a very considerable

rise in the significance accorded to *consensus* or agreement." A. W. B. Simpson, "Innovation in Nineteenth Century Contract Law," *Law Quarterly Review* 91 (1975): 247, 267.

37. See generally, Roscoe Pound, "The Role of Will in Law," *Harvard Law Review* 68 (1954): 1; E. Allan Farnsworth, "The Past of Promise," *Columbia Law Review* 69 (1969): 576. For a review of the demise of the will theory of contract see, John D. Calamari and Joseph M. Perillo, *Contracts*, 3d ed. (St. Paul, Minn.: West Publishing Co., 1987).

38. "The phrase first appeared in English usage in 1825, and is literally translated by the imperative 'let do.' The popular understanding of it was that individuals, especially businesspersons, should be free of all government restraint to pursue their own selfish interests." Rondo Cameron, *A Concise History of Economic History of the World* (New York: Oxford University Press, 1989), 213; Adam Smith, *Inquiry and Causes of the Wealth of Nations* (1776; reprint, New York: The Modern Library, 1937).

39. "[I]t is said that the paramount public policy is that *freedom of contract* is not to be interfered with lightly, and it is the court's duty to sustain the legality of a contract in whole or in part whenever it can do so." *American Jurisprudence, Contracts*, 2d ed. 17 (1991), 264 (emphasis added). "The fundamental basis of American contract law is that parties should have absolute 'freedom of contract' unless some overriding public policy concern restricts that freedom." Larry A. DiMatteo, "Depersonalization of Personal Service Contracts: The Search for a Modern Approach to Assignability," *Akron Law Review* 27 (1994): 407, 411. See also, *Bene v. New York Life Ins. Co.*, 87 S.W.2d 979 (Ark. 1935); *Cimmins and Pierce Co. v. Kidder Peabody Acceptance Corp.*, 185 N.E. 383 (Mass. 1933); *Tharp v. Allis-Chalmers Mfg. Co.*, 81 P.2d 703 (N.M. 1938).

40. Grant Gilmore, *The Death of Contract* (Columbus: Ohio State University Press, 1974), 40 (emphasis added).

41. "Intention is regarded as the keystone of contract law." Calamari and Perillio, *Contracts*, 8.

42. James Gordley, *The Philosophical Origins of Modern Contract Doctrine* (Oxford: Clarendon Press, 1991), 7–8.

43. David P. Dougherty, "Error Revisited: The Louisiana Revision of Error as a Vice of Consent in Contracting," *Tulane Law Review* 62 (1988): 717–18. For an analysis of the notion of subjective rights and "objective juridical situations" in Roman law see, Geoffrey Samuel, "Epistemology, Propaganda and Roman Law: Some Reflections on the History of the Subjective Right," *Journal of Legal History* 10 (1989): 161. The author states that "the Roman objective view of *ius*, which originally meant legal connection, became a subjective form of individual sovereignty." Ibid., 167.

44. For a concise and clear exposition of the evolution and meaning of ancient ritual and practice see, Steven Lukes and Andrew Scull, eds., *Durkheim and The Law* (Oxford: Basil Blackwell, 1983), 196–200.

45. Ibid., 213.

46. "Contract by ritual was secured by magic and sacred processes . . . in the consensual form the given word acquired the same security and the same objectivity through the effect of the law alone." Ibid., 211. Durkheim argues that "had it not been for the existence of the contract by solemn ritual, there would be no notion of the contract by mutual assent." Ibid.

47. Merton L. Ferson, "The Formation of Simple Contracts," *Cornell Law Quarterly* 9 (1924): 402, 407, as quoted in Randy E. Barnett, ". . . And Contractual Consent," *Southern California Interdisciplinary Law Journal* 3 (1993): 412, 435n. 38.

48. Macneil, *New Social Contract*, 59–60 (emphasis added).

49. The notion of will has been incorporated into other theories of contract. Professor Fried incorporates the notion of will in his "promise theory" of contract. "So long as we see contractual obligation as based on promise, . . . the focus of the inquiry is on the *will of the parties.*" Fried, *Contract As Promise*, 4.

50. Richard A. Posner, *The Problems of Jurisprudence* (Cambridge: Harvard University Press, 1990), 25.

51. Gilmore, *Death of Contract*, 8 (emphasis added).

52. Roscoe Pound, *Jurisprudence* 5 (St. Paul, Minn.: West Publishing Co., 1959), 209, citing, Planiol, *Traite elemrntaire de droit civil* (1932), vol.2, sec. 986.

53. U.N. Convention on Contracts for the International Sale of Goods, Art. 18 (2), U.N. Doc. A/CONF.97/18 (1980).

54. Clarence D. Ashley, "Should There Be Freedom of Contract?," *Columbia Law Review* 4 (1904): 423, as quoted in Morton J. Horwitz, *The Transformation of American Law, 1870–1960* (New York: Oxford University Press, 1992), 38.

55. Horwitz, 35.

56. See, e.g., E. Allan Farnsworth, "Precontractual Liability and Preliminary Agreements: Fair Dealing and Failed Negotiations," *Columbia Law Review* 87 (1987): 217.

57. Macneil, *New Social Contract*, 8–9. "Promises are inherently fragmentary." Ibid., 8.

58. 118 N.E. 214 (New York, 1917).

59. Ibid. (emphasis added). See also, *McCall Co. v. Wright*, 117 N.Y.S. 775 (1909); *Moran v. Standard Oil Co.*, 105 N.E. 217 (New York, 1914).

60. Ibid., 9.

61. Paul A. Kolers, "Perception and Representation," *Annual Review of Psychology* 34 (1983): 129, 146.

62. "Necessarily confusing therefore is the structure of natural language; polysemy, multiple interpretations assignable to a single word, makes natural language nonnotational." Ibid., 146–47.

63. Karl Llewellyn, *The Case Law System in America*, ed. Paul Gewirtz (Chicago: University of Chicago Press, 1989), 74n. 1.

64. Ibid., 74.

65. For a fuller discussion of the notion of "presentiation" see, Ian R. Macneil, "Restatement (Second) of Contracts and Presentiation," *Virginia Law Review* 60 (1974): 589.

66. Macneil, *New Social Contract*, 9.

67. Ibid.

68. See chapter 4, notes 69–104 and accompanying text.

69. "Problems of intentionality . . . seem to be soluble if one puts aside their subjective aspect." Thomas Nagel, *Mortal Questions* (Cambridge: Cambridge University Press, 1979), 201.

70. Fried, *Contract As Promise*, 75 (emphasis added).

71. Atiyah, "Contracts, Promises," 193, 209 (emphasis added).

72. Barnett, ". . . And Consent," 412, 427.

73. Ibid., 429.

74. Holmes, *Common Law*, 242.

75. Arthur L. Corbin, "Discharge of Contracts," *Yale Law Journal* 22 (1919): 513, 515, as quoted in Horwitz, *Transformation of American Law*, 50.

76. See, e.g., Uniform Commercial Code, sec. 1–102(3) (obligation of reasonableness); sec. 1–204 (reasonable time); sec. 1–205 (course of dealing and usage of trade); sec. 2–204(3) (manifested intent); sec. 2–305(1)(c) (reasonable price term); sec. 2–306 (output, requirements, and exclusive dealings); sec. 2–308 (place of delivery); sec. 2–503 (tender of delivery) (1995).

77. Nagel, *Mortal Questions*, 201.

78. Dennis M. Patterson, "The Pseudo-Debate Over Default Rules in Contract Law," *Southern California Interdisciplinary Law Journal* 3 (1993): 235, 243.

79. "Where there is no agreement, the court should supply a term which comports with community standards of fairness and policy rather than analyze a hypothetical model of the bargaining process." *Restatement (Second) of Contracts* (1981), sec. 204, Comment *d.*, as quoted in Patterson, "The Psuedo-Debate Over Default Rules," 249.

80. See above notes 38–42 and accompanying text.

81. See above notes 4, 13, and 14 and accompanying text.

82. See generally, Richard Craswell, "Contract Law, Default Rules, and the Philosophy of Promising," *Michigan Law Review* 88 (1989): 489. See also, Charles J. Goetz and Robert E. Scott, "The Limits of Expanded Choice: An Analysis of the Interactions Between Express and Implied Contract Terms," *California Law Review* 73 (1985): 261.

83. See chapter 6, notes 1–41 and accompanying text.

84. See chapter 6, notes 64–76 and accompanying text.

85. There is no separate substantive area known as the law of satisfaction, however, the norm of satisfaction can be seen throughout the law of contract. It can be found pervasively in the areas of performance and material breach.

86. The central tenet of Holmes's jurisprudential thought was that the inevitable process of legal development was *from* a starting point at which rules of law are based on . . . judgments about subjective moral fault or culpability *toward* an end point at which the original moral content . . . will have disappeared and the subjective state of mind of the defendant will become irrelevant.
    Gilmore, *Death of Contract*, 41.

87. If in contract . . . the actual state of the parties' minds is relevant, then each litigated case must become an extended factual inquiry into what was intended. . . . If, however, we can restrict ourselves to the externals, then the factual inquiry will be much simplified and in time be dispensed with altogether as the courts accumulate precedents about recurring types of permissible and impermissible conduct. By this process questions, originally perceived as questions of fact, will resolve themselves into questions of law.
    Ibid., 42.

88. Benjamin N. Cardozo, *The Nature of the Judicial Process* (New Haven: Yale University Press, 1921), 20, 23, 30–31, 34.

89. Ibid., 19, 31, and 43.

90. Ibid., 89.

91. Ibid., 102.

92. "The traditions of our jurisprudence commit us to the objective standard." Ibid., 106.

93. "A jurisprudence that is not constantly brought into relation to objective or external standards incurs the risk of degenerating into a jurisprudence of mere sentiment." Ibid.

94. The search for objective truth is "beyond the reach of human faculties." Ibid., 168.

95. Ibid., 136.

96. Ibid.

97. Lon L. Fuller, "Consideration and Form," *Columbia Law Review* 41 (1941): 799, 801 (emphasis added).

98. These channels or forms of contract are not static. See, e.g., Charles L. Knapp, "Enforcing the Contract to Bargain," *New York University Law Review* 44 (1969): 673. Professor Knapp introduces the concept of a *contract to bargain*. This is an unrecognized area of contract law somewhere between noncontractual negotiations and a complete contract. He argues for the granting of relief in instances where parties have manifested a commitment to bargain in good faith with the purpose of completing a contract. "[C]ontracts do not spring, full-blown, from the collective brows of the parties." Ibid., 727.

99. George K. Gardner, "An Inquiry Into the Principles of the Law of Contracts," *Harvard Law Review* 46 (1932): 1, 25.

100. Fuller, "Consideration and Form," 802.

101. Professor Fuller believed that the expression of intention was a type of contractual formality. "[E]ven the requirement . . . that the intention of the parties be express, rather than implied or tacit, is in essence a requirement of form." Ibid., 806.

102. "He who is compelled to do something which will furnish a satisfactory memorial of his intention will be induced to deliberate. . . . In this way the party is induced to canalize his own intention." Ibid., 803.

103. Ibid.

104. Ibid.

105. Ibid., 807.

106. Ibid., 808.

107. "Any such uncompromising *objective* method of interpreting an act would be incomprehensible." Ibid.

CHAPTER 3

1. David Granfield, *The Inner Experience of Law: A Jurisprudence of Subjectivity* (Washington, D.C.: Catholic University, 1988), 14.

2. R. B. Vermeesch and K. E. Lindgren, *Law of Australia*, 2d ed. (Sydney: Butterworths, 1973), 133.

3. Henry Sumner Maine, *Ancient Law* (Boston: Beacon Press, 1963).

4. "Lastly, the consensual contracts emerge, in which the mental attitude of the contractors is solely regarded, and external circumstances have no title to notice *except as evidence of inward undertaking.*" Ibid., 328 (emphasis added).

5. See generally, N. Goodman, "On Thoughts Without Words," *Cognition* (1982): 10.

6. Paul A. Kolers, "Perception and Presentation," *Annual Review of Psychology* 34 (1983): 129, 155.

7. Justice Holmes succinctly states that the "law has nothing to do with the actual state of the parties' minds. In contract, as elsewhere, it must go by externals, and judge parties by their conduct." Oliver Wendell Holmes, *The Common Law*, ed. M. DeWolfe-Howe (Boston: Little, Brown, and Co., 1963), 242.

8. Grant Gilmore, *The Death of Contract* (Columbus: Ohio State University Press, 1974), 42–43. It should be noted that the subjective-objective dialectic has a long history. One should not automatically suppose that the subjective approach preceded the objective one. The objective approach has a lineage as long as its subjective counterpart. Immanuel Kant's necessarily subjective notion of duty recognizes the objective nature of the need to obey the law. Kant notes that imperatives or commands are "formulas expressing the relation of objective laws of volition in general to the subjective imperfection of [the] will of the rational being." Immanuel Kant, *Foundations of the Metaphysics of Morals*, trans. L. W. Beck (New York: Macmillan, 1985), 31. He concludes that "nothing remains which can determine the will objectively except the law, and nothing subjectively except pure respect for this practical law." Ibid., 17.

9. W. von Leyden, *Aristotle on Equality and Justice* (New York: St. Martin's Press, 1985), 89.

10. Ibid., 110.

11. Ibid., 97.

12. "[T]he nature of that reasonableness which Sir Frederick Pollock, like Coke and Blackstone before him, claims as the historic ideal of the common law." George K. Gardner, "An Inquiry Into the Principles of the Law of Contracts," *Harvard Law Review* 46 (1932): 1, 3.

13. Clarke B. Whittier, "The Restatement of Contracts and Mutual Assent," *California Law Review* 17 (1929): 441, 442. See generally, *Restatement (Second) of Contracts* (1981), sec. 69.

14. Ibid., 448.

15. "The meaning that will determine legal effect is that which is arrived at by objective standards; one is bound, not by what he subjectively intends, but by what he leads others reasonably to think that he intends." Arthur L. Corbin, "Cardozo on the Law of Contracts," *Harvard Law Review* 52 (1939): 446. See generally, *Globe Steel Abrasive Co. v. National Metal Abrasive Co.*, 101 F.2d 489 (6th Cir. 1939); *Crossland v. Kentucky Blue Grass Seed Grower's Coop Ass'n*, 103 F.2d 565 (6th Cir. 1939); *Remington-Rand Business Service, Inc. v. Walter J. Peterson Co.*, 58 F.2d 11 (6th Cir.1932); *Ken-Rad Corp. v. R. C. Bohannan, Inc.*, 80 F.2d 251 (6th Cir. 1935).

16. Arthur L. Corbin, *Corbin on Contracts* (St. Paul, Minn.: West Publishing Co., 1952), sec.106, p. 156.

17. "The objective theory of contracts dictates that a contract shall have the meaning that a reasonable person would give it under the circumstances under which it was made, if he knew every-

thing he should plus everything the parties actually knew." W. David Slawson, "The Futile Search for Principles for Default Rules," *Southern California Interdisciplinary Law Journal* 3 (1993): 29, 38.

18. Ibid., 39.

19. See, e.g., *Uniform Commercial Code,* sec. 2–305 ("reasonable price at time of delivery"); 2–306 ("no quantity unreasonably disproportionate"); 2–307 ("where the circumstances give either party"); 2–309 ("time for shipment or delivery . . . shall be a reasonable time"); 2–609 ("reasonable grounds for insecurity").

20. *Restatement,* sec. 65 ("reasonableness of medium of acceptance"); sec. 90 ("promise reasonably inducing action or forbearance"); sec. 162(2) ("misrepresentation is material if it would be likely to induce a reasonable person"); sec. 228 ("if such a reasonable person in the position of the obligor would be satisfied").

21. "True laws of meaning presumably are so rare because they are out of step with the modern understanding that language always gains its meaning from contexts." Slawson, "Futile Search," 40.

22. 200 F. 287 (S.D.N.Y. 1911).

23. Ibid., 293–94 (emphasis added).

24. Courts will generally objectively imply contractual intent based upon the totality of the circumstances. "Courts look to the intent and the *surrounding circumstances* of the parties when forming a contract." Thomas P. Egan, "Equitable Doctrines Operating Against the Express Provisions of a Written Contract," *Depaul Business Law Journal* 5 (1993): 261, 311 (emphasis added). The implication of intent is widely accepted as a prerogative of the courts because the parties "with hindsight will tend to the interpretation that best suits their interests." Howel Lewis, "Letters of Comfort," *New Law Journal* 139 (1989): 339.

25. Patrick S. Atiyah, *Essays on Contract* (Oxford: Clarendon Press, 1986), 4 (emphasis added).

26. 1 W. L. R. 1403 (C.A. 1974).

27. Ibid.

28. Ibid., 1408 (emphasis added).

29. Lon Fuller, "Consideration and Form," *Columbia Law Review* 41 (1941): 799. See also, *Restatement (Second)* (1981), sec. 72, Comment *c.*

30. For a discussion of the "operative words" of contract see, Larry A. DiMatteo and René Sacasas, "Credit and Value Comfort Instruments: Crossing the Line from Assurance to Legally Significant Reliance and Toward a Theory of Enforceability," *Baylor Law Review* 47 (1995): 357.

31. Fuller, "Consideration and Form," 800, quoting John Austin, "Fragments—On Contracts," *Lectures on Jurisprudence,* 4th ed. 2 (1879), 939–44.

32. Ibid., 802.

33. The Roman *stipulatio* was a type of ceremonial procedure in which parties participated in order to imbue their promises with a binding force. "[S]*tipulatio* was the verbal contract and was the most solemn and formal of all contracts in [the Roman] system of jurisprudence." *Black's Law Dictionary,* 5th ed. (St. Paul, Minn.: West Publishing Co., 1979), 1268–69.

34. It was a ceremonial transfer of land used prior to the filing of deeds. "It was livery . . . where the parties went together upon the land, and there a twig . . . or other symbol was delivered in the name of the whole." Ibid., 843.

35. See generally, *Restatement (Second)*, sec. 95–97 and Introductory Note. See also, *Mobil Oil Corp. v. Wolfe*, 252 S.E.2d 809 (N.C. 1979); *Twining v. National Mortgage Corp.*, 302 A.2d 604 (Md. 1973).

36. Fuller, "Consideration and Form," 801 (emphasis added). Citing Jhering, Fuller notes that "legal formalities relieve the judge of an inquiry *whether* a legal transaction was intended, and . . . *which* was intended." Ibid.

37. See, e.g., *Restatement (Second)*, sec. 26 (Preliminary Negotiations). "A manifestation of willingness to enter into a bargain is not an offer if the person to whom it is addressed knows or has reason to know that the person making it does not intend to conclude a bargain until he has made a further manifestation of intent." The further manifestation of intent may be the formal exchange of a written contract.

38. 1 W. L. R. 1403, 1410 (C.A. 1974).

39. "A promise . . . which induces an action or forbearance is binding if injustice can be avoided only by enforcement of the promise." *Restatement (Second)*, sec. 90(1).

40. 629 N.E.2d 214, 218 (Ill. 1994).

41. *Restatement (Second)*, sec. 75. Professor Egan explains the rise of the "bargain principle":

> The strict bargain principle of contract law developed in response to the rise of the free market. The bargain principle's real appeal was its ease of administration. Theorists and courts found that rigid rules applied in an *objective manner* required a lot less inquiry and thought than attempting to inject equity and fairness into a consensual transaction.

Egan, "Equitable Doctrines," 311 (emphasis added).

42. "In modern times the enforcement of bargains . . . has been extended to the wholly executory exchange in which promise is exchanged for promise. . . . The promise is enforced by virtue of the fact of bargain, without more." Ibid., sec. 75, Comment *a*. The *Restatement*'s bargain principle (section 75) and its adoption of promissory estoppel (section 90) was the product of the scholarly "duel" between Samuel Williston and Arthur Corbin, a staunch believer in reliance theory. For an interesting account of this debate see Gilmore, *Death of Contract*.

43. *Restatement (Second)*, sec. 17. Apparent consent is sufficient to bind a party even if lack of actual consent can be proved. "[I]t is clear that a mental reservation of a party to a bargain does not impair the obligation it purports to undertake." Ibid., Comment *a*.

44. Harvey McGregor, *Contract Code* (Milano: Sweet and Maxwell, 1993), sec. 571.

45. Kenneth J. Goldberg, "Lender Liability and Good Faith," *Boston University Law Review* 68 (1988): 653, 669 (emphasis added). The scope of reliance's reach can be seen in cases where negotiations and discussions have not been reduced to formalized contract. An example of this would be the use of "comfort instruments" in the world of commerce and finance. These are generally instruments in letter form lacking the formalities of contract and lacking contractual intent by the writer. Nonetheless, it is the hope of the comfort letter writer to induce another party to act or forebear. Such was the case in *Nimrod Marketing v. Texas Energy*. While in the process of bargaining for a construction contract, the defendant sent a letter to its purchasing agent notifying him of its "hope" to begin construction by a certain date. Based on the letter and without a "formal" contract the plaintiff began to make purchases in preparation for the construction. The court held that the defendant was liable for the plaintiff's expenses because it "clearly had knowl-

edge of the special circumstances" and that the plaintiff had "relied on the comfort instrument." 769 F.2d 1076, 107–80 (5th Cir. 1985). See generally, DiMatteo and Sacasas, "Credit and Value Comfort Instruments." For a review of detrimental reliance and promissory estoppel, see generally, Lon Fuller and William Perdue, "The Reliance Interest in Contract Damages: 1 [2]," *Yale Law Journal* 46 (1936): 52 and *Yale Law Journal* 46 (1937): 373; Benjamin F. Boyer, "Promissory Estoppel: Principles From Precedents," *Michigan Law Review* 50 (1952): 639; Note, "Once More Into The Breach: Promissory Estoppel and Traditional Damage Doctrine," *University of Chicago Law Review* 37 (1970): 559; Jay M. Feinman, "The Meaning of Reliance: A Historical Perspective," *Wisconsin Law Review* (1984): 1371; Charles L. Knapp, "Reliance in the Revised Restatement: The Proliferation of Promissory Estoppel," *Columbia Law Review* 81 (1981): 52. Compare, Phuong Pham, "The Waning of Promissory Estoppel," *Cornell Law Review* 79 (1994): 1263. See also, Randy E. Barnett and Mary E. Becker, "Beyond Reliance: Promissory Estoppel, Contract Formalities, and Misrepresentation," *Hofstra Law Review* 15 (1987): 443.

46. See generally, *Restatement (Second)*, sec. 75; Grant Gilmore, *The Ages of American Law* (New Haven: Yale University Press, 1977); Gilmore, *The Death of Contract*; Melvin A. Eisenberg, "The Bargain Principle and Its Limits," *Harvard Law Review* 95 (1982): 741. See also, Wallace K. Lightsey, "A Critique of the Promise Model of Contract," *William and Mary Law Review* 26 (1984): 45. Compare, Randy E. Barnett, "A Consent Theory of Contract," *Columbia Law Review* 86 (1986): 269.

47. Fuller and Perdue, "Reliance Interest: 1," 52.

48. Fuller and Perdue, "Reliance Interest: 2," 373.

49. See, e.g., Feinman, "Meaning of Reliance," 1373; Robert Childress and Jack Garamella, "Law of Restitution and the Reliance Interest in Contract," *Northwestern Law Review* 64 (1969): 433.

50. See note 76 below.

51. *Restatement (Second)*, sec. 90, Comment *b*.

52. Ibid., sec. 90, Comment *d*.

53. Corbin, *Contracts*, sec. 200, p. 290.

54. For an interesting exposé of the Williston-Corbin debate on the bargain-reliance poles of contract as represented by sections 75 and 90 of the *Restatement*, see Gilmore, *The Death of Contract*.

55. Corbin, *Contracts*, sec. 200, p. 289.

56. The promisor "should have reasonably expected to induce the action or forbearance." *Restatement (Second)*, sec. 90(1).

57. "Section 90 of the Restatement provides in effect that serious reliance may under some circumstances make binding a promise for which nothing has been given or promised in exchange." Fuller and Perdue, "Reliance Interest: 2," 373, 401.

58. Professor Macneil refers to surrounding circumstances as the "tacit assumptions" of contract. Ian Macneil, *The New Social Contract* (New Haven: Yale University Press, 1980), 24. Professor Macneil states that such "assumptions may range from general ones such as trust to the highly specific, such as assumptions about particular and precise trade usages."

59. *Hillas and Co. v. Arcos*, 147 L.T. 503, 513 (1932).

60. "The strict bargain principle of contract law developed in response to the rise of the free market. The bargain principle's real appeal was its ease of administration," Egan, "Equitable Doctrines," 311.

61. See, e.g., Robert S. Summers, "General Equitable Principles Under Section 1–103 of the *Uniform Commercial Code*," *Northwestern University Law Review* 72 (1978): 906; *Uniform Commercial Code*, sec. 1–203 (duty of good faith); *Restatement (Second)*, sec. 205 (duty of fair dealing).

62. Lloyd's Bank Canada, No. 18929/87, 1991 Ont. C. J. Lexis, *23.

63. See generally, DiMatteo and Sacasas, "Credit and Value Comfort Instruments."

64. See generally, "Symposium on the Restatement (Third) of Suretyship," *William and Mary Law Review* 34 (1993): 985; Arthur A. Stearns, *The Law of Suretyship*, 5th ed. (1951); *Uniform Commercial Code*, sec. 3–416(1) and (2).

65. 1924 All E.R. 245 (Ct. App. 1923).

66. Ibid., 255.

67. John D. Calamari and Joseph M. Perillo, *Contracts*, 3d ed. (St. Paul, Minn.: West Publishing Co., 1990), 17.

68. Queen's Bench, affirmed, Court of Appeals (Commercial Court) (Transcript Assoc. 1985).

69. Wolfgang Hering, "The Commercial Laws of the Federal Republic of Germany," *Digest of Commercial Laws of the World*, ed. Lester Nelson (New York: Oceana Publications, 1992), 62.

70. This informalism is reflected in the fact that "a merchant's guarantee is valid even if given only verbally." Dennis Campbell, ed., *Legal Aspects of Doing Business in Western Europe* (St. Paul, Minn.: West Publishing Co., 1983), 216.

71. "They are at liberty to *agree* to variants of accepted legal instruments or to develop entirely new ones." Ibid.

72. L. Proscour, "France," in *Legal Aspects*, ed. Campbell, 302.

73. Hering, "Commercial Laws," 206.

74. 45 N.W.2d 537, 542 (Minn. 1950), quoting, *Magee v. Scott and Holston Lumber Co.*, 80 N.W. 781, 782 (Minn. 1899).

75. See note 35 and accompanying text in chapter 5.

76. The concept of good faith has a long tradition in English common law. When one party possesses specialized knowledge she has a duty to disclose it under the principle of *uberrimae fidei*, of the utmost good faith. The expansiveness of these normative concepts was noted by Professor Knapp. "The two grand principles . . . good faith and unconscionability . . . state a principle of abstract justice capable of application in an infinite variety of factual situations." Knapp, "Reliance in the Revised Restatement," 53, 81.

77. "There is a normal assumption that a business transaction is not meaningless and that the words have a purpose." *Chelsea Industries, Inc. v. Accuray Leasing Corp.*, 699 F.2d 58, 60 (1st Cir. 1983). See also, *Cincinnati Enquirer, Inc. v. American Security and Trust Co.*, 160 N.E.2d 392, 398 (Ohio 1958).

78. *Kleinwort Benson Ltd. v. Malaysia Mining Corp. Bhd.*, 1 W.L.R. 799 (1988).

79. See, e.g., *U.S. v. Seckinger*, 397 U.S. 203 (1970).

80. Sheldon W. Halpern, "Application of the Doctrine of Commercial Impracticability: Searching for 'The Wisdom of Solomon,'" *University of Pennsylvania Law Review* 135 (1987): 1123.

81. "The contractual fiction of presumed intent allows one to assume that the excuse arises from the terms of the contract itself rather than from . . . judicial legislation." Ibid., 1127–28. "While espousing the need for a doctrine of excuse predicated on the mutual intent of the parties, the courts replaced a finding of actual intent with the fiction of presumed intent to condition performance." Ibid., 1140.

82. See, *Uniform Commercial Code*, sec. 2–615; Halpern, "Doctrine of Commercial Impracticability," 1146–54.

83. "[A] party's performance is made impracticable . . . by the occurrence of an event the nonoccurrence of which was a *basic assumption* on which the contract was made. . . ." *Restatement (Second)*, sec. 261, Comment *b.*, states that the "fact the event was foreseeable, or even foreseen, does not compel a conclusion that its nonoccurrence was not a basic assumption."

84. Halpern argues that in practice the principle of foreseeability has remained a judicial favorite. "The Code's and Restatement's apparently *subjective* search for actual intent has not in fact displaced the centrality of *objective* foreseeability." Halpern, "Doctrine of Commercial Impracticability," 1148 (emphasis original). It is unclear whether the code and the restatement do indeed adopt a subjective approach as indicated by Professor Halpern. Comment *e.*, entitled "Subjective and objective impracticability," states that the proper focus is whether the performance can objectively be rendered, not whether it is impracticable in terms of the particular party. The notion of "basic assumption" is nonetheless a party-specific analysis. It may be that both objective and subjective approaches are reconcilable because there are two factors at work: the subjective, party-specific approach of basic assumption and the objective, occurrence-centered approach. The two can be used to answer two different questions. The first is whether the occurrence is one that was a basic assumption of the contract at the time of formation. The second is whether the occurrence is indeed a type to render performance impracticable.

85. Lord Denning, *The Discipline of Law* (London: Butterworths, 1979), 41–53.

86. Calamari and Perillo, *Contracts*, secs., 2–7, p. 33.

87. 62 N.Y. 256 (1875).

88. "The defendant is *precluded* from asserting" a lack of actual assent. Ibid.

89. Ibid., 257 (emphasis added).

90. Frederick Pollock, *Principles of Contract*, 10th ed. (London: Stevens and Sons, 1936), 245, as quoted by J. P. Vorster, *Law Quarterly Review* 103 (1987): 274, 277n. 24.

91. Gardner, "Principles of the Law of Contracts," 4–8.

92. This is the famous case of mutual mistake regarding the shipment of cotton from India to England involving two ships named Peerless. 2 H. and C. 906 (1864).

93. Gardner, 6.

94. "[T]he line between a contractual claim and a quasi-contractual claim based on unjust enrichment is often indistinct." *Restatement (Second)* sec. 19, Comment *a.*

95. Ibid., sec. 200, Comment *b.* See generally, Edwin W. Patterson, "The Interpretation and Construction of Contracts," *Columbia Law Review* 64 (1964): 833.

96. Ibid., sec. 2, Comment b.

97. An alternative issue in the art of objective interpretation is whether it should be an interpretation of the community or of the parties. "The objective of interpretation in the general law of contracts is to carry out the understanding of the parties rather than to impose obligations on them contrary to their understanding." Ibid., sec. 201, Comment *c*. See generally, E. Allan Farnsworth, "Meaning in the Law of Contracts," *Yale Law Journal* 76 (1967): 939.

98. For an elaboration on this school of thought see Edward Yorio and Steve Thel, "The Promissory Basis of Section 90," *Yale Law Journal* 101 (1991): 111.

99. "In the Holmesian revision foreseeability was not enough; there must have been a deliberate and conscious assumption of the risk by the contract-breaker." Gilmore, *Death of Contract*, 52.

100. "Proceedings at Fourth Annual Meeting," *American Law Institute Proceedings* 4 (1926): 93, as quoted in,Yorio and Thel "Promissory Basis,"126.

101. Charles Fried, *Contract As Promise* (Cambridge: Harvard University Press, 1981), 25n.

102. Gilmore, *Death of Contract*, 92.

103. Ibid., 61.

104. Fried, *Contract As Promise*, 4.

105. Professor Gilmore asserts that "damages in contract have become indistinguishable from damages in tort." *Death of Contract*, sec. 8, p. 88.

106. William Howarth, "The Meaning of Objectivity in Contract," *Law Quarterly Review* 100 (1984): 265 and J. P. Vorster, "A Comment on the Meaning of Objectivity in Contract," *Law Quarterly Review* 103 (1987): 274.

107. Howarth, "Meaning of Objectivity," 266.

108. "Both of these perspectives provide a rationale for resolving disputes between the subjective views actually held by the parties whilst doing the minimum damage to the ideal of freedom of contract." Ibid., 280.

109. It may be argued that as a promisor knows what he wants to promise, he should be under a duty to ensure that his intention is correctly understood and that the promise should accordingly be viewed from the perspective of a reasonable promisee. However, it may be argued with equal force that a promisee knows what he wants from the promisor and that the promisee is therefore bound to make sure the promisor understands what he wants from him.
Vorster, "A Comment," 283n. 51.

110. Arthur A. Leff, "Contract As Thing," *American University Law Review* 19 (1970): 131, 138.

111. "What results is neither's will; it is somehow a combination of those desires." Ibid.

112. Ibid., 286n. 71, quoting; *Smith v. Hughes*, 6 Q.B. 597 (1871).

113. Ibid.

114. 1 A.C. 854 (1983).

115. Ibid., 914, as quoted in Howarth, "Meaning of Objectivity," 284.

116. Atiyah, *Essays on Contract*, 13.

117. Howarth sees objectivity in its detached form as giving a "greater scope for judicial intervention and the imposition of agreement upon the parties contrary to their intentions." Howarth, "Meaning of Objectivity," 280.

118. The *Restatement (Second)* refers to the notion of the acts of contracting. Acts or operative acts of contracting generally refers to the act of promising or manifestations of conduct in which an intent to contract may be implied. Section 1, Comment *b*. states that "contract . . . denotes the act or acts of promising." It then qualifies this statement by stating that "operative acts other than promise" may also create a contractual obligation. See, sec. 1, Comment *d*. The notion that the communication of assent may be exercised by other than words is further explained in section 19, "Conduct as Manifestation of Assent."

119. Totality of circumstances implies that there are numerous elements other than the spoken or written word that are relevant to issues of formation and interpretation. "A wide variety of elements of the total situation may be relevant to the interpretation of [contractual] conduct." *Restatement (Second)*, sec. 19, Comment *a*.

120. 6 CHESHIRE 481 (Mass. 1834).

121. Ibid., 493 (emphasis added).

122. Denning, *Discipline of Law,* 32–53 (the construction of contracts).

123. Ibid., 42. Lord Denning likens this problem to the *ejusdem generis* rule used in contractual and statutory construction. This rule holds that when general words are used in conjunction with words of a more particular or specific meaning, "such general words are not to be construed in their widest extent." *Black's Law Dictionary*, 464.

124. Ibid.

125. "Even if the contract is absolute in its terms, nevertheless if it is not absolute in intent, it will not be held absolute in effect." Ibid.

126. Ibid., 38, quoting, Lord Radcliffe in *Davis Contractors Ltd. v. Fareham Urban District Council*, A.C. 696 at 728 (1956).

127. Karl N. Llewellyn, *The Common Law Tradition* (Boston: Little, Brown, and Co., 1960), 364.

128. Ibid., 365.

129. Ibid., 371 (emphasis original).

130. Ibid., 370 (emphasis added).

131. *Restatement (Second)*, sec. 211, Comment *c*. (emphasis added).

132. Fried, *Contract As Promise*, 72.

133. Ibid.

134. Ibid., 73.

135. Richard E. Speidel, "Unconscionability, Assent and Consumer Protection," *University of Pittsburgh Law Review* 31 (1970): 359, 361.

136. *Uniform Commercial Code,* sec. 2–302, Comment 1 (1995).

137. The two types of assent are discussed by Professor Speidel, "Unconscionability," 361–67.

138. "[O]r should have exploited an opportunity to shop comparatively." Ibid., 363.

139. Phillip S. James, *English Law*, 9th ed. (London: Butterworths, 1976), 238–39.

140. "Certainty of contract" generally holds that the parties must have agreed or have provided a basis for the determination of the "essential" terms of the contract. "[A] contract can only be complete

if all essential terms have been agreed upon; for there can be no agreement if any such terms remain to be settled." Ibid., 208.

141. The standardization of contract has long been the subject of scholarly research. Llewellyn refers to Isaacs' 1917 work as the first "pioneering" scholarly paper on the subject. See generally, Nathan Isaacs, "The Standardizing of Contracts," *Yale Law Journal* 27 (1917): 34. See also, Todd Rakoff, "Contracts of Adhesion: An Essay in Reconstruction," *Harvard Law Review* 96 (1983): 1174; W. David Slawson, "The New Meaning of Contract: The Transformation of Contracts by Standard Forms," *University of Pittsburgh Law Review* 46 (1984): 21. Compare, Andrew Burgess, "Consumer Adhesion Contracts and Unfair Terms," *Anglo-American Law Review* 15 (1986): 255.

142. Llewellyn, *Common Law Tradition*, 367.

143. Contract law is set on its head when the terms of a contract are in direct conflict. The courts face an enforcement dilemma where there is clear contractual intent to contract coupled with an exchange of written instruments possessing conflicting terms. Beale and Dugdale, venture this response; "A court faced with a clearly unresolved conflict of terms on the one hand but a clear intention to contract on the other might decide that there was a contract containing those terms which had been agreed, and dismiss the remainder of the conditions." Hugh Beale and Tony Dugdale, "Contracts Between Businessmen: Planning and the Use of Contractual Remedies," *British Journal of Law and Society* 2 (1975): 45, 50. This article represents the findings of interviews with engineering manufacturers in the city of Bristol, England. See also, Stuart Macaulay, "Noncontractual Relations in Business," *American Sociological Review* 28 (1963): 45.

144. Llewellyn, *Common Law Tradition*, 371.

145. "The boiler is assented to en bloc . . . on the implicit assumption . . . that its terms are . . . not manifestly unreasonable and unfair." Ibid. Llewellyn's blanket assent may well violate one of his own admonitions: "Covert tools are never reliable tools." Ibid., 365.

146. Richard E. Speidel, "Contract Law: Some Reflections Upon Commercial Context and the Judicial Process," *Wisconsin Law Review* (1967): 822, 829.

147. Stephen Hedley offers the following definition of the "intent to create legal relations" unrelated to the *Uniform Commercial Code*. "When the courts ask whether contractual intent is present . . . they mean [d]oes what the parties intended qualify as a contract? . . . intent to create legal relations is simply one subdivision of contractual intent." Stephen Hedley, "Keeping Contract In Its Place—*Balfour v. Balfour* and the Enforceability of Informal Agreements," *Oxford Journal of Legal Studies* 5 (1985): 391, 403.

148. Speidel, "Reflections Upon Commercial Context," 830. Professor Speidel notes that this affixation of liability to simple intent to create may only be feasible in specific, clearly defined categories of contracts. Quoting Fuller and Braucher: "Legal consequences can be said to be directly derived from the intention of the parties only where that intention runs in terms which coincide roughly with the categories of the law, when, in other words, the parties' intention is capable of answering the question which the law proposes." Ibid., 831 n.34, citing Lon Fuller and Robert Braucher, *Basic Contract Law*, 2d ed. (St. Paul, Minn.: West Publishing Co., 1964), 67.

149. *Bach v. Friden Calculating Mach. Co.*, 155 F.2d 361, 365 (6th Cir. 1946).

150. "This insistence that the parties must of had some intention forces the courts to invent an intention . . . one that leads to the most reasonable result." Hedley, "Keeping Contract in Its Place," 393–94.

151. Ibid., 396, citing Macaulay, "Noncontractual Relations in Business," 45.

152. Beale and Dugdale, "Contracts Between Businessmen," 48.

153. Ibid., 49.

154. See notes 160–63 below and accompanying text for a further examination of the notion and role of the default rules of contract.

155. . . . where contracts are made informally by telephone or simple exchange of letters. Here only the primary obligations would be planned expressly but the parties to such contracts often held *unexpressed assumptions* about the way in which obligations would be adjusted or enforced, relying upon trade custom or a gentlemen's agreement with the other contracting party.

   Beale and Dugdale, "Contracts Between Businessmen," 48.

156. Another argument offered regarding the waning importance of intent is that the reasonable person is a creation of values and not of objective facts. It is a device used to forward not what *was* considered to be reasonable by the contracting parties at the time of contracting but what is considered reasonable by the court in hindsight. Hedley, "Keeping Contract in Its Place," 398.

157. Morton J. Horwitz, *The Transformation of American Law, 1870–1960* (New York: Oxford University Press, 1992), 37.

158. Ibid., 48. Professor Horwitz singles out the growth of the corporate form of doing business as the other force behind the rise of the objective theory. "The corporate form forced judges to objectivize legal concepts, to look for the reliance of a reasonable person rather than the actual subjective command of a principal." Ibid.

159. The "objective theory of contract could no longer be regarded as simply the best practical approximation of the actual will of the parties." Ibid., 50.

160. Randy E. Barnett, "The Sound of Silence: Default Rules and Contractual Consent," *Virginia Law Review* 78 (1992): 821, 825. See generally, Ian Ayres and Robert Gertner, "Filling Gaps in Incomplete Contracts: An Economic Theory of Default Rules," *Yale Law Journal* 99 (1989): 87.

161. Ibid., 826.

162. The "overall consent . . . operates to justify the selection of particular default rules." Ibid., 827. See also, Randy E. Barnett, "The Internal and External Analysis of Concepts," *Cardozo Law Review* 11 (1990): 525.

163. Barnett, "The Sound of Silence," 829 (emphasis added).

164. Ibid., 855.

165. Ibid., 857.

166. "The use of conventionalist default rules bring the parties' actual or subjective consent closer to the meaning that they objectively manifest to each other." Barnett, ". . . And Contractual Consent," *Southern California Interdisciplinary Law Journal* 3 (1993): 412, 431.

167. Barnett, "The Sound of Silence," 859n. 81. See also, E. Allan Farnsworth, *Contracts*, 2d ed. (Boston: Little, Brown, and Co. 1990), sec. 7.9, pp. 502–11.

168. Ibid., 504.

169. Ibid., 505n. 12. 59 A.2d 524 (Conn. 1948).

170. 254 N.Y. 179 (1930) (Justice Cardozo writing for a unanimous Court of Appeals).

171. Ibid., 183.

172. "Alternative shades of meaning may remain. There is still a true contract, whichever shade shall be accepted." Ibid., 185.

173. Ibid., 183.

174. Slawson, "Search for Principles," 38.

175. "To be a law of meaning . . . a law must provide a meaning different from the meaning that the objective theory of contracts would provide." Ibid.

176. Samuel Williston and George J. Thompson, *Selections From Williston on Contracts*, rev. ed. (1938), sec. 21, p. 18.

177. He proclaimed that the subjective theory "is foreign to the common law and . . . is intrinsically objectionable." Ibid.

178. Corbin, *Contracts*, 157.

179. *Chelsea Industries, Inc. v. Accuray Leasing Corp.*, 699 F.2d 58, 60 (1st Cir. 1983).

180. An example is in the area of the assignability of personal service contracts:

> The early common law took a strictly logical view in regard to the assignability of contract rights and duties. Since a contract is essentially a personal relationship voluntarily entered into by the parties to it, it follows as a logical deduction that one of the parties should not be allowed to destroy that relationship by introducing a third person onto it in his place without the *consent* of the other party.

Grover C. Grismore, "Effect of a Restriction in Assignments in a Contract," *Michigan Law Review* 31 (1933): 299. The parties to any contract may subjectively affix the "personal service" label to it and thus make it per se nonassignable. "It is competent for the parties to make any contract a personal one no matter what the subject-matter." *Frissell et ux. v. Nichols*, 114 So. 431, 434 (Fla. 1927). See also, *Boston Ice Co. v. Potter*, 123 Mass. 28 (1877). See generally, Larry A. DiMatteo, "Depersonalization of Personal Service Contracts: The Search For A Modern Approach to Assignability," *Akron Law Review* 27 (1994): 407.

181. One may look to the notion of the "fairness of the exchange" as an example of the cyclical nature of contract. In the nineteenth century a contract had to be fair in order to be enforceable. Early twentieth century contract doctrine discarded the importance of a determination of the adequacy of the consideration. In more recent times the importance of the fairness of the exchange has regained a foothold with the adoption of such notions as implied good faith, the duty to adjust long-term contracts, analysis of relative bargaining powers, and unconscionability.

182. One commentator states that the evolution of contracts reveals a "pattern that is cyclical and not a process of linear change." James Oldham, "Reinterpretations of 18th-Century English Contract Theory: The View from Lord Mansfield's Trial Notes," *Georgetown Law Journal* 76 (1988): 1949, 1983.

183. See generally, Samuel Williston, "Mutual Assent in the Formation of Informal Contracts," *Illinois Law Review* 14 (1919): 85.

184. "Actual mental assent is not essential to the formation of an informal contract enforceable as a bargain." *Restatement (Second)*, sec. 19, Comment *d*.

185. "The element of agreement is sometimes referred to as the 'meeting of the minds.' The parties to most contracts give actual as well as apparent assent . . . ." Ibid., sec. 17, Comment *c*.

186. Ibid., secs. 202 and 203.

187. Ibid., sec. 202(1).

188. Ibid., (3)(a).

189. Ibid., (3)(b).

190. Ibid., (5). See also, ibid., Comment *g*. and sec. 203.

191. 1 All E. R. 220 (C.A. 1942).

192. Ibid.

193. The court of appeals stated the issue as follows: "[D]oes it prevent there being a contractual relationship merely because the Upton brigade, which responds to that request and render services, thinks, at the time it starts out . . . that the farm in question is in its area . . .?" Ibid.

194. "There is no escape from the legal liability . . . the defendant gave the order for the fire brigade he wanted, and he got it." Ibid., 221.

195. 3 All E.L.R. 566 (K.B. 1939).

196. Ibid.

197. Ibid. (emphasis added). The difference in value for the goods sold per piece was approximately one-third the value of being sold per pound. One may argue that the unilateral mistake did not render the contract meaningless. The court, however, relied heavily upon the fact that evidence showed that prior negotiations had made reference to "price per piece." Thus, the subjective, what the promisor actually intended, is given sway in the rescission or reformation of the contract.

198. Ibid., 566 and 568 ("must have realised").

199. *Restatement (Second)*, sec. 200, Comment *b*.

200. Taken from Illustration 1. of the *Restatement (Second)*, sec. 21, Comment *a*. In contrast to the case of frolic, the general presumption is that if the parties intend to make a contract, then it is the duty of the court to reasonably imply what is needed to "complete" the contract. "If the parties intend to make a contract and there is a reasonably certain basis for granting an appropriate remedy, such alternative [or missing] terms do not invalidate the contract." Ibid., sec. 34, Comment *a*.

201. 3 All E.R. 25, 32 (1993).

202. 3 All E.R. 824, 829 (1974).

203. "They were envisaging that, once the tenant signed, then he would be entitled to a counterpart." Ibid.

204. David Vernon, *Contracts: Theory and Practice* (New York: M. Bender, 1980), 2–10.

205. The area of "mistake" is another fertile ground for the courts' analysis of the subjective intent or understandings of the parties. See the often-cited case of *Raffles v. Wichelhaus*, 2 H and C 906 (1864) (mutual mistake) (the case of the ships Peerless).

206. See chapter 6.

207. John N. Adams and Roger Brownsword, *Understanding Contract Law*, 2d ed. (London: Fontana Press, 1994), 57. The term "communal" is added because the meaning being referred to is not the actual meaning given by either one of the contracting parties or by the objective reasonable person. It is a meaning which is a product of the interaction and communication between two contracting parties. For a philosophical explanation of inter-subjective meaning see, Charles Taylor, *Philosophy and The Human Sciences* (New York: Cambridge University Press, 1985), 28–43.

208. Ibid.

209. For purposes of this article "acting party" is the party to a contract whose action or intent is being examined. The "receiving party" is the observing party or the party to which the action or intent is being communicated or directed. In the course of the exchange of promises, the parties to a contract are both acting and receiving parties. For a variant of intersubjectivity see, *Smith v. Hughes*, 6 Q.B. 597 (1871). "The judge left to the jury the question whether the plaintiff had believed the defendant to believe . . . ." Ibid.

210. Karl N. Llewellyn, "What Price Contract?—An Essay in Perspective," *Yale Law Journal* 40 (1931): 704, 705n. 1.

211. Jürgen Habermas, *The Theory of Communicative Action 1* (Boston: Beacon Press, 1984), 34.

212. Seyla Benhabib, *Critique, Norm, and Utopia* (New York: Columbia University Press, 1986), 238.

213. Ibid.

214. P. F. Strawson, *Skepticism and Naturalsim: Some Varieties* (New York: Columbia University Press, 1985), 75–77.

215. Ibid., 240.

216. Robert L. Young, "Intentions, Interpretations, and Misunderstandings," *Sociological Spectrum* 15 (1995): 161, 162–63 . See generally, Heider Fritz, *The Psychology of Interpersonal Relations* (New York: Wiley and Sons, 1958); Maurice Merleau-Ponty, *The Primacy of Perception*, trans. Colin Smith (Evanston, Ill.: Northwestern University Press, 1964).

217. 6 L.R. 597 (QB 1871).

218. For a review of the law of mistake see generally, *Restatement (Second)*, sec. 151–55; Calamari and Perillo, *Contracts*, secs. 9–25 to 9–30; Edward H. Rabin, "A Proposed Black-Letter Rule Concerning Mistaken Assumptions in Bargain Transactions," *Texas Law Review* 45 (1967): 1273.

219. Adams and Brownsword, *Understanding Contract Law*, 72.

220. Ibid. (emphasis added).

221. 3 All E.R. 566 (1939).

222. Adams and Brownsword, *Understanding Contract Law*, 73.

CHAPTER 4

1. *Black's Law Dictionary*, 4th ed. (St. Paul, Minn.: West Publishing Co., 1968), 1431.

2. Richard E. Speidel, "Unconscionability, Assent and Consumer Protection," *University of Pittsburgh Law Review* 31 (1970): 359, 363.

3. Arthur L. Corbin, "Offer and Acceptance, and Some of the Resulting Legal Relations," *Yale Law Journal* 26 (1917): 169, 205. See also, *Jacob Johnson Fish Co. v. Hawley*, 150 Wis. 578 (1912). The reasonable person and its application as found in tort law is explained in William L. Prosser, *Torts* 4th ed.(St. Paul, Minn.: West Publishing, 1971), §§ 32 and 33 at 149–80.

4. Thomas Aquinas, *Summa Theologiae* 1a2ae.1–20, as reprinted in Timothy McDermott, ed., *Selected Philosophical Writings* (Oxford: Oxford University Press, 1993), 419 (emphasis added).

5. John Finnis, *Natural Law and Natural Rights* (Oxford: Clarendon Press, 1980), 88.

6. Prosser, *Torts* at § 32, p. 151.

7. Ibid.

8. Patricia Smith, *The Nature and Process of Law* (New York: Oxford University Press, 1993), 450, quoting, Prosser, *Torts*.

9. Kent Greenawalt, *Law and Objectivity* (New York: Oxford University Press, 1992), 262n. 36.

10. John Dewey, *How We Think* (Buffalo, N.Y.: Prometheus Press, 1910), 214.

11. Greenawalt, *Law and Objectivity*, 246.

12. Ibid., 248.

13. Ibid., 251–52 (emphasis added).

14. W. David Slawson, "The Futile Search for Principles for Default Rules," *Southern California Interdiscipliniary Law Journal* 3 (1993): 29, 38.

15. Ont. C. J. Lexis 1015 (1991).

16. Ibid.

17. *Zidenburg v. Greenberg*, Ont. C. J. Lexis 2157 (Gen. Div. 1993).

18. *Hoosier Energy Rural Elec. v. Amoco Tax Leasing*, 34 F.3d 1310, 1317 (7th Cir. 1994).

19. *Restatement (Second) of Contracts* (1981), § 201, Comment *b*.

20. Ibid., § 201, Comment *a*.

21. 667 P.2d 174 (Alaska 1983).

22. Ibid., 182, citing, *Meredith Corp. v. Design and Lithography Center, Inc.*, 614 P.2d 414 (Idaho 1980) (emphasis added).

23. 91 Cal. Rptr. 489 (1970).

24. *Mattei v. Hopper*, 330 P.2d 625 (Calif. 1958).

25. Weisz, 91 Cal Rptr. at 492.

26. 968 F.2d 273 (2nd Cir. 1992).

27. Ibid., 276.

28. Comment *b* states a general preference for an objective standard but makes an exception for third-party determinations. "[T]o the extent that it is practicable to apply an objective test of reasonable satisfaction, such a test will be applied. The situation differs from that where the satisfaction of a third party such as an architect, surveyor, or engineer is concerned." *Restatement (Second)*, § 228, Comment *b*.

29. 968 F.2d 273, 277 (1992).

30. 375 F. Supp. 482, 484 (E. D. Tenn. 1973). See also, *Real Estate Management, Inc. v. Giles*, 293 S.W.2d 596 (Tenn. 1956).

31. Ibid.

32. This term was used specifically in a case involving the doctrine of excuse. The allocation of risk between the two parties to a contract is to be "determined by the totality of the circumstances, including the comparative abilities of the parties to make informed judgments as to the extent of the risk; each party's interest in avoiding the risk; and the extent to which that interest was a factor in the negotiation of the contract." In re Westinghouse Elec. Corp. Uranium Contracts Litig., 517 F. Supp. 440, 456 (E.D.Va. 1981), as quoted in, Sheldon W. Halpern, "Application of the Doctrine of Commercial Impracticability: Searching for 'The Wisdom of Solomon'" *University of Pennsylvania Law Review* 135 (1987): 1149n. 106. The English Sale of Goods Act of 1979 expressly states that the determination of when title to goods passes "regard shall be had to the terms of the contract, the conduct of the parties and the circumstances of the case." Ibid., § 17(2).

33. *Artex, Inc. v. Omaha Edible Oils, Inc.*, 436 N.W.2d 146, 150 (Neb. 1989).

34. "A written contract which is expressed in clear and unambiguous language is not subject to interpretation or construction." Ibid. See also, *Bedrosky v. Hiner*, 430 N.W.2d 535 (Neb. 1988); *Fisbeck v. Scherbarth, Inc.*, 428 N.W.2d 141 (Neb. 1988); *Lueder Constr. Co. v. Lincoln Electric Sys.*, 424 N.W.2d 126 (Neb. 1988).

35. Statements may be categorized into four categories: mere (noncontractual) puff, condition precedents, representations, and contractual terms. See generally, Robert Lowe, *Commercial Law*, 5th ed. (London: Sweet and Maxwell, 1976), 157–66.

36. "The intention of the parties can only be deduced from the totality of the evidence." Ibid., quoting, Heilbut, *Symons v. Buckleton*, [1913] A.C. 30, 51.

37. *Towne v. Eisner*, 245 U.S. 418, 425 (1918) (emphasis added).

38. *Restatement (Second)*, § 20, Comment *b*.

39. "Uncertainties in the meaning of words are ordinarily greatly reduced by the contexts in which they are used." Ibid., § 201, Comment *b*.

40. The *Second Restatement* provides that the courts may look at "the transaction . . . in all its length and breadth." Ibid., § 212, Comment *b*.

41. Ibid., § 223, Comment *b*.

42. "Where there is tacit agreement or a common tacit assumption . . . interpretation may be enough" for the court to supply an essential term. Ibid., § 204, Comment *c*.

43. Ibid., § 200, Comments *a*. and *b*.

44. Ibid., § 204.

45. Ibid., § 214, Comment *b*.

46. *Uniform Commercial Code* § 1–205(1) (1990). Comment One elaborates on the interpretation of meaning as party-specific.

47. "The parties themselves know best what they have meant by their words of agreement and their action under that agreement is the best indication of what that meaning was." Ibid., § 2–208, Official Comment 1.

48. *Restatement (Second)*, § 212, Comment *c*.

49. Ibid., Comment *a*.

50. Ibid., § 19, Comment *c*. (emphasis added).

51. "The phrase manifestation of intention adopts an external or objective standard for interpreting conduct." Ibid., § 2, Comment *b*.

52. Ibid., § 23, Comment *a*.

53. Ibid., § 19, Comment *c*.

54. Ibid.

55. 2 H.L. 235, 241 (1974).

56. Ibid., 252.

57. Ibid., 261.

58. Ibid., 268.

59. Richard E. Speidel, "Some Reflections Upon Commercial Context and the Judicial Process," *Wisconsin Law Review* (1967): 822. "The sovereign . . . is free to recognize that imperfect communities that operate beneath the umbrella of the greater community have a role to play in their own governance." Robert S. Miller, "America Singing: The Role of Custom and Usage in the Thoroughbred Horse Business," *Kentucky Law Review* 74 (1986): 781, 796. See generally, James Q. Whitman, "Why Did the Revolutionary Lawyers Confuse Custom and Reason?" *University of Chicago Law Review* 58 (1991): 1321 (a review of the mingling and evolution of custom, reason, and the common law from their historical antecedents in the Middle Ages to the time of the American Revolution). The breeding ground for usage and custom are generally found in smaller communities within a societal or national umbrella. Examples include professional groups, trade unions and associations, and business associations. Custom and practice can also be found in a supranational community. The notion of the *lex mercatoria* or law merchant in international trade and business is such an example. See, e.g., Keith Highet, "The Enigma of the Lex Mercatoria," *Tulane Law Review* 63 (1989): 613. See generally, N. Horn and C. Schmitthoff, eds., *The Transnational Law of International Commercial Transactions* (Boston: Kluwer, 1982).

60. Martin P. Golding, "Jurisprudence and Legal Philosophy in Twentieth-Century America—Major Themes and Developments," *Journal of Legal Education* 36 (1986): 441, 446 (emphasis added).

61. 162 Cal. Rptr. 52 (Ct. App. 1979). See also, *Masterson v. Sine*, 436 P.2d 561 (Cal. 1968).

62. *Uniform Commercial Code*, § 1–205(2). See generally, Elizabeth Warren, "Trade Usage and Parties in the Trade: An Economic Rationale for an Inflexible Rule," *University of Pittsburgh Law Review* 42 (1981): 515.

63. Ibid., Comment 4. See, e.g., *Lipshultz v. Gordon Jewelry Corp.*, 373 F. Supp. 375 (S.D. Tex. 1974). "[P]rovisions [may be] unclear and ambiguous to a layman, such language is nevertheless clear to those cognizant of the customs, practices, usages and terminology in the diamond industry." Ibid., 388. See also, *Eskimo Pie Corp. v. Whitelawn Diaries, Inc.*, 284 F. Supp. 987 (S.D.N.Y. 1968).

64. "Both ways and norms of business practice may be firm at the center, but hazy at the edge; they offer little sureness to guide in dealing with the outside and unusual case." Karl N. Llewellyn, "What Price Contract?—An Essay in Perspective," *Yale Law Journal* 40 (1931): 704, 722.

65. 373 F. Supp. 375, 387 (S.D. Tex. 1974) (emphasis added). The development of custom and usages as sources of law can be seen in the development of international customary law.

> If standard contracts, standard clauses or rules on the interpretation of contract clauses are published by semi-official international agencies such as the International Chamber of Commerce, the de facto recognition and use of such contractual patterns and rules may lead to a new commercial custom . . . [and may] help to create international customary law.

Horn and Schmitthoff, *Transnational Law,* 20 and 138, as quoted in Ralph H. Folsom, Michael W. Gordon, and John A. Spanogle, Jr., *International Business Transactions* (St. Paul, Minn.: West Publishing Co., 1986), 93.

66. *Restatement (Second)*, § 19, Comment *b*.

67. Ibid.

68. "Reason to know depends on the words or other conduct, but also on the circumstances, including previous communications of the parties and the usages of their community or line of business." Ibid., § 26, Comment *a*.

69. For example, "[W]hat is reasonable depends on the circumstances; it may be reasonable to hold a nonmerchant to mercantile standards if he is represented by a mercantile agent." Ibid., § 221, Comment *b*.

70. Unfair Contract Terms Act, § 4(1) (1977).

71. Ibid., § 27(2)(a).

72. "The question is what time would be thought satisfactory to the offeror by a reasonable person in the position of the offeree." Ibid., § 41, Comment *b*.

73. Ibid., § 222, Comment *b*.

74. See generally, Dale B. Furnish, "Custom as a Source of Law," *American Journal of Comparative Law* 30 (1982): 31.

75. 22 Tenn. 493 (1842).

76. Ibid., 514–15 (emphasis added).

77. W. von Leyden, *Aristotle on Equality and Justice* (New York: St. Martin's Press, 1985), 82 (emphasis added).

78. Karl Llewellyn, *The Common Law Tradition* (Boston: Little, Brown, and Co., 1960), 367.

79. Llewellyn further states that "at law one begins with the words, not with the practice." Llewellyn, "What Price Contract?" 722–23n. 45.

80. Ibid.

81. 567 N.E. 2d 1 (Ill. App. 1990).

82. Ibid., 4.

83. Ibid.

84. Ibid., 5.

85. Ibid., 6.

86. Ibid.

87. Ibid., 7.

88. "Few judges have the specialized skill in such matters . . . and juries are notoriously out of touch with such matters." Zipporah B. Wiseman, "The Limits of Vision: Karl Llewellyn and the Law of Contracts," *Harvard Law Review* 100 (1987): 465, 513.

89. There is an "indisputable advantage in having issues of business facts and trade custom decided by experts in the trade involved." Philip G. Phillips, "A Lawyer's Approach to Commercial Arbitration," *Yale Law Journal* 44 (1934): 31, 40–41, as quoted in Wiseman, "Limits of Vision," 465, 511n. 206. Although this is not Llewellyn's statement, the fact that he cited Phillip's article is evidence that it explains his belief on the subject of the use of expert evidence.

90. Ibid., 513.

91. The *Restatement (Second)*, §§ 222(1) and (3) states that "a usage is [something] having such regularity of observance . . . as to justify an expectation that it will be observed . . . [it] gives meaning to or supplements or qualifies [an] agreement."

92. "In . . . contract cases, the court is trying to determine whether an actor knew a practice well enough that one can assume he made a judgment with respect to it." Miller, "America Singing," 801.

93. Greenawalt, *Law and Objectivity*, 77.

94. Ibid., 166. Reasonableness can be seen as a product of a society's sense of morality. Greenawalt reviews the relationship between law and cultural morality. Ibid., 165–70.

95. John D. Calamari and Joseph M. Perillo, *Contracts*, 2d ed. (St. Paul, Minn.: West Publishing Co., 1977), 329.

96. For an enlightening exposé on the uses and limitations of language, see, James B. White, *The Legal Imagination* (Chicago: University of Chicago Press, 1985). "The description of an event can go on forever and still be incomplete. What is said is only part of what happens." Ibid., 3.

97. Dewey, *How We Think*, 175.

98. White, *The Legal Imagination*, 5.

99. Words are initially taken at their common meanings "unless a special meaning is attributed by trade custom or local usage." Harvey McGregor, *Contract Code* (Milano: Dott. A. Giuffrè Editore, 1993), § 111. This a model code drafted on behalf of the English Law Commission.

100. The latent ambiguity of words was recognized even in the realm of words imbued with technical meaning. "An ambiguous word or phrase is one capable of more than one meaning when viewed objectively by a reasonably intelligent person who has examined the context of the entire agreement and who is cognizant of the customs, practices, usages and terminology as generally understood in the particular trade or business." *Lipschutz v. Gordon Jewelry Corp.*, 373 F.Supp. 375, 388 (S.D.Tex. 1974), quoting, *Eskimo Pie Corp. v. Whitelawn Diaries, Inc.*, 284 F.Supp. 987, 994 (S.D.N.Y. 1968).

101. Von Leyden, *Aristotle on Equality and Justice*, 108.

102. *Restatement (Second)*, § 201, Comment *a* (emphasis added). "If an established meaning is given to a word, the courts should adhere to it, for it is presumed that that is the meaning that the parties have given it." *Wickman Tools v. Schuler A.G.*, 2 A.C. 235, 240 (1974). See also, *The Michael Angelos*, 1 Q.B. 164 (1971).

103. "Where a contract is unambiguous, no need exists to resort to other means of interpretation, and the effect must be given to the parties' intent as indicated by the language itself." Hoosier Energy,

34 F. 3d 1310, 1318n. 4, quoting, *Samuels v. Wilder*, 871 F.2d 1346, 1351 (7th Cir. 1989), citing, *Leslie Fay, Inc. v. Rich*, 478 F.Supp. 1109, 1113 (S.D.N.Y. 1979).

104. Oliver Wendell Holmes, "The Theory of Legal Interpretation," *Harvard Law Review* 12 (1899): 417, 418–19 (emphasis added).

105. "In the case of speech it is possible . . . to utter words intending them to mean something other than which they mean; but so long as the words are uttered with some intent they are uttered intentionally." David Goddard, "The Myth of Subjectivity," *Oxford Journal of Legal Studies* 7 (1987): 263, 267.

106. *Wickman Tools v. Schuler A.G.*, 2 A.C. 235, 243 (1974).

107. Ibid., 272 (emphasis added).

108. White, *The Legal Imagination*, 109.

109. 1 Q.B. 44, 62–63 (1976).

110. Ibid., 61.

111. *Arcos, Limited v. E.A. Ronaasen*, [1933] A.C. 470, 474.

112. Ibid., 475.

113. "It must be apparent that such is its purpose and intention." [1967] A.C. 361, 392–93.

114. Ibid., 363 (emphasis added).

115. Ibid., 398–99 (emphasis added).

116. Ibid., 427 (emphasis added). See also, *Bunge Corp. v. Tradex SA*, 2 All E.R. 513 (1981); The Moorcock 14 P.D. 64 (1889).

117. [1893] A.C. 351, 357.

118. "One may safely say that the parties cannot have contemplated that a clause should have so wide an ambit as in effect to deprive one party's obligations of all contractual force." *Suisse Atlantique*, above note 63, p. 432. One may fashion another argument that such a contract could be held to be illusory. If one party can be insulated from any liability for breach, then we are at the threshold of noncontract.

119. Ibid., 434.

120. Ian Macneil, *Contracts* (Mineola, N.Y.: Foundation Press, 1971), 279.

121. Ibid.

122. For a further look at the notion of the "essence" of contract see notes 59–67 above and accompanying text.

123. Warren Schmaus, "Explanation and Essence in the Rules of Sociological Method and the Division of Labor in Society," *Sociological Perspectives* 38 (1995): 57.

124. Macneil, *Contracts*, 279.

125. Ibid.

126. Hoffman F. Fuller, "Mistake and Error in the Law of Contracts," *Emory Law Journal* 33 (1984): 41. See also, G. C. Chesire, "Mistake as Affecting Contractual Consent," *Law Quarterly Review* 60 (1944): 175.

127. Ibid., 91 (emphasis added).

128. Ibid.

129. Arthur Leff, "Contract as a Thing," *American University Law Review* (1970): 131.

130. Patrick S. Atiyah, "Contracts, Promises and the Law of Obligations," *Law Quarterly Review* 94 (1978): 193, 197.

131. Professor Frug offers a definition of reification. It is the "reduction of human ideas to the status of things and the consequent . . . treatment of the things as if they were ideals themselves." Gerald E. Frug, "The Ideology of Bureaucracy in American Law," *Harvard Law Review* 97 (1984): 1276, 1294.

132. Robert S. Summers, "Lon L. Fuller's Jurisprudence and the Possibility It Was Much Influenced by G. W. F. Hegel," *Cornell Law Forum* 10 (1983): 9, 12.

133. Ibid.

134. Ibid., 280.

135. Ibid.

136. See generally, Richard E. Speidel, "The Revision of Article 2 of the *Uniform Commercial Code:* Contract Formation and Modification Under Revised Article 2," *William and Mary Law Review* 35 (1994): 1305.

137. Michael I. Meyerson, "The Reunification of Contract Law: The Objective Theory of Consumer Form Contracts," *University of Miami Law Review* 47 (1993): 1263, 1279, citing, W. David Slawson, "The New Meaning of Contract: The Transformation of Contracts Law by Standard Forms," *University of Pittsburgh Law Review* 46 (1984): 21.

138. Professor Meyerson asserts that at least in the consumer form transaction the courts must move away from the form and interpret the contract through the expectations of a reasonable consumer. "Courts must examine the circumstances surrounding the transaction to determine the consumer's objective understanding." Ibid., 1300. That is, there is a reinstallation of the totality of the circumstances analysis found elsewhere in contracts. Meyerson also intimates that the reasonable person analysis should be done through the eyes of the form-giver. "[A] consumer's assent to a contract should be determined by how a reasonable person in the other party's position would ascertain the consumer's intent as manifested through words and deeds." Ibid., 1325–26. He concludes that the "courts should examine both what the consumer actually knew and what knowledge is properly attributable to the consumer." Ibid.

139. "The preference is for standards and agreement in fact rather than some limited concept of promise." Richard E. Speidel, "The New Spirit of Contract," *Journal of Law and Commerce* 2 (1982): 193, 199.

140. Thomas Egan, "Equitable Doctrines Operating Against the Express Provisions of a Written Contract," *DePaul Business Law Journal* 5 (1993): 261, 312. Professor Macneil poses a response to the growth in the relational nature and complexity of contracts. "[One] response is to develop an overall structure of contract of greater general applicability than now exists and to merge the details and the structure of transactional contract into that overall structure." Ian Macneil, "Restatement (Second) of Contracts and Presentiation" *Virginia Law Review* 60 (1974): 589, 597.

174

141. "When rights and obligations cannot be traced to an express contract, but instead relate back to an informal and often long-term relationship . . . it is difficult to find real consent to the duties imposed by courts." Peter Linzer, "Uncontracts: Context, Contorts and the Relational Approach," *Annual Survey of American Law* (1988): 139, 142, as cited, Randy E. Barnett, "The Sound of Silence: Default Rules and Contractual Consent," *Virginia Law Review* 78 (1992): 821, 823n. 6.

142. "In many cases we become aware of our intentions only by realizing after the fact that we did not intend for our actions to be interpreted the way they were." Robert L. Young, "Intentions, Interpretations, and Misunderstandings," *Sociological Spectrum* 15 (1995): 161, 165.

143. Gidon Gottlieb, "Relationalism: Legal Theory for a Relational Society," *University of Chicago Law Review* 50 (1983): 567, 568. Professor Gottlieb distinguishes three different aspects of the use of legal rules: the "external aspect," the "internal aspect," and the "relational aspect." Ibid., 568, 573–74.

144. Ian R. Macneil, *New Social Contract* (New Haven, Conn.: Yale University Press, 1979), 25.

145. "Nested within the overall consent to be legally bound that justifies the enforcement of default rules, is another consent based on tacit assumptions that unavoidably colors the meaning of what parties make explicit." Randy E. Barnett, ". . . And Contractual Consent," *Southern California Interdisciplinary Law Journal* 3 (1993): 430

146. This insight has been gleaned from Professor Macneil's work on relational contracts. Macneil, *New Social Contract*, 49–50.

147. James Gordley, *The Philosophical Origins of Modern Contract Doctrine* (Oxford: Clarendon Press, 1991), 241.

CHAPTER 5

1. Stephen Hedley, "Keeping Contract in Its Place—*Balfour v. Balfour* and the Enforceability of Informal Agreements," *Oxford Journal of Legal Studies* 5 (1985), 391, 415.

2. Jacques Ellul, *The Theological Foundation of Law* (Garden City, N.Y.: Doubleday and Co., 1960), 18.

3. James Gordley, *The Philosophical Origins of Modern Contract Doctrine* (Oxford: Clarendon Press, 1991), 246.

4. Roscoe Pound listed four strains in what has become known as the school of sociological jurisprudence. The four strains included the historical, the sociological, the philosophical, and the analytic. See generally, Roscoe Pound, *Outlines of Jurisprudence* (Cambridge: Harvard University Press, 1943).

5. Maurice De Wulf, *History of Medieval Philosophy*, trans. Ernest Messenger (London: Nelson Press, 1938), 289.

6. Ibid., 283 (emphasis added).

7. Ibid., 286.

8. Harold J. Berman, *Faith and Order: The Reconciliation of Law and Religion* (Atlanta: Scholar's Press, 1993), 38n. 3 (emphasis added).

9. See generally, Guido Le Bras, "Canon Law," in *The Legacy of the Middle Ages*, ed. Charles G. Crump and Ernest F. Jacobs (Oxford: Clarendon Press, 1926).

10. Steven Lukes and Andrew Scull, eds., *Durkheim and the Law* (New York, N.Y.: St. Martin's Press, 1983), 209.

11. Ibid., 200.

12. Berman, *Faith and Order*, 45.

13. Lukes and Scull, *Durkheim and the Law*, 210.

14. Roscoe Pound, *Jurisprudence* 5 (St. Paul, Minn.: West Publishing Co., 1959), 199.

15. "The consensual contract alone was able at a single stroke to create the two-way track of bonds that we find in any reciprocal agreement." Lukes and Scull, *Durkheim and The Law*, 216–17.

16. Ibid., 217.

17. Francis B. Sayre, "Mens Rea," *Harvard Law Review* 45 (1932): 974, 980.

18.   The late scholastics analyzed contractual consent by applying Aristotelian and Thomistic ideas about the human intellect and will. Out of that analysis came the proposition that duress, mistake, and fraud can invalidate contractual consent. The Romans had known that the parties must consent to form a contract. The late scholastics organized the Roman rules into doctrines and provided them with a theory.

Gordley, *Origins of Modern Contract Doctrine*, 82. This was the beginning of the contractual defenses that are based upon the reality of intent as discussed in chapter 7.

19. "The obligations of religion and of law in the field of promises were in medieval times almost indistinguishable." Sir David H. Parry, *The Sanctity of Contracts in English Law* (London: Stevens and Sons, 1959), 6.

20. Ibid., 8 (emphasis added).

21. Ibid., 13 and 18.

22. Thomas Aquinas, *Summa Theologiae*, 1a2ae.90–1, as reprinted in Timothy McDermott, trans., *Selected Philosophical Writings* (Oxford: Oxford University Press, 1993), 421.

23. Ibid., 420.

24. Pierre De Touroulan, *Philsosophy in the Development of Law*, trans. Martha McC. Read (New York: Macmillan Co., 1922), 179.

25. Equally important as religion was the belief in magic. Victims of promise breakers were thought to possess the ability to cast a curse over their debtors. The sorcerer became a creation of the collective consciousness. The belief in the sorcerer can be analogized to the modern belief in the *magical* powers of the reasonable person. Both are community-driven beliefs used to support the juridical function. Ibid.

26. Irwin A. Horowitz and Thomas E. Willging, *The Psychology of Law* (Boston: Little, Brown, and Co., 1984), 22.

27. One theologian asserts, "What good does a law do when it merely interprets social conditions without giving them direction?" Ellul, *Theological Foundation of Law*, 128–29.

28. Ibid., 32–33. "The history of law becomes the history of juridical aims, that is, the history of the philosophy of law." Ibid., 32.

29. Grant Gilmore, *The Ages of American Law* (New Haven, Conn.: Yale University Press, 1977), 56.

30. Gordley, *Origins of Modern Contract Doctrine*, 230.

31. Ibid.

32. "If all promises are binding, why does the promise need to be accepted?" Ibid., 79.

33. It is the "commonsense view . . . that mental and physical events mutually influence one another." John Hospers, *An Introduction to Philosophical Analysis*, 3d ed. (Englewood Cliffs, N.J.: Prentice-Hall, 1988), 254.

34. "The parties willed a certain normative relationship . . . ." Ibid., 241.

35. Ibid.

36. 14 PD 64, 68 (1889), as quoted in Lord Dennning, *The Discipline of Law* (London: Butterworths, 1979), 35 (emphasis added).

37. Ibid., 40–41.

38. 55 Ll. L. Rep. 159 (House of Lords 1936).

39. Ibid., 173, as quoted, *Hongkong Fir Shipping C. Ltd. v. Kawasaki Kisen Kaisha Ltd.*, 2 Q.B. 26, 37 (1962) (emphasis added).

40. Ibid.

41. H. Trevor-Roper, "The Intellectual World of Sir Thomas More," *The American Scholar* (winter 1978/1979): 19, 26.

42. In reference to More's *Utopia* Professor Trevor-Roper touches upon this definitional dilemma. "Divided souls have long agonies, but they also have moments of great productive fusion." Ibid., 28.

43. Kent Greenawalt, *Law and Objectivity* (New York: Oxford University Press, 1992), 75.

44. Hospers, *Introduction to Philosophical Analysis*, 248.

45. Lukes and Scull, *Durkheim and the Law*, 224 (emphasis added). See generally, Émile Durkheim, *Professional Ethics and Civic Morals*, trans. C. Brookfield (New York: St. Martin's Press, 1957); Émile Durkheim, *The Rules of the Sociological Method*, trans. W.D. Halls (London: McMillan, 1982); Émile Durkheim, *The Division of Labor in Society* (London: McMillan, 1984).

46. The notion of sympathy can be seen as the underlying cause for the development of doctrines and rules that negate contract enforcement. These rules are often found in the areas of capacity, reality of consent and illegality. "The feelings of sympathy that we usually have for our fellow-creatures are outraged when suffering is inflicted on someone when it is no way deserved." Ibid., 223.

47. Ibid., 227.

48. Ibid.

49. See generally, Patrick S. Atiyah, *Essays on Contract* (Oxford: Clarendon Press, 1986); Patrick S. Atiyah, "Contract and Fair Exchange," *University of Toronto Law Journal* 35 (1985): 1.

50. Ibid., 226.

51. "When we sympathize with another, we open our hearts to his or her subjective predicament, rather than our minds to his or her behavioral choices and preferences." Robin West, "Disciplines, Subjectivity, and Law," in *The Fate of Law*, ed. Austin Sarat and Thomas R. Kearns (Ann Arbor:

University of Michigan Press, 1991), 53. For an example of the long history of the role of sympathy in knowledge acquisition see, Adam Smith, *The Theory of Moral Sentiments* (London: Oxford University Press, 1971), as cited in West, "Disciplines, Subjectivity and Law."

52. "We assume as certain many things which, on closer scrutiny, are found to be so full of apparent contradictions that only a great amount of thought enables us to know what it is that we really may believe." Bertrand Russell, *The Problems of Philosophy* (Indianapolis: Hackett, 1912), 7.

53. Ibid., 8.

54. David Granfield, *The Inner Experience of Law: A Jurisprudence of Subjectivity* (Washington, D.C.: Catholic University Press, 1988), 20.

55. Ibid., 21.

56. "In a jurisprudence of subjectivity, we value reality so highly that we do not limit ourselves to a detached objectivity; subjectivity, properly understood and responsibly used, is a necessary component and safeguard of objectivity." Ibid., 3.

57. Cornelius F. Murphy, *Descent Into Subjectivity* (Wakefield, N.H.: Longwood Academic Press, 1990), 8.

58. Ibid., 12.

59. Ibid., 29.

60. See generally, John Rawls, *A Theory of Justice* (Cambridge: Belknap Press of Harvard, 1971).

61. Gerald E. Frug, "A Critical Theory of Law," *Legal Education Review* 1 (1989): 43, 47 (emphasis added).

62. Ibid. See generally, Ludwig Wittgenstein, *Philosophical Investigations*, trans. G. Anscombe, 3d ed. (Oxford: Basil Blackwell, 1958).

63. "It is the structure of meaning which makes it possible for us to see and understand the world. In intentionality, the dichotomy between subject and object is partially overcome." Rollo May, *Love and Will* (New York: Dell, 1969), 225.

64. Ibid., 236.

65. Ibid., 236 and 237.

66. We "cannot perceive something until we can conceive it." Ibid., 237.

67. De Tourtoulan, *Philosophy in the Development of Law*, 207.

68. Ibid., 226.

69. "The group can have but a single consciousness. From it the individuals imbibe their beliefs, and consequently these beliefs are always allowable and obligatory." Ibid., 184.

70. Calvin S. Hall and Gardner Lindzey, *Theories of Personality*, 2d ed. (New York: John Wiley and Sons, 1970), 194.

71. Paul A. Kolers, "Perception and Representation," *Annual Review of Psychology* 34 (1983): 129, 136.

72. "An event later in time will interfere with the perception of an earlier one." This is known as backward masking. Ibid., 136.

73. Ibid., 155.

74. The relation of the objective and subjective theories of contract can be analogized to the psychological notion of coding. "The relation between the world of objects (the presented world) and schemes for ordering or arranging the objects (the representing world)." Ibid., 156.

75. William S. Laufer and Steven D. Walt, "The Law and Psychology of Precedent," in *Handbook of Psychology and Law*, ed. Dorothy K. Kagehiro and William S. Laufer (New York: Springer-Verlag, 1992), 42, quoting, *Helvering v. Hallock*, 309 U.S. 106, 119 (1940).

76. A number of studies have differentiated a number of types of starie decisis. Examples include "personal stare decisis" (consistency with own decisions), "local stare decisis" (consistency with decisions of other members of the court), and "traditional stare decisis." Ibid., 43.

77. Ibid., 41.

78. Horowitz and Willging, *Psychology of Law*, 18, 19.

79. "Lawyers . . . may find the objective approach used by social scientist too concrete and unyielding." Ibid., 36.

80. Gilmore, *Ages of American Law,* 35.

81. 41 U.S. 1 (1842). It was overturned in *Erie R. Co. v. Tompkins*, 304 U.S. 64 (1938).

82. Gilmore, *Ages of American Law*, 34. See also, Cardozo's "methods of sociology," Benjamin N. Cardozo, *The Nature of the Judicial Process* (New Haven, Conn.: Yale University Press, 1921), 30–93. Professor Gilmore renders a synthesis of the "method of sociology." Judges, "at least in a situation where he finds nothing else to guide him [that being a precedent], is to take into account the effect of his decision on social or economic conditions." Gilmore, 76.

83. Ibid., 34.

84. Ibid.

85. It is what Gilmore calls the "bleak and terrifying universe where the function of law is to channel private aggressions . . . so that they correspond with the actual feelings and demands of the community." Ibid., 49, partially quoting Oliver Wendell Holmes, *The Common Law*, ed. Mark DeWolfe-Howe (Boston: Little, Brown, and Co., 1963), 36.

86. Ibid., 54.

87. "In my view, it is a mistake to think that one has to choose between the firm ground of objectivity and the abyss of subjectivity as the only explanations for legal decision-making." Frug, "A Critical Theory of Law," 52. See also, Gerald E. Frug, "The Ideology of Bureaucracy in American Law," *Harvard Law Review* 97 (1984): 1277; Duncan Kennedy, "Toward a Critical Phenomenology of Judging," *Legal Education Review* 36 (1986): 518. For examples of the more traditional study of the objective-subjective distinction see, e.g., Betty Mensch, "Freedom of Contract as Ideology," *Stanford Law Review* 3 (1981): 753; Robert W. Gordon, "Unfreezing Legal Reality: Critical Approaches to Law," *Florida State Law Review* 15 (1987): 195.

88. Ibid., 52–53.

89. Owen M. Fiss, "Objectivity and Interpretation," *Stanford Law Review* 34 (1982): 739.

90. Fiss promises that a "recognition of the interpretive dimensions of adjudication and the dynamic character of all interpretive activity and its capacity to relate constructively the *subjective* and *objective* will deepen our understanding of law." Ibid., 740 (emphasis added).

91. Ibid., 745. Fiss argues that the interpretive community of judges is bonded not by shared views but "by virtue of a commitment to uphold and advance the rule of law itself." Ibid., 746.

92. Interpretation . . . makes law possible. We can find in this conceptualization a recognition of both the subjective and the objective—the important personal role played by the interpreter in the mean-giving process, and yet the possibility of an inter-subjective meaning rooted in the idea of the disciplining rules and of the interpretive community. Ibid., 750.

93. Ibid., 745. Fiss states that "bounded objectivity is the only kind of objectivity to which the law . . . ever aspires," ibid., citing Charles Taylor, "Interpretation and the Sciences of Man," *Review of Metaphysics* 24 (1971): 3.

94. De Tourtoulan concisely states that "law is a social affair." De Tourtoulan, *Philosophy in the Development of Law*, 179.

CHAPTER 6

1. Thomas Nagel, *Mortal Questions* (Cambridge: Cambridge University Press, 1979), 201.

2. See generally, *Restatement (Second) of Contracts* (1981), §18. See also, *Uniform Commercial Code*, § 2–204(3).

3. G. Schaber and C. Rohwer, *Contracts* (St. Paul, Minn.: West Publishing Co., 1975), 9.

4. See, e.g., *Hadley v. Baxendale*, 156 E. R. 145 (1854) (the use of reasonableness in determining contract damages). See also, *Victoria Laundry Ltd. v. Newman Industries Ltd.*, 2 K.B. 528 (1949). See generally, John D. Calamari and Joseph M. Perillo, *Contracts,* 2d ed. (St. Paul, Minn.: West Publishing Co., 1977), 523–25.

5. The *Uniform Commercial Code's* gap-filling provisions have codified the reasonable person standard regarding the implication of specific contractual terms. See, e.g., *Uniform Commercial Code* §§ 2–103(1)(b) and 2–305(1)(c). See generally, James White and Robert S. Summers, *Uniform Commercial Code*, 3d ed. (St. Paul, Minn.: West Publishing Co., 1990).

6. Satisfaction is an element in all contracts whether transactional or relational. Contractual remedies largely revolve around the shortcomings of a given performance. This is true whether the contract is for the performance of services, the manufacture and delivery of goods, or the payment of money.

7. See below notes 64–75 and accompanying text.

8. *Uniform Commercial Code*, § 2–102(1)(b).

9. J. F. O'Connor, *Good Faith in English Law* (Brookfield, Vt.: Gower, 1990), 40.

10. See, Convention on Contracts for the International Sale of Goods (CISG) at Article (1). The United Nations Convention on Contracts for the International Sale of Goods also adopts a good faith requirement in the interpretation of its provisions.

11. Fritz Enderlein and Dietrich Maskow, *International Sales Law* (New York: Oceana, 1992), 56–57.

12. The *Restatement (Second) of Contracts* states that "an interpretation is preferred under which the condition [of satisfactory performance] occurs if such a reasonable person in the position of the obligor would be satisfied." *Restatement (Second),* § 228.

13. See, e.g., *Misano di Navigazione, SpA v. U.S.*, 968 F.2d 273 (2d Cir. 1992); *Action Engineering v. Martin Marietta Aluminum*, 670 F.2d 456 (3d Cir. 1982); *Mattei v. Hopper*, 330 P.2d 625 (Cal. 1958). See generally, E. Allan Farnsworth, *Contracts*, 2d ed. (Boston: Little, Brown, and Co., 1990), 585.

14. *Restatement (Second)*, § 228, Comment *b*. (emphasis added).

15. Ibid., illustration 4.

16. Ibid.

17. 330 P.2d 625 (Cal. 1958). See also, *Tiffany v. Pacific Sewer Pipe Co.*, 182 P. 428 (Cal. 1919) (leasing); *Brenner v. Redlick Furniture Co.*, 298 P. 62 (Cal. 1931); *Quinn v. Daly*, 133 N.E. 290 (Ill. 1921) (determining reliability of a purchaser); *Stribling v. Ailion*, 157 S.E.2d 427 (Ga. 1967) (creditworthiness).

18. See, e.g., *In re Estate of Hollingsworth*, 560 P.2d 348 (Wash. 1977). See also, *Restatement (Second)*, § 228 (1981). "[A]n interpretation is preferred . . . if such a reasonable person ... would be satisfied." Comment *b*. is entitled "Preference For Objective Standard." Ibid.

19. 558 N.E.2d 677 (Ill. 1990).

20. Ibid., 682 (emphasis added).

21. See note 13 above (fancy, taste, or judgment).

22. 446 N.E. 2d 535, 538 (Ill. 1983).

23. Ibid., 539 (emphasis added). See also, *Wood Machine Co. v. Smith*, 15 N.W.2d 906 (Mich. 1983).

24. Don Wiesner, "Specifications: Technical or Performance? Legal Characterizations," *Commercial Law Journal* 97 (1992): 32.

25. Ibid.

26. 717 F.2d 413 (7th Cir. 1983).

27. Ibid., 417.

28. Ibid., 415. This rationale was also used by Justice Cardozo in implying a "duty of reasonable efforts" into an exclusive agency contract. "We are not to suppose that one party was to be placed at the mercy of the other." *Wood v. Lucy, Lady Duff-Gordon*, 118 N.E. 214 (N.Y. 1917). See also, *Hearn v. Stevens and Bros.*, 97 N.Y.S. 566 (1906); *Russell v. Allerton*, 15 N.E. 391 (N.Y. 1888).

29. Latin for "legal fiction," *Black's Law Dictionary*, 5th ed. (St. Paul, Minn.: West Publishing Co., 1979), 514.

30. 968 F.2d 273 (2d Cir. 1992).

31. "When a contract conditions performance upon the satisfaction of one party . . . courts generally require performance of a reasonable person." Ibid., 274. Other cases supporting the preference for a reasonable person standard see, e.g., *Haymore v. Levinson*, 328 P.2d 307 (Utah 1958); *Bruner v. Hegyi*, 183 P. 369 (Cal. 1919).

32. Judge Jerome Frank acknowledges this conflict between the law's desire for objective consistency and law's desire for justice. "[M]ost judges are too common-sensible to allow . . . for the appearance of an abstract consistency, to bring about obviously unjust results. Accordingly, courts not infrequently have departed from the objective theory when necessary to avoid what they have considered an unfair decision. . . ." *Ricketts v. Pennsylvania R. Co.*, 153 F.2d 757 (2d Cir. 1946).

33. The field that Judge Frank was viewing was that of unequal bargaining powers between employer and employee in general. More specifically, the scrutiny to be applied to the enforceability of releases signed by such employees. Ibid., 769.

34. In *Nohcra Communications* the court further surmises that the rejection must "not be prompted by caprice or *bad faith*." *Nohcra Communications v. AM Communications*, 909 F.2d 1007, 1011 (7th Cir. 1990) (emphasis added).

35. *Restatement (Second)* §205, comment *a*. (emphasis added). See also, § 205, Comment *e*. (Good faith in enforcement). (Lists a number of violations of the duty of good faith including "rejection of performance for unstated reasons.")

36. *Uniform Commercial Code*, § 2–103(1)(b) (1990) (emphasis added). See also, *Uniform Commercial Code*, § 1–201(19) (good faith). See generally, Robert S. Summers, "The General Duty of Good Faith," *Cornell Law Review* 67 (1982): 810; Eric G. Andersen, "Good Faith in the Enforcement of Contracts," *Iowa Law Review* 73 (1988): 299; Steven Burton, "More on Good Faith Performance of a Contract," *Iowa Law Review* 69 (1984): 497.

37. 162 Cal. Rptr. 52 (Ct. App. 1979).

38. Ibid., 54 (emphasis added).

39. Professor Farnsworth notes that "words such as . . . sole judgment help to show that subjective satisfaction was intended." Farnsworth, *Contracts*, 583n. 35. Professor Farnsworth cites *Ard Dr. Pepper Bottling Co. v. Dr. Pepper Co.*, 202 F.2d 372 (5th Cir. 1953); *Gibson v. Cranage*, 39 Mich. 49 (1878); *Fursmidt v. Hotel Abbey Holding Corp.*, 200 N.Y.S.2d 256 (1960).

40. *Larwin-Southern*, 162 Cal. Rptr. 52 (Ct. App. 1979), 59. Compare, *Bruner v. Hegyi*, 183 P. 369 (Cal. 1919); *Hawkins v. Graham*, 21 N.E. 312 (Mass. 1889); *Doll v. Noble*, 22 N.E. 406 (N.Y. 1889); *Duplex Safety Boiler Co. v. Garden*, 4 N.E. 749 (N.Y. 1886); *Haymore v. Levinison*, 328 P.2d 307 (Utah 1958), as cited in Farnsworth, *Contracts*, 583n. 36. These cases show that courts have generally applied a reasonable satisfaction standard if the express language in the contract leaves any room for doubt.

41. *Larwin-Southern*, 59 (emphasis added).

42. *Ricketts*, 761 (concurring opinion).

43. *Misano di Navigazione*, 274.

44. See chapter 7 (economic duress) and chapter 8 (mens rea).

45. The "doctrine of *renvoi*" is a circular doctrine found in conflicts of law. "A doctrine under which the court in resorting to a foreign law adopts the rules of the foreign law as to conflict of laws, which rules may in turn refer the court to the law of the forum." *Black's Law Dictionary*, 4th ed. (St. Paul, Minn.: West Publishing Co., 1968), 1462.

46. The difference ultimately may be as great as the answer given to the wag's inquiry as to the difference between a difference of kind and of degree: "A difference of kind is itself . . . a difference of degree. It is merely a violent difference of degree." Glanville Williams, "Language and The Law," *Law Quarterly Review* 61 (1945): 179, 191–92.

47. 153 F.2d 757 (2d Cir. 1946).

48. Ibid., 760.

49. Ibid. "Williston to whom all subjectivity was anathema, insisted that the external [manifestations] of the parties will, no matter how mistaken, result in a contract . . . ." Ibid., 762n. 15. Samuel Williston, "The Formation of Contracts," *Illinois Law Review* 14 (1919): 89.

50. Charles Fried, *Contract As Promise* (Cambridge: Harvard University Press, 1981). "The promise principle . . . is the moral basis of contract law, is that principle by which persons may impose on themselves obligations where none existed before. Security of the person, stability of property, and the obligation of contract were for David Hume the bases of a civilized society." Ibid., 1.

51. Ibid., 17.

52. *Ricketts v. Pennsylvania R. Co.*, 762–63n. 15.

53. Kant acknowledges the great appeal of such inclinations to do justice. "[Such] claims are so impetuous and yet so plausible." Immanuel Kant, *Foundations of the Metaphysics of Morals*, trans. L. W. Beck (New York: Macmillan, 1985), 21.

54. Ibid. (emphasis added).

55. Ibid., 17–18n. 2.

56. Ibid., 72–73.

57. Ibid., 55–56.

58. Benjamin N. Cardozo, *The Nature of the Judicial Process* (New Haven: Yale University Press, 1921), 139–40.

59. 153 F. 2d 757, 764–65 (2d Cir. 1946).

60. Ibid., 762. Judge Frank offered a rationale for the all or nothing approach of the objectivist. "[A]dvocacy of the objective standard in contracts appears to have represented a desire for legal symmetry, legal uniformity, a desire seemingly prompted by aesthetic impulses." Ibid.

61. Ibid., 761.

62. Ibid. (emphasis added).

63. *Uniform Commercial Code*, §2–601 (emphasis added).

64. Zipporah B. Wiseman, "The Limits of Vision: Karl Llewellyn and the Law of Contracts," *Harvard Law Review* 100 (1987): 465, 510.

65. O'Connor, *Good Faith in English Law*, 2.

66. Ibid., 37.

67. "Where . . . the intentions of the parties regarding performance are not discernible . . . it becomes impossible to define substantial performance." *J.R. Sinnott Carpentry, Inc. v. Phillips*, 443 N.E.2d 597, 604 (Ill. 1982). See also, *First National Bank of Oak Lawn v. Minke*, 425 N.E.2d 11 (Ill. 1981).

68. *Jacob and Youngs v. Kent*, 129 N.E. 889, 891 (N.Y. 1921).

69. *Restatement (Second)* § 237, Comment *d*.

70. Ibid., § 241.

71. Ibid., § 241(a), (b), and (d).

72. "Substantial performance is never properly invoked unless the promisee has obtained to all intents and purposes all benefits which he reasonably anticipated under the contract." *Franklin E. Penny Co. v. United States*, 524 F.2d 668, 677 (Ct. Claims 1975), quoting, In *Re Kinney*

Aluminum Co., 78 F.Supp. 565, 568 (S.D.Cal. 1948). For a brief analysis of the associated doctrine of *de minimis*, see *Hessel v. O'Hearn*, 977 F.2d 299 (7th Cir. 1992). "The doctrine is closely related to ameliorative doctrines such as substantial performance." Ibid., 304.

73. Ibid., § 241(e).

74. *National Wrecking Co. v. Midwest Term Corp.*, 601 N.E.2d 999, 1005 (Ill. 1992). See also, *Broncata v. Timbercrest Estates, Inc.*, 241 N.E.2d 569 (Ill. 1968).

75. 16 A. 36 (Pa. 1888), as quoted in Arthur L. Corbin, *Corbin on Contracts* (St. Paul, Minn.: West Publishing Co., 1952), 663n. 20.

CHAPTER 7

1. Herman Hesse, *Siddhartha* (New York: New Directions, 1951), 143.

2. *Non compos mentis* translates into "not of sound mind," *Black's Law Dictionary*, 6th ed. (St. Paul, Minn.: West Publishing Co., 1990), 1051.

3. See, e.g., *First Nat'l Bank of Freehold v. Rutter*, 106 A. 371 (N.J. 1919) (the common law held that married woman did not possess the capability to contract).

4. See generally, T. Jaeger, "Contracts: Convicts, Legal Capacity to Contract and Alienate Property," *Cornell Law Quarterly* 5 (1920): 320.

5. *Civiliter mortuus* is the "condition of one who has lost his [or her] civil rights and capacities, and is considered civilly dead in law," *Black's Law Dictionary*, 246.

6. "Until very recent times economic or commercial pressures were almost entirely ignored by the common law." Patrick S. Atiyah, *The Law of Contract*, 4th ed. (Oxford: Clarendon Press, 1989), 287.

7. For the first mention of the doctrine see, Y.B. 20 and 21 Edw. I 318 (1292). The historical age of majority was considered to be twenty-one. This can be traced to feudal times where the "art of war" both in the length of the training period and the "strength of mature men" dictated the use of the age of twenty-one as a practical age for adulthood. Bernard F. Cataldo, Cornelius W. Gillam, Frederick G. Kempin, Jr., John M. Stockton, and Charles M. Weber, *Introduction to Law and the Legal Process* (New York: John Wiley and Sons, 1965), 515. See also, T. E. James, "The Age of Majority," *American Journal of Legal History* 4 (1960): 22. The common law age of majority has been lowered to eighteen years of age. See generally, C. Sanger and E. Willemsen, "Minor Changes: Emancipating Children in Modern Times," *University of Michigan Journal of Law Reform* 25 (1992): 239.

8. *Petition of Yonnone,* 339 N.Y.S.2d 212, 214 (1972). This ability to avoid a contract is commonly referred to as the "right of disaffirmance." See, e.g., *Halbman v. Lemke*, 298 N.W.2d 562, 564 (Wis. 1980).

9. R. Richardson, "Children and the Recorded-Message Industry: The Need for a New Doctrine," *Virginia Law Review* 72 (1986): 1325, 1332–33.

10. I. Mehler, "Infant Contractual Responsibilty: A Time for Reappraisal and Realistic Adjustment?" *Kansas Law Review* 11 (1963): 361, 373. See also, Note, "Statutory Problems in the Law of

Minors' Contracts," *Columbia Law Review* 48 (1948): 272. For a discussion of the civil law equivalent see, M. Dugas, "The Contractual Capacity of Minors: A Survey of the Prior Law and the New Articles," *Tulane Law Review* 62 (1988): 745.

11. R. Braucher, "Freedom of Contract and the Second Restatement," *Yale Law Journal* 78 (1969): 598.

12. "Disaffirmance" is defined as "[t]he repudiation of a former transaction." *Black's Law Dictionary*, 462. The practical result of a minor's disaffirmance is a voiding of the contract without being required to pay damages or restitution.

13. George Clark, *Summary of American Law* (Rochester: Lawyer's Co-Operative Publishing Co., 1949).

14. *Restatement (Second) of Contracts* (1981), §1.

15. See generally, S. Williston and W. Jaeger, *A Treatise on the Law of Contracts*, 3d ed. (Mount Kisco, N.Y.: Daker, Voorhis, 1959), § 18.

16. "Where form is not observed, a nullity of the act is inferred." *Black's Law Dictionary*, 652.

17. Note, "Liability of an Infant for Fraudulent Misrepresentation." *Yale Law Journal* 31 (1921): 201.

18. *Zouch v. Parsons*, 3 Burr. 1794.

19. 209 A.2d 730 (N.H. 1965).

20. Ibid., 732.

21. See generally, *Pankas v. Bell*, 198 A.2d 312 (Pa. 1964) (applied the benefits doctrine to a case involving equitable relief); *Valencia v. White*, 654 P.2d 287 (Ariz. 1982). See also, R. Regan, "Restitution in Minor's Contracts in California," *Hastings Law Journal* 19 (1968): 1199.

22. *Berglund v. American Multigraph Sales Co.*, 160 N.W. 191, 193 (Minn. 1916).

23. *Pettit v. Liston*, 190 P. 660 (Or. 1920).

24. Ibid., 662.

25. "[I]t is generally recognized that the purpose of the infancy law doctrine is the protection of minors from foolishly squandering their wealth." *Halbman v. Lemke*, 298 N.W.2d 562, 564 (Wis. 1980). See also, *Kiefer v. Fred Howe Motors, Inc.*, 159 N.W.2d 288 (Wis. 1968). For the historical antecedent of the doctrine see, James Kent, *Commentaries on American Law*, J. Gould, 14th ed. (St. Paul, Minn.: West Publishing Co., 1896), 356.

26. S. Williston and Jaeger, *Law of Contracts*, § 238 (emphasis added).

27. 105 A. 201 (N.J. 1918).

28. Ibid., 203.

29. See generally, James, "The Age of Majority," 22–23.

30. 273 A.2d 408 (N.J. Super. Ct 1971).

31. Ibid., 440.

32. 188 N.E. 726 (N.Y. 1934).

33. Ibid., 728.

34. Ibid.

35. 250 N.E.2d 898 (Ohio Ct. App. 1969).

36. *Tuck v. Payne*, 17 S.W.2d 8 (Tenn. 1929).

37. 250 N.E. 2d ed. 898, 900.

38. "Emancipation" is the severing of the parental-child relationship in which the severance is recognized under law. See, e.g., *Glover v. Glover*, 319 S.W.2d 238 (Tenn. Ct. App. 1958).

39. Merrick v. Stephens, 377 S.W.2d 713, 720 (Mo. Ct. App. 1960).

40. Williston and Jaeger, *Law of Contracts*, § 254.

41. See, e.g., *New York Arts and Cultural Affairs Law* (McKinney 1984), § 35.03.

42. See, e.g., *New York Insurance Law* (McKinney 1985), § 3207(a) (prevents disaffirmance by anyone over the age of fourteen of an insurance contract); *North Carolina General Statutes* (1984), § 39–13.2 (ability to finance the purchase of real estate); *Virginia Code Annotated* (Michie 1993), § 11–8 (ability to contract for federal benefits).

43. *Kiefer v. Fred Howe Motors*, 158 N.W.2d 288, 293 (Wis. 1968) (dissent) (emphasis added). See also, R. Edge, "Voidability of Minors' Contracts: A Feudal Doctrine in a Modern Economy," *Georgia Law Review* 1 (1967): 205.

44. Harvey McGregor, *Contract Code* (Milano: Dott. A. Giuffrè Editore, 1993), § 541(1) .

45. Ibid., 542.

46. Ian Macneil, "The Many Futures of Contracts," *Southern California Law Review* 47 (1974): 691, 785.

47. John Finnis, *Natural Law and Natural Rights* (Oxford: Clarendon Press, 1989), 88.

48. John D. Calamari and Joseph M. Perillo, *Contracts*, 2d ed. (St. Paul, Minn.: West Publishing Co., 1979), 233.

49. 522 S.W.2d 679, 688 (Tenn. 1975).

50. In his book *Ancient Law* Henry Sumner Maine championed the cause of historical and comparative jurisprudence. Fredrick Pollock writes that Maine showed that "legal ideas and institutions have a real course of development as much as the genera and species of living creatures." Henry Sumner Maine, *Ancient Law* (Boston: Beacon Press 1963), xiv.

51. William Zelermeyer, *Legal Reasoning: The Evolutionary Process of Law* (Englewood Cliffs: Prentice-Hall, 1960), 3.

52. Thomas Egan, "Equitable Doctrines Operating Against the Express Provisions of a Written Contract," *DePaul Business Law Journal* 5 (1993): 261, 311.

53. 2 Q.B. 163 (C.A. 1967).

54. Ibid., 172.

55. See, e.g., Richard Spiedel, "The New Spirit of Contract," *Journal of Law and Commerce* 2 (1982): 193. This expanded analysis of objectivity has at times been expressed as the "new spirit" of contracts.

56. *Restatement (Second)*, §205. See also, *Uniform Commercial Code*, §§ 1–102(3), 1–201(19), and 1–203.

57. Charles Knapp, "Reliance in the Revised Restatement: The Proliferation of Promissory Estoppel," *Columbia Law Review* 81 (1981): 52, 78.

58. Patrick S. Atiyah, *Essays on Contract* (Oxford: Clarendon Press, 1986), 95.

59. Georgio Del Vecchio, *Philosophy of Law*, trans. Thomas O. Martin (Washington, D.C.: Catholic University, 1953), 419.

60. Ibid. (emphasis added).

61. See generally, E. Allan Farnsworth, *Contracts*, 2d ed. (Boston: Little, Brown, and Co., 1990), § 4.16n. 10. See also, Dawson, "Economic Duress—An Essay in Perspective," *Michigan Law Review* 45 (1947): 253. (An agreement reached under duress is generally not considered to be void. It is voidable by the party who suffered the duress.) See generally, Arthur Corbin, *Contracts* (St. Paul, Minn.: West Publishing Co., 1952), § 146.

62. Karl N. Llewellyn, "What Price Contract?—An Essay in Perspective," *Yale Law Journal* 40 (1931): 704, 728n. 49.

63. 157 Cal. App.3d 1154, 204 Cal. Rptr. 86 (1984).

64. Ibid., 1158.

65. Ibid. See also, *Totem Marine T. and B. v. Alyeska Pipeline, Etc.*, 584 P.2d 15 (Alaska 1978).

66. "Freedom of contract" policy rationales are buzzwords for the belief that parties in a free market system should be given a wide range of freedom in their contractual relations. See generally, Braucher, "Freedom of Contract."

67. 157 Cal. App.1154 at 1155.

68. Ibid.

69. R. Cross and J.W. Harris, *Precedent in English Law*, 4th ed. (New York: Oxford University Press, 1991), 214.

70. 2 Q.B. 617, 625 (1966).

71. Atiyah, *Essays on Contract*, 285–86.

72. Professor Atiyah points out that contractual relationships are inherently characterized by "constraints" and pressure. Therefore, the dividing line between legitimate and illegitimate pressure is the crucial issue in the law of duress. Ibid., 285.

73. Ibid.

74. Ibid., 289.

75. Ibid., 290–91. See, e.g., *North Ocean Shipping Ltd. v. Hyundai Construction Co.*, Q.B. 705 (1989); *Atlas Express Ltd. v. Kafco Ltd.*, 1 All ER 641 (1989), ibid., n. 5.

76. 1 Q.B. 31, 56 (1961).

77. R. H. Coase, "The Problem of Social Cost," *Journal of Law and Economics* 3 (1960): 1, 15, as quoted in Carl J. Dahlman, "The Problem of Externality," *Journal of Law and Economics* 22 (1979): 141, 147. Dahlman lists the following examples of transaction costs: "search and information costs, bargaining and decision costs, policing and enforcement costs." Ibid., 148.

78. Ibid., 151.

79. Willaim L. Prosser, *Torts* (St. Paul, Minn.: West Publishing Co., 1941), § 92.

80. See, e.g., *Travelers Ins. Co. v. Anderson*, 210 F. Supp. 735 (W.D.S.C. 1962); *Comunale v. Traders and Gen. Ins. Co.*, 328 P.2d 198 (Cal. 1958). For the expansion of bad faith breach into other areas

see, e.g., *Seaman's Direct Buying Service v. Standard Oil Co.*, 686 P.2d 1158 (Cal. 1984). Compare, *Foley v. Interactive Data Co.*, 765 P.2d 373 (Cal. 1988). See generally, E. Allan Farnsworth, "Developments in Contract Law During the 1980's: The Top Ten," *Case Western Reserve Law Review* 41 (1990): 203, 204–6; Note, "Extending the Bad Faith Tort Doctrine to General Commercial Contracts," *Boston University Law Review* 65 (1985): 355; Note, "Tort Remedies for Breach of Contract: The Expansion of Tortious Breach of the Implied Covenant of Good Faith and Fair Dealing into the Commercial Realm," *Columbia Law Review* 86 (1986): 377.

81. Dahlman, "The Problem of Externality," 161.

82. Elizabeth Warren, "Trade Usage and Parties in the Trade: An Economic Rationale for an Inflexible Rule," *University of Pittsburgh Law Review* 42 (1981): 515.

83. 83 Ill. 33, 36 (1867), as quoted in Warren, "Trade Usage and Parties in the Trade," 533.

84. See generally, Eugene F. Mooney, "Old Kontract Principles and Karl's New Kode: An Essay on the Jurisprudence of Our New Commercial Law," *Villanova Law Review* 11 (1966): 213.

CHAPTER 8

1. See, e.g., Michael Garner, "The Role of Subjective Benefit in the Law of Unjust Enrichment," *Oxford Journal of Legal Studies* 10 (1990): 42. The author analyzes a subjective component of the law of restitution. The benefactor of another's act may attach subjective valuation to something received that may be objectively worthless. The author argues that if subjective devaluation is permitted due to factors such as personal taste, then subjective "revaluation" should be permitted in order to prove a case of unjust enrichment. The author concludes that objective determination of enrichment is preferred but he poses a subjective caveat. If a defendant acknowledges a benefit that cannot be found objectively, then "enrichment [should] be determined subjectively." Ibid., 65. Professor Helmholz examined the importance of subjective intent in the area of adverse possession. The tying of adverse possession to a statutory period of time renders it a prime candidate for the domain of pure objectivity. Professor Helmholz argues that the law's claim to objectivity is an illusion. "Honest possession" is viewed in practice differently than the possessor who acts with full knowledge. Despite the black letter law's acceptance of any type of possession as being adverse, "questions of subjective intent . . . [is] a fact of life." R. H. Helmholz, "Adverse Possession and Subjective Intent," *Washington University Law Quarterly* 61 (1983): 331, 358.

2. For example, in order for there to be a theft of goods, "there must be the intent to permanently deprive the owner of the goods." *State v. Wood*, 435 P.2d 857, 859 (Ariz. 1968).

3. John H. Wigmore, "Responsibility for Tortious Acts," *Harvard Law Review* 7 (1884): 315, 441, as quoted in Francis B. Sayre, "Mens Rea," *Harvard Law Review* 45 (1932): 974, 976n. 4.

4. Mens rea has also been translated to mean guilty intent. Phillip S. James, *English Law*, 9th ed. (London: Butterworths, 1976), 150.

5. P. J. Fritzgerald, *Salmond on Jurisprudence*, 12th ed. (London: Sweet and Maxwell, 1966), 366. "The mens rea and the actus reus must concur to constitute a true crime." Rollin M. Perkins, *Criminal Law*, 2d ed. (Mineola, N.Y.: Foundation Press, 1969), 834. Mens rea should not be confused with

the concept of motive. "[M]otive in the penal law is distinguished from intention (mens rea) . . . Given a motive, [however,] a given intention can be inferred." Patricia Smith, *The Nature and Process of Law* (New York: Oxford University Press, 1993), 574–75, quoting Jerome Hall, *General Principles of Criminal Law*, 2d ed. (Indianapolis: Bobbs-Merrill, 1960). "[T]he defendant's motivation may be an important evidentiary clue to what special mens rea, if any, was formed." Stephen J. Morse, "The Guilty Mind: Mens Rea," in *Handbook of Psychology and Law*, ed. Dorothy K. Kagehiro and William S. Laufer (New York: Springer-Verlag, 1992), 209. The dialectic can also be seen at work in the roles of the actus reus and mens rea requirements. The former being the objective component, the outward manifestation of a criminal activity. The latter being the subjective element of the guilty mind.

6. "[M]ens rea differs from crime to crime. In murder it is malice aforethought; in burglary it is intent to commit . . . ; in uttering a forged instrument it is knowledge." Perkins, *Criminal Law*, 743. There is a distinction between general criminal intent and specific intent or mens rea. The former is the notion that the accused intended to perform the actus reus. Some crimes, however, require an additional finding of a specific state of mind or intent. Examples include intent to defraud, malice, knowledge, willfulness, wantonness, and recklessness. Ibid., 762–83. "The word willful means no more than an inderdicted act, that is, a forbidden act that is done deliberately and with knowledge." *McClanahan v. United States*, 230 F. 2d 919, 924 (5th Cir. 1956).

7. Strict liability or absolute crimes are rare and generally disfavored. An example would be regulatory crimes such as the mislabeling of hazardous substances. "Because moral fault is absent in these cases, these crimes typically carry little stigma and light punishment." Morse, "The Guilty Mind," 207n. 2.

8. "Thus if one intentionally does some unlawful act on a man which she did not realize, but which a reasonable person would realize, is highly likely to cause death . . . , this is enough to render her guilty of murder." Ibid., 370.

9. Ibid., 371.

10. "Since . . . the latter task [of proving subjective intent] is flatly impossible the conflict between the opposing views is really no more than one of degree." James, *English Law*, 151.

11. "It is well established that [the principle of paternalism] justifies ignoring a child's consent in relation to activity which society judges harmful to children." Roger Leng, "Consent and Offences against the Person," *Criminal Law Review* (July 1994): 480, 483.

12. Ibid., 483.

13. "Subjective awareness of guilt is a prerequisite for criminal . . . liability." Richard Mahoney, "Memory and Mens Rea: The Defence of Forgotten Possession," *Criminal Law Quarterly* 32 (1989): 43.

14. Ibid., 40.

15. Similarities can also be seen in the devices used to find intent in both contract and criminal laws. The contract doctrines of presumed and constructive intent are also found in the criminal law. In the 1884 case of *Harrison v. Commonwealth* the court held that criminal intent can be presumed from the criminal act. "A man is to be taken to intend what he does, or that which is the neces-

sary and natural consequence of his act." 79 Va. 374, 377 (1884), as quoted in Perkins, *Criminal Law*, 748.

16. "The civil judge and juror are in no different predicament than anyone else, notably the criminal judge and juror. Yet the latter must arrive at plausible beliefs about what was true inwardly (subjectively) respecting certain accused persons." Richard Bronaugh, "Agreement, Mistake, and Objectivity in the Bargain Theory of Contract," *William and Mary Law Review* 18 (1976): 213, 247.

17. John W. Salmond, *Jurisprudence*, 12th ed. (London: Sweet and Maxwell, 1966), § 82, 351.

18. Steven Lukes and Andrew Scull, eds., *Durkheim and the Law* (New York: St. Martin's Press, 1983), 221.

19. "An act is the result of the exercise of the will." *Duncan v. Landis*, 106 F. 839, 848 (3d Cir. 1901). See generally, Perkins, *Criminal Law*, 551.

20. Ibid.

21. For a discussion of the notions of direct intention and oblique intention see, R.A. Duff, "Intentions Legal and Philosophical," *Oxford Journal of Legal Studies* 9 (1989): 76. The author discusses the difference between consequential and nonconsequential types of intentionality. "The criminal law should distinguish direct from oblique intention only when there is some significant difference in responsibility between one who directly intends the relevant effect and one who foresees it as a certain side-effect of her intended action." Ibid., 85.

22. Perkins, *Criminal Law*, 923.

23. Ibid., 939–40.

24. James Macdonald and Carol Beck-Dudley, "Are Deontology and Teleology Mutually Exclusive?" *Journal of Business Ethics* 13 (1994): 615, 616.

25. Professor Marshall proffers that contract law focuses upon the intent of the document or intendment and not upon the actual intent of the parties to the document. "The treatment of intendment as if it were intention is a pragmatic solution to the problem of the meaning of parties to a document. It better meets the needs of society . . . than would an attempt to find intention in fact." James Marshall, *Intention—In Law and Society* (New York: Funk and Wagnalls, 1968), 170.

26. Morse, "The Guilty Mind," 212.

27. "If we know what a person wishes to happen (motive) and that he has the capacity (means) to accomplish it, and if he has the opportunity . . . we say he intends to act. This is the formula for proving by circumstantial evidence the commission of a crime." Marshall, *Intention*, 137.

28. *McClanahan v. United States*, 230 F. 2d 919, 923 (5th Cir. 1956).

29. *Luther v. State*, 98 N.E. 640, 642 (Ind. 1912).

30. 1 A.E.L.R. 813 (C.C.A. 1947).

31. "The guilty intent cannot be presumed, and must be proved." Ibid., 817.

32. Marshall, *Intention*, 138.

33. F. 245, 247 (1882).

34. Ibid., 248.

35. Ibid., 249.

36. Andrew S. Butler, "An Objective or Subjective Approach to the Right to be Informed of the Right to Counsel? A New Zealand Perspective," *Criminal Law Quarterly* 36 (1994): 317, 319.

37. Ibid., 323

38. Ibid., 328.

39. Ibid.

40. These different approaches are discussed in an English law review article. See, James Gobert, "Corporate Criminality: New Crimes for the Times," *Criminal Law Review* (October 1994): 722.

41. "Designated officials are thought to be so identified with the company that they embody its *mind* and *will.*" Ibid., 723.

42. Ibid., 729.

43. Marshall, *Intention*, 140.

44. Ibid.

45. Stephen A. Reiss, "Prosecutorial Intent in Constitutional Criminal Procedure," *University of Pennsylvania Law Review* 135 (1987): 1365.

46. Ibid., 1477.

47. 19 C.C.C. 2d 154, 160 (1974), as quoted in Peter Rosenthal, "Duress in Criminal Law," *Criminal Law Quarterly* 32 (1989): 199, 206–7.

48. Professor Rosenthal ventures that it is common sense to allow evidence of duress to affect the trier of fact's reasonable doubt determination. The duress may create a reasonable doubt as to mens rea. Ibid., n. 37 and accompanying text.

49. The use of agents to forward one's contractual interests precedes the development of common law contracts. "The concept of one person's authority to enter into contractual relations on behalf of another was recognized under English common law by the end of the thirteenth century. Steven N. Bulloch, "Fraud Liability Under Agency Principles: A New Approach," *William and Mary Law Review* 27 (1986): 301, citing, W. Holdsworth, *A History of English Law*, 3d ed. 8 (London: Methuen, 1926), 222–23.

50. "We have to search for the mechanism of our law in life as it actually is, rather than fit the life we live to *a priori* rules of rigid legal systems." Harold J. Laski, "The Basis of Vicarious Liability," *Yale Law Journal* 26 (1916): 105, 113.

51. Ibid., 119 (emphasis original).

52. Ibid.

53. Ibid., 121.

54. *Restatement (Second) of Agency* (1958), § 1 and 15 (emphasis added).

55. Jethro K. Lieberman and George J. Siedel, *Business Law and the Legal Environment*, 3d ed. (San Diego: Harcourt, Brace, and Javanovich, 1992), 841.

56. 172 N.W.2d 317 (Minn. 1969). See generally, *Restatement of Agency*, § 64 (emphasis added).

57. See generally, Randy E. Barnett, "Squaring Undisclosed Agency Law with Contract Theory," *California Law Review* 75 (1987): 1969. "This situation is strikingly similar to the problem of explaining the objective interpretation of contracts." Ibid., 1996.

58. Bulloch, "Fraud Liability Under Agency Principles," 308.

59. Lieberman and Siedel, *Business Law*, 842 (emphasis added).

60. "The third person must *believe* that the agent is authorized." *Restatement of Agency*, § 8, Comment *c*. (emphasis added).

61. Ibid., § 8 A. Compare, § 35 (incidental authority).

62. "The liability results purely from the relation." Ibid., § 8 A., Comment *b*. "[T]he power is based neither upon the consent of the principal nor upon his manifestations." Ibid.

63. "Where certain customs prevail, the agent has implied authority to act in accordance with such customs, provided that they are reasonable and lawful." Robert Lowe, *Commercial Law*, 5th ed. (London: Sweet and Maxwell, 1976), 27.

64. "Unless he indicates otherwise, a principal engaged in business represents to his agents that he knows the business usages of the locality in which he regularly does business." *Restatement of Agency*, 10, Comments *b*. and *c*.

65. Ibid., § 26, Comment *a*.

66. See, notes 31-57 and accompanying text in chapter 4 of this work.

67. Ibid., § 34, Comment *a*.

68. Ibid., 33, Comment *a*. (bounded by the principal's will as manifested).

69. Macdonald and Beck-Dudley, "Deontology and Teleology," 620.

70. Perkins, *Criminal Law*, 741.

71. Human action is usually a result of a number of motives, some of which may be at variance. "Seldom does it happen, that a man's conduct stands exposed to the action of no more than one motive." Amnon Goldworth, ed., *Deontology* (New York: Oxford University Press, 1983), 112.

72. Ibid., 621.

73. Alan H. Goldman, *Moral Knowledge* (London: Routledge, 1988), 55.

74. Ibid., 61.

75. Kant provides an "analysis of the contents of judgments of obligation that could be objectively binding, valid for all rational agents as such, irrespective of their subjective feelings and beliefs." Ibid., 92.

76. James Gordley, *The Philosophical Origins of Modern Contract Doctrine* (Oxford: Clarendon Press, 1991), 233.

77. "[If] promises are binding because one cannot will the violation of a promise as universal law, then it would seem that all promises should be treated the same way." Ibid., 236-37.

78. Goldworth, *Deontology*, 109 (emphasis original).

79. "Intentions, considered in respect of the consequences." Ibid.

80. Professor Kronman describes the deontological-teleological perspectives of judicial decision-making. The law of precedent and deference to opinions of prestigious judges are seen as a utilitarian device for reducing the costs of judicial decision-making. Stare decisis is directly correlated to the predictability of law. Predictability serves utilitarian ends by allowing private parties to plan and structure their contractual relationships more efficiently. Predictability can also be

seen as serving deontological objectives. See generally, Anthony T. Kronman, "The Problem of Judicial Discretion," *Journal of Legal Education* 36 (1981): 481.

81. U.N. Doc. A/CONF.97/18 (1980) (CISG).

82. Ibid., Article 8(1).

83. Article 8(1) states that subjective intent is to be the means of interpretation "where the other party knew or could not have been unaware what that intent was." Ibid.

84. Paul Amato, "U.N. Convention on Contracts for the International Sale of Goods—The Open Price Term and Uniform Application: An Early Interpretation by the Hungarian Courts," *Journal of Law and Commerce* 13 (1993): 1, 7.

85. Thus actual knowledge of the receiving party is not required. If the statement or conduct of the other party is such that a reasonable person would have been made aware of her intent, then that is sufficient. "When one party clearly expresses his intent through a legal act, the addressee cannot pretend to have insufficient knowledge of that intent." Fritiz Enderlein and Dietrich Maskow, *International Sales Law* (New York: Oceana, 1992), 63.

86. CISG, Article 8(2).

87. One commentator states that the "subjective element relates to a person of the same type as the other party, the addressee." The *individualization* of this analysis requires an inquiry into the party's enterprise, the country of his place of business, knowledge and experience of prior dealings, and the customary business forms existing in his country.

88. Article 8(3) makes more explicit the totality of the circumstances approach. "[D]ue consideration is to be given to all relevant circumstances." CISG, Article 8(3).

89. Ibid.

90. "The subjective and objective elements of each case have to be taken into account." Enderlein and Maskow, *International Sales Law*, 66.

CHAPTER 9

1. William James, *Pragmatism* (Buffalo: Prometheus Books, 1991), 7.

2. Georgio Del Vecchio, *Philosophy of Law*, trans. Thomas O. Martin (Washington, D.C.: Catholic University Press, 1953), 430.

3. Benjamin N. Cardozo, *The Nature of the Judicial Process* (New Haven: Yale University Press, 1921), 103–4 (emphasis added).

4. Immanuel Kant, *Foundations of the Metaphysics of Morals*, trans. L. Beck, (New York: Macmillan, 1985), 21.

5. Oliver Wendell Holmes, "The Path of the Law," *Harvard Law Review* 10 (1897): 457.

6. "[J]udges generally have a choice among competing principles and their choices are based on personal attitudes and values, not anchored in precedent." Irwin A. Horowitz and Thomas E. Willging, *The Psychology of Law* (Boston: Little, Brown, and Co., 1984), 27.

7. John Dewey, *How We Think* (Buffalo, N.Y.: Prometheus Press, 1910), 26.

8. "The primary restraint on judges is the compelling need to articulate a principled decision, one that resides in logic independent of the result of the case at issue." Ibid.

9. Jon O. Newman, "Between Legal Realism and Neutral Principles: The Legitimacy of Institutional Values," *California Law Review* 72 (1984): 200, 215.

10. "It is pertinent, in deciding whether to adopt a rule that turns on a person's intent, to assess, however intuitively, how likely we are to determine intent correctly." Ibid., 213. For a discussion on rule application and judicial justification see, David Lyons, "Justification and Judicial Responsibility," *California Law Review* 72 (1984): 178. The importance of rules varies from case to case. There are easy cases and there are hard cases. The harder cases are often less susceptible to the application of rules of law, and rules vary as to their functionality and scope. "Some rules are too vague for routine application, rules can conflict, and sometimes no established rule is available." Ibid.

11. The "obligation created by the demand for stare decisis is institutional." Samuel I. Shuman, "Justification of Judicial Decisions," *California Law Review* 59 (1971): 715, 721.

12. Ibid., 717.

13. Ibid., 721.

14. George K. Gardner, "An Inquiry Into the Principles of the Law of Contracts," *Harvard Law Review* 46 (1932): 1, 39.

15. Ibid.

16. Ibid.

17. 37 Sup. Ct. Rptr. 524, 531 (1916).

18. "[Judges] easily sacrifice a deduction which naturally follows according to the rules of the syllogism, but which their circle of friends and acquaintances would not ratify." Pierre De Tourtoulan, *Philosophy in the Development of Law*, trans. Martha McC. Read (New York: Macmillan Co., 1922), 192.

19. Ibid.

20. Paul Gerwirtz, Introduction to Llewellyn's *The Case Law System in America* (Chicago: University of Chicago Press, 1989), xviii.; Stanley Fish, "Working on the Chain Gang: Interpretation in Law and Literature," *Texas Law Review* 60 (1982): 551. See also, Kent Greenawalt, *Law and Objectivity* (New York: Oxford University Press, 1992), 84–85 (the authority of the interpretive community).

21. "By failing to adhere to basic norms that define his role within the legal system, he has performed an act that is determinately, objectively wrong under the law, and he has violated his promise to fulfill the judge's role." Greenawalt, *Law and Objectivity*, 89.

22. Ibid., xix.

23. Ibid., 78.

24. Ibid., 89.

25. Ibid., 76.

26. Ibid., 79.

27. Ibid., 10.

28. Ibid. (emphasis added).

29. "Whatever leeways of discretionary choice . . . must accommodate the community's common convictions." Cornelius F. Murphy, *Descent Into Subjectivity* (Wakefield, N.H.: Longwood Academic Press, 1990), 62. See generally, Ronald Dworkin, *Taking Rights Seriously* (Cambridge: Harvard University Press, 1977); Ronald Dworkin, "Judicial Discretion," *Journal of Philosophy* 60 (1963): 624.

30. Ibid., 116.

31. "Out of one and the same mass of facts, each of us, based on individual experience, decides what the facts are." Greenawalt, *Law and Objectivity*, 53.

32. Ibid., 79 (emphasis original).

33. James, *Pragmatism*, 12.

34. "Jural objectivity arises out of subjective creativity." Murphy, *Descent Into Subjectivity*, 192.

35. Arthur T. Vanderbilt, *Judges and Jurors: Their Functions, Qualifications and Selection* (Boston: Boston University Press, 1956), 20n. 67.

36. Patricia Smith, *The Nature and Process of Law* (New York: Oxford University Press, 1993), 138.

37. Cardozo, *Nature of the Judicial Process*, 43.

38. Ibid., 45.

39. Ibid., 74 and 141.

40. "Objectivity always depends on subjectivity." Ibid.

41. "Only if we are conscious of our experiencing, understanding, *judging*, and *deciding* can we guarantee the objectivity of results." David Granfield, *The Inner Experience of Law: A Jurisprudence of Subjectivity* (Washington, D.C.: Catholic University Press, 1988), 3.

42. Martin P. Golding, "Jurisprudence and Legal Philosophy in Twentieth Century America—Major Themes and Developments," *Journal of Legal Education* 36 (1986): 441, 465. See generally, Jerome Frank, "What Courts Do in Fact?" *Illinois Law Review* 26 (1932): 645; John Dickinson, "Legal Rules: Their Function in the Process of Decision," *University of Pennsylvania Law Review* 79 (1931): 833.

43. Professor Kronman explains the position of the "free creativity" of judicial interpretation as a residual of rule application.

   The idea that there is an irreducible element of free creativity, of interpretative freedom, in the adjudicative process which is left over so to speak, after one has taken account of all the rules that might conceivably bear on the case at hand is today an idea so familiar, so patently obvious. . . .

   Anthony T. Kronman, "The Problem of Judicial Discretion," *Journal of Legal Education* 36 (1986): 481.

44. Kent Greenawalt, "Discretion and Judicial Decision: The Elusive Quest for the Fetters that Bind Judges," *Columbia Law Review* 75 (1975): 359, 360 ("for the judge is legally bound by some external standard"). See generally, Dworkin, "Judicial Discretion," 624; Ronald Dworkin, "Social Rules and Legal Theory," *Yale Law Journal* 81 (1972): 855; Rolf Sartorius, "Social Policy and Judicial Legislation," *American Philosophy Quarterly* 8 (1971): 151.

45. Ibid., 396 (emphasis added).

46. Rupert Cross and J. W. Harris, *Precedent in English Law*, 4th ed. (New York: Oxford University Press, 1991), 217.

47. "When authoritative standards yield no clear answers . . . and when more than one result will widely be regarded as a satisfactory fulfillment of his judicial responsibilities . . . as far as the law is concerned, the judge has discretion to decide between them." Greenawalt, "Discretion and Judicial Decision," 378.

48. (1989) Q.B. 488, as discussed in Cross and Harris, *Precedent in English Law*, 222.

49. Greenawalt, "Discretion and Judicial Decision," 397.

50. The judge acknowledges "the reaction of other people is an anticipated fact." Duncan Kennedy, "Freedom and Constraint in Adjudication: A Critical Phenomenology," *Journal of Legal Education* 36 (1986): 518, 521.

51. Ibid., 561.

52. Ibid., 559.

53. The notion of collegial decision making has been explored by a number of legal commentators. Ronald Dworkin speaks of law as a collective enterprise in which judges act as novelists writing successive chapters of a chain novel. Ronald Dworkin, *A Matter of Principle* (Cambridge: Harvard University Press, 1985), as cited, Joshua P. Davis, "Cardozo's Judicial Craft and What Cases Come to Mean," *New York University Law Review* 68 (1993): 777, 810.

54. Ibid., 813.

55. Robert S. Summers, "Lon L. Fuller's Jurisprudence and the Possibility It Was Much Influenced by G. W. F. Hegel," *Cornell Law Forum* 10 (1983): 9, 12.

56. Melvin A. Eisenberg, "The Responsive Model of Contract Law," *Stanford Law Review* 36 (1984): 1107, 1160.

57. Gerald E. Frug, "The Ideology of Bureaucracy in American Law," *Harvard Law Review* 97 (1984): 1276.

58. Ibid., 1288. This term was borrowed from the work of Jacques Derrida. See, Jacques Derrida, *Of Grammatology*, trans. Gayatri Spivak (Baltimore, M.D.: Johns Hopkins University Press, 1967).

59. Ibid., 1290.

60. Ibid., 1292.

61. Ibid., 1291. See also, Gerald E. Frug, "The City as a Legal Concept," *Harvard Law Review* 93 (1980): 1059.

62. Richard Bronaugh, "Agreement, Mistake, and Objectivity in the Bargain Theory of Contract," *William and Mary Law Review* 18 (1976): 213, 244.

63. Ibid., 251.

64. Eisenberg, "Responsive Model of Contract," 1111–12.

65. Karl N. Llewellyn, "What Price Contract?—An Essay in Perspective," *Yale Law Journal* 40 (1931): 704, 750–51.

66. James, *Pragmatism*, 75.

67. De Tourtoulan, *Philosophy in the Development of Law*, 208.

68. Lewis Sargentich, "Sympathy as a Legal Structure," *Harvard Law Review* 105 (1992): 1961.

69. Lynne N. Henderson, "Legality and Empathy," *Michigan Law Review* 85 (1987): 1574.

70. Sargentich, "Sympathy as a Legal Structure," 1968.

71. Gardner, "Inquiry into the Principles of Contract," 3.

72. Robin West, "Disciplines, Subjectivity, and Law," in *The Fate of Law*, ed. Austin Sarat and Thomas R. Kearns (Ann Arbor: University of Michigan Press, 1991), 154.

73. Ibid., 152.

74. M. Eisenberg, "The Bargain Principle and Its Limits," *Harvard Law Review* 95 (1982): 741, 801.

75. Sargentich, "Sympathy as a Legal Structure," 1969, 1973, 1975–76 (emphasis added).

76. In explaining the workings of causality in the law, De Tourtoulan asserts that the "application of abstract formulas to concrete situations is a special labor. The method of objective science is based upon the *degree of subjectivity* which the objective cause undergoes through it." De Tourtoulan, *Philosophy in the Development of Law*, 72 (emphasis added).

Chapter 10

1. Robin West, "Disciplines, Subjectivity, and Law," in *The Fate of Law*, ed. Austin Sarat and Thomas R. Kearns (Ann Arbor: University of Michigan Press, 1991), 157.

2. David Granfield, *The Inner Experience of Law: A Jurisprudence of Subjectivity* (Washington, D.C.: Catholic University Press, 1988), 23.

3. See generally, Paul Redding, *Hegel's Hermeneutics* (Ithaca: Cornell University Press, 1996). See also, Charles Taylor, *Hegel* (Cambridge: Cambridge University Press, 1975).

4. Granfield, *Inner Experience of Law*, 23.

5. Benjamin N. Cardozo, *The Nature of the Judicial Process* (New Haven: Yale University Press, 1921), 110.

6. Ibid.

7. Melvin A. Eisenberg, "The Responsive Model of Contract Law," *Stanford Law Review* 36 (1984): 1107, 1167.

8. R. H. Helmholz, "Adverse Possession and Subjective Intent," *Washington University Law Quarterly* 61 (1983): 331, 358.

9. Herbert A. Simon, *Reason in Human Affairs* (Stanford: Stanford University Press, 1983), 20.

10. Cornelius F. Murphy, *Descent into Subjectivity* (Wakefield, N.H.: Longwood Academic Press, 1990), 4.

11. Frederick Perls, Ralph E. Hefferline, and Paul Goodman, *Gestalt Therapy* (New York: Julian Press, 1951), 23.

12. Dennis M. Patterson, "Law's Pragmatism: Law as Practice and Narrative," *Virginia Law Review* 76 (1990): 937, 941.

13. Ibid., 940.

14. 1 All E. R. 512 (C.A. 1990).

15. Ibid.

16. Ibid., 524.

17. See generally, Robert S. Summers, "The Technique Element in Law," *California Law Review* 59 (1971): 733; Hans Kelsen, *General Theory of Law and State* (New York: Russell and Russell, 1961); Hans Kelsen, "Law as a Specific Social Technique," *University of Chicago Law Review* 9 (1941): 75.

18. Professor Summers explains that the technique element in law is the study of "How does the law do what it does?" Ibid. Ultimately, the dialectic is more concerned with the question of how then the questions of why or when. Summers lists five basic techniques that are utilized in law: grievance-remedial, penal, administrative-regulatory, public benefit conferral, and private arranging. Ibid., 736.

19. Ibid., 742.

20. Ibid.

21. Roscoe Pound, "Fifty Years of Jurisprudence," *Harvard Law Review* 51 (1938): 444, 453.

22. Jon O. Newman, "Between Legal Realism and Neutral Principles: The Legitimacy of Institutional Values," *California Law Review* 72 (1984): 200, 205.

BIBLIOGRAPHY

Adams, John N., and Roger Brownsword. *Understanding Contract Law*. 2d ed. London: Fontana Press, 1994.

Aquinas, Thomas. *Selected Philosophical Writings*. Translated by Timothy McDermott. Cambridge: Oxford University Press, 1993.

Atiyah, Patrick S. "Contracts, Promises and the Law of Obligations." *Law Quarterly Review* 94 (1978): 193.

————. *Essays on Contract*. Oxford: Clarendon Press, 1986.

————. *The Law of Contract*. 4th ed. Oxford: Clarendon Press, 1989.

Barnett, Randy E. ". . . And Contractual Consent." *Southern California Interdisciplinary Law Journal* 3 (1993): 421.

————. "The Internal and External Analysis of Concepts." *Cardozo Law Review* 11 (1990): 525.

————. "The Sound of Silence: Default Rules and Contractual Consent." *Virginia Law Review* 78 (1992): 821.

————. "Squaring Undisclosed Agency Law with Contract Theory." *California Law Review* 75 (1987): 1969.

Beale, Hugh, and Tony Dugdale. "Contracts Between Businessmen: Planning and the Use of Contractual Remedies." *British Journal of Law and Society* 2 (1975): 45.

Berman, Harold J. *Faith and Order: The Reconciliation of Law and Religion*. Atlanta: Scholar's Press, 1993.

Bernstein, Richard J. *Beyond Objectivism and Relativism: Science, Hermeneutics, and Praxis*. Philadelphia: University of Pennsylvania Press, 1983.

Birmingham, Robert L. "Holmes on 'Peerless': *Raffles v. Wichelhaus* and the Objective Theory of Contract." *University of Pittsburgh Law Review* 47 (1985): 183.

Braucher, Richard. "Interpretation and Legal Effect in the Second Restatement of Contracts." *Columbia Law Review* 81 (1981): 13.

————. "Freedom of Contract and the Second Restatement." *Yale Law Journal* 78 (1969): 598.

Bronaugh, Richard. "Agreement, Mistake, and Objectivity in the Bargain Theory of Contract." *William and Mary Law Review* 18 (1976): 213.

Bulloch, Steven N. "Fraud Liability Under Agency Principles: A New Approach." *William and Mary Law Review* 27 (1986): 301.

Burton, Steven J. *Principles of Contract Law*. St. Paul, Minn.: West Publishing Co., 1995.

Butler, Andrew S. "An Objective or Subjective Approach to the Right to Counsel? A New Zealand Perspective." *Criminal Law Quarterly* 36 (1994): 317.

Calamari, John D., and Joseph M. Perillo. *Contracts*. 3d ed. St. Paul, Minn.: West Publishing Co., 1987.

Cardozo, Benjamin N. *The Nature of the Judicial Process*. New Haven: Yale University Press, 1921.

Cataldo, Bernard F., Cornelius W. Gillam, Frederick G. Kempin, John M. Stockton, and Charles M. Weber. *Introduction to Law and the Legal Process*. New York: John Wiley and Sons, 1965.

Charny, David. "Hypothetical Bargains: The Normative Structure of Contract Interpretation." *Michigan Law Review* 89 (1991): 1815.

Corbin, Arthur L. *Corbin on Contracts*. 2d ed. St. Paul, Minn.: West Publishing Co., 1952.

————. "Offer and Acceptance, and Some of the Resulting Legal Relations." *Yale Law Journal* 26 (1917): 169.

Craswell, Richard. "Contract Law, Default Rules, and the Philosophy of Promising." *Michigan Law Review* 88 (1989): 489.

Danzig, Richard. *The Capability Problem in Contract Law*. Mineola, N.Y.: Foundation Press, 1978.

Davis, Joshua P. "Cardozo's Judicial Craft and What Cases Come to Mean." *New York University Law Review* 68 (1993): 777.

Del Vecchio, Georgio. *Philosophy of Law*. Translated by Thomas O. Martin. 8th ed. Washington, D.C.: Catholic University Press, 1953.

De Moor, Anne. "Contract and Agreement in English and French Law." *Oxford Journal of Legal Studies* 6 (1986): 275.

Denning, Lord. *The Discipline of Law*. London: Butterworths, 1979.

De Tourtoulan, Pierre. *Philosophy in the Development of Law*. Translated by Martha McC. Read. New York: Macmillian Co., 1922.

Dewey, John. *How We Think*. Buffalo, N.Y.: Prometheus Press, 1910.

De Wulf, Maurice. *History of Medieval Philosophy*. Translated by Ernest Messenger. London: Thomas Nelson and Sons, 1938.

DiMatteo, Larry A. "Deconstructing the Myth of the Infancy Law Doctrine: From Incapacity to Accountability." *Ohio Northern University Law Review* 21 (1994): 481.

———. "Depersonalization of Personal Service Contracts: The Search for a Modern Approach to Assignability." *Akron Law Review* 27 (1994): 407.

DiMatteo, Larry A., and René Sacasas. "Credit and Value Comfort Instruments: Crossing the Line from Assurance to Legally Significant Reliance and Toward a Theory of Enforceability." *Baylor Law Review* 47 (1995): 357.

Duff, R.A. "Intentions Legal and Philosophical." *Oxford Journal of Legal Studies* 9 (1989): 76.

Dworkin, Gerald. *The Theory and Practice of Autonomy*. New York: Cambridge University Press, 1988.

Eisenberg, Melvin A. "The Bargain Principle and Its Limits." *Harvard Law Review* 95 (1982): 741.

———. *The Nature of the Common Law*. Cambridge: Harvard University Press, 1988.

———. "The Responsive Model of Contract Law." *Stanford Law Review* 36 (1984): 1107.

Egan, Thomas P. "Equitable Doctrines Operating Against the Express Provisions of a Written Contract." *DePaul Business Law Journal* 5 (1993): 261.

Ellul, Jacques. *The Theological Foundation of Law*. Garden City, N.Y.: Doubleday and Co., 1960.

Enderlein, Fritz, and Dietrich Maskow. *International Sales Law*. New York: Oceana 1992.

Farnsworth, E. Allan. *Contracts*. 2d ed. Boston: Little, Brown, and Co., 1990.

———. "Good Faith Performance and Commercial Reasonableness Under the Uniform Commercial Code." *University of Chicago Law Review* 30 (1963): 666.

———. "Meaning in the Law of Contracts." *Yale Law Journal* 76 (1967): 939.

———. "Precontractual Liability and Preliminary Agreements: Fair Dealing and Failed Negotiations." *Columbia Law Review* 87 (1987): 217.

Finnis, John. *Natural Law and Natural Rights*. Oxford: Clarendon Press, 1980.

Fiss, Owen M. "Objectivity and Interpretation." *Stanford Law Review* 34 (1982): 739.

Fried, Charles. *Contract As Promise*. Cambridge: Harvard University Press, 1981.

Fritzgerald, P. J. *Salmond on Jurisprudence*. 12th ed. London: Sweet and Maxwell, 1966.

Frug, Gerald E. "A Critical Theory of Law." *Legal Education Review* 1 (1989): 43.

———. "The Ideology of Bureaucracy in American Law." *Harvard Law Review* 97 (1984): 1276.

Fuller, Hoffman F. "Mistake and Error in the Law of Contracts." *Emory Law Journal* 33 (1984): 41.

Fuller, Lon, and William Perdue. "The Reliance Interest in Contract Damages: 1." *Yale Law Journal* 46 (1936): 52.

———. "The Reliance Interest in Contract Damages: 2." *Yale Law Journal* 46 (1937): 373.

Gadamer, Hans-Georg. *Hegel's Dialectic*. Translated by P. Christopher Smith. New Haven: Yale University Press, 1976.

Gardner, George K. "An Inquiry Into the Principles of the Law of Contracts." *Harvard Law Review* 46 (1932): 1.

Gilmore, Grant. *The Death of Contract*. Columbus: Ohio State University Press, 1974.

———. *The Ages of American Law*. New Haven: Yale University Press, 1977.

Gobert, James. "Corporate Criminality: New Crimes for the Times." *Criminal Law Review* (October 1994): 722.

Goddard, David. "The Myth of Subjectivity." *Oxford Journal of Legal Studies* 7 (1987): 263.

Goetz, Charles J., and Robert E. Scott. "The Limits of Expanded Choice: An Analysis of the Interactions Between Express and Implied Contract Terms." *California Law Review* 73 (1985): 261.

Golding, Martin P. "Jurisprudence and Legal Philosophy in Twentieth-Century America—Major Themes and Developments." *Journal of Legal Education* 36 (1986): 441.

Goldman, Alan H. *Moral Knowledge*. London: Routledge, 1990.

Goldworth, Amnon, ed. *Deontology*. New York: Oxford University Press, 1983.

Gordley, James. *The Philosophical Origins of Modern Contract Doctrine*. Oxford: Clarendon Press, 1991.

Granfield, David. *The Inner Experience of Law: A Jurisprudence of Subjectivity*. Washington, D.C.: Catholic University Press, 1988.

Greenawalt, Kent. *Law and Objectivity*. New York: Oxford University Press, 1992.

———. "Discretion and Judicial Decision: The Elusive Quest for the Fetters that Bind Judges." *Columbia Law Review* 75 (1975): 359.

Hall, Calvin S., and Gardner Lindzey. *Theories of Personality*. 2d ed. New York: John Wiley and Sons, 1970.

Hall, Kermit L., William M. Wiecek, and Paul Finkelman. *American Legal History*. New York: Oxford University Press, 1991.

Halpern, Sheldon W. "Application of the Doctrine of Commercial Impracticability: Searching for the 'Wisdom of Solomon.'" *University of Pennsylvania Law Review* 135 (1987): 1123.

Hedley, Stephen. "Keeping Contract in Its Place—*Balfour v. Balfour* and the Enforceability of Informal Agreements." *Oxford Journal of Legal Studies* 5 (1985): 391.

Helmholz, R. H. "Adverse Possession and Subjective Intent." *Washington University Law Quarterly* 61 (1983): 331.

Holmes, Oliver Wendell. *The Common Law*. Edited by Mark DeWolfe-Howe. Boston: Little, Brown, and Co., 1963.

———. "The Theory of Legal Interpretation." *Harvard Law Review* 12 (1899).

Horowitz, Irwin A., and Thomas E. Willging. *The Psychology of Law*. Boston: Little, Brown, and Co., 1984.

Horwitz, Morton J. *The Transformation of American Law, 1870-1960*. New York: Oxford University Press, 1992.

Howarth, William. "The Meaning of Objectivity in Contract." *The Law Quarterly Review* 100 (1984): 265.

James, Phillip S. *English Law*. 9th ed. London: Butterworths, 1976.

James, William. *Pragmatism*. Buffalo: Prometheus Books, 1991.

Kagehiro, Dorothy K. and William S. Laufer, eds. *Handbook of Psychology and Law*. New York: Springer-Verlag, 1992.

Kant, Immanuel. *Foundations of the Metaphysics of Morals*. Translated by Lewis W. Beck. New York: Macmillan, 1985.

Kennedy, Duncan. "Freedom and Constraint in Adjudication: A Critical Phenomenology." *Journal of Legal Education* 36 (1986): 518.

Knapp, Charles L.. "Reliance in the Revised Restatement: The Proliferation of Promissory Estoppel." *Columbia Law Review* 81 (1981): 52.

Kolers, Paul A. "Perception and Representation." *Annual Review of Psychology* 34 (1983): 129.

Kronman, Anthony T. "Precedent and Tradition." *Yale Law Journal* 99 (1990): 1029.

———. "The Problem of Judicial Discretion." *Journal of Legal Education* 36 (1986): 481.

LaFave, Wayne R., and Austin W. Scott. *Criminal Law*. St. Paul, Minn.: West Publishing Co., 1972.

Laski, Harold J. "The Basis of Vicarious Liability." *Yale Law Journal* 26 (1916): 105.

Llewellyn, Karl N. *The Case Law System in America*. Edited by Paul Gewirtz. Chicago: University of Chicago Press, 1989.

———. *The Common Law Tradition*. Boston: Little, Brown, and Co., 1960.

———. "What Price Contract?—An Essay in Perspective." *Yale Law Journal* 40 (1931): 704.

Lowe, Robert. *Commercial Law*. 5th ed. London: Sweet and Maxwell, 1976.

Lukes, Steven, and Andrew Scull, eds. *Durkheim and the Law*. New York: St. Martin's Press, 1983.

Macaulay, Stuart. "Non-contractual Relations in Business." *American Sociological Review* 28 (1963): 45.

Macneil, Ian R. *Contracts*. Mineola, N.Y.: Foundation Press, 1971.

———. "The Many Futures of Contracts." *Southern California Law Review* 47 (1974): 691.

———. *The New Social Contract*. New Haven: Yale University Press, 1980.

———. "Restatement (Second) of Contracts and Presentiation." *Virginia Law Review* 60 (1974): 589.

Maine, Henry Sumner. *Ancient Law*. Boston: Beacon Press, 1963.

Marshall, James. *Intention—In Law and Society*. New York: Funk and Wagnalls, 1968.

May, Rollo. *Love and Will*. 1969. Reprint, New York: Dell Publishing Co., 1989.

McGregor, Harvey. *Contract Code*. Milano: Dott. A. Giuffrè Editore, 1993.

Miller, Robert S. "America Singing: The Role of Custom and Usage in the Thoroughbred Horse Business." *Kentucky Law Journal* 74 (1986): 781.

Muris, Timothy J. "The Costs of Freely Granting Specific Performance." *Duke Law Journal* (1982): 1053.

Murphy, Cornelius F. *Descent Into Subjectivity*. Wakefield, N.H.: Longwood Academic Press, 1990.

Nagel, Thomas. *Mortal Questions*. Cambridge: Cambridge University Press, 1979.

Newman, Jon O. "Between Legal Realism and Neutral Principles: The Legitimacy of Institutional Values." *California Law Review* 72 (1984): 200.

O'Connor, J. F. *Good Faith in English Law*. Brookfield, Vt.: Gower, 1990.

Oldham, James. "Reinterpretations of 18th-Century English Contract Theory: The View from Lord Mansfield's Trial Notes." *Georgetown Law Journal* 76 (1988): 1949.

Parry, David H. *The Sanctity of Contracts in English Law*, rev. ed. London: Stevens and Sons, 1959.

Patterson, Dennis M. "The Pseudo-Debate Over Default Rules in Contract Law." *Southern California Interdisciplinary Law Journal* 3 (1993): 235.

———. "Law's Pragmatism: Law as Practice and Narrative." *Virginia Law Review* 76 (1990): 937.

Perkins, Rollin M. *Criminal Law*. 2d ed. Mineola, N.Y.: Foundation Press, 1969.

Pollock, Frederick. *Principles of Contract*. 10th ed. London: Stevens and Sons, 1936.

Posner, Richard A. *The Problems of Jurisprudence*. Cambridge: Harvard University Press, 1990.

Pound, Roscoe. *An Introduction to the Philosophy of Law*. New Haven: Yale University Press, 1954.

———. "Fifty Years of Jurisprudence." *Harvard Law Review* 51 (1938): 444.

———. *Jurisprudence*. Vol. 5. St. Paul, Minn.: West Publishing Co., 1959.

Prosser, William L. *Torts*. 4th ed. St. Paul, Minn.: West Publishing Co., 1971.

Reiss, Steven A. "Prosecutorial Intent in Constitutional Criminal Procedure." *University of Pennsylvania Law Review* 135 (1987): 1365.

Russell, Bertrand. *The Problems of Philosophy*. Indianapolis: Hackett, [1912] 1990.

Sargentich, L. "Sympathy as a Legal Structure." *Harvard Law Review* 105 (1992): 1961.

Shell, G. Richard. "Contracts in the Modern Supreme Court." *California Law Review* 81 (1993): 431.

Shuman, Samuel I. "Justification of Judicial Decisions." *California Law Review* 59 (1971): 715.

Simon, Herbert A. *Reason in Human Affairs*. Stanford: Stanford University Press, 1983.

Simpson, A.W. B. "Innovation in Nineteenth Century Contract Law." *Law Quarterly Review* 91 (1975): 247.

Slawson, W. David. "The New Meaning of Contract: The Transformation of Contracts Law by Standard Forms." *University of Pittsburgh Law Review* 46 (1984): 21.

―――. "The Futile Search for Principles for Default Rules." *Southern California Interdisciplinary Law Journal* 3 (1993): 29.

Smith, Patricia. *The Nature and Process of Law*. New York: Oxford University Press, 1993.

Speidel, Richard E. "Contract Law: Some Reflections Upon Commercial Context and the Judicial Process." *Wisconsin Law Review* (1967): 822.

―――. "The New Spirit of Contract." *Journal of Law and Commerce* 2 (1982): 193.

―――. "Unconscionability, Assent and Consumer Protection." *University of Pittsburgh Law Review* 31 (1970): 359.

Summers, Robert S. "The General Duty of Good Faith." *Cornell Law Review* 67 (1982): 810.

―――. "Lon L. Fuller's Jurisprudence and the Possibility It Was Much Influenced by G. W. F. Hegel." *Cornell Law Forum* 10 (1983): 9.

―――. "The Technique Element in Law." *California Law Review* 59 (1971): 733.

Von Leyden, W. *Aristotle on Equality and Justice*. New York: St. Martin's Press 1985.

Vorster, J. P. "A Comment on the Meaning of Objectivity in Contract." *The Law Quarterly Review* 103 (1987): 274.

Warren, Elizabeth. "Trade Usage and Parties in the Trade: An Economic Rationale for an Inflexible Rule." *University of Pittsburgh Law Review* 42 (1981): 515.

West, Robin. "Disciplines, Subjectivity, and Law." In *The Fate of Law*, edited by Austin Sarat and Thomas R. Kearns. Ann Arbor: University of Michigan Press, 1991.

Whitman, James Q. "Why Did the Revolutionary Lawyers Confuse Custom and Reason?" *University of Chicago Law Review* 58 (1991): 1321.

White, James B. *The Legal Imagination*. Chicago: University of Chicago Press, 1985.

Whittier, Clarke B. "The Restatement of Contracts and Mutual Assent." *California Law Review* 17 (1929): 441.

Williston, Samuel. "Mutual Assent in the Formation of Informal Contracts." *Illinois Law Review* 14 (1919): 85.

Williston, Samuel, and William Jaeger. *A Treatise on the Law of Contracts.* 3d ed. Mount Kisco, N.Y.: Baker, Voorhis, 1959.

Wiseman, Zipporah B.. "The Limits of Vision: Karl Llewellyn and the Law of Contracts." *Harvard Law Review* 100 (1987): 465.

Yorio, Edward, and Steve Thel. "The Promissory Basis of Section 90." *Yale Law Journal* 101 (1991): 111.

Young, Robert L. "Intentions, Interpretations, and Misunderstandings." *Sociological Spectrum* 15 (1995): 161.

Zelermeyer, William. *Legal Reasoning: The Evolutionary Process of Law.* Englewood Cliffs: Prentice-Hall, 1960.

INDEX

action of deceit, 147n. 3
actions in covenant, 11
actus reus, 116, 118, 188n. 5, 189n. 6
Adams, John N., 50
ad idem, 150n. 34
agency. *See* law of agency
American law: basis of, 151n. 39; evolution
of, 107–8; nineteenth-century, 32, 37,
62, 88, 100; and the reasonable person
standard, 53–55, 60, 61, 62, 63; on state
of mind, 120; twentieth-century, 23, 41,
44, 53–55, 60–63, 92–93, 95, 104, 119,
122. *See also* law
analogue, 87
Ancient Law (Maine), 21, 107, 186n. 50
arational. *See* subjectivism
Arcos, Limited v. E.A. Ronaasen, 172n. 100
Aristotle: on a basis for reasonableness, 22,
129; on language, 65; on law and custom
or behavior, 62; as a teleologist, 125
*Ashville Investments Ltd. v. Elmer Contractors
Ltd.*, 134–35
assault: judicial, 103–6; legislative, 106–7
assent: apparent, 40, 166n. 185; blanket, 38,
39, 40; Llewellyn on the duality of,
38–42, 108; manifestation and, 11–12,
22, 58; mutual, 11, 12, 13–14, 22, 31,
35, 38, 40, 58, 69, 86, 92, 103, 151n.

46; and the reasonable person standard,
40; specific, 108; Whittier on, 22. *See
also* LLewellyn
assumpsit, writ of, 7, 78, 147nn. 2–3
Atiyah, Patrick S., xiv; on duress, 187n.
72; on promise as a contract basis, 8–9;
on fairness of exchange, 14, 36–37, 83;
on the undue influence duality, 111,
112
Atkin, Lord, 81
attributives, 125
Augustine (Saint), 75
Australian law, 21
authority: actual, 122–23; implied, 122–23
autonomy, 8, 87

Bach v. Friden Calculating Mach. Co., 41
backward masking, 178n. 72
bad faith, 86, 94, 113, 182n. 34
bargain, 25–26, 27, 41, 110, 153n. 79; contract to, 154n. 98; demise of, 80; objectivity of, 137; principle, 157nn. 41, 42,
159n. 60; theory, 103, 137
Barnett, Randy E.: on consent, 43; on default
rules, 14–15; second-order problem of
knowledge of, 42–45
Beale, Hugh, 42, 163n. 143
Beasley v. St. Mary's Hosp. of Centralia, 93

207

benefit rule, 103
Bernstein, Richard J., 146n. 26
bilateral monopoly, 112
bill of sale, 24
Blackburn, Lord, 36, 111
Blackpool & Fyde Aero Club v. Blackpool Borough Council, 48
Blackstone, William, 22, 155n. 12; restrictionism of, 7
boilerplate. *See* contract
Bowen, Lord, 80
Boyce v. Doyle, 104
Braucher, Richard, 102, 163n. 148
breach of contract, 10–11, 32–33, 77–78, 99, 147n.3; bad faith, 113; determined by will, 92; fundamental, 66, 67, 173n. 107; main purpose rule and, 66–68. *See also* promise
Britton v. Turner, 37
Bronaugh, Richard, 137
Brownsword, Roger, 50
Bunge Corp. v. Tradex SA, 173n. 105
Burton, Steven J., 8
Butler, Andrew S., 120

Campbell v. Rockerfeller, 44
Canadian law, 53, 121
canon law, 75, 76, 77, 98
Cardozo, Benjamin N.: on agency, 181n. 28; on the binary relationship of the subjective and objective, 141; conception of law of, 17; on contract reading, 44–45; on discourse, 13; echoes Kantian objectivism, 97; on judicial discretion, 133–34; method of philosophy of, 17–18; on objective and subjective change, 17–18; on performance, 99; on the role of judge, 129; subjectivism of, 129, 133–34
categories of facts, 132. *See also* fact patterns
Cehave N. V. v. Bremer, 66

certainty of contract, 87, 162n. 140
Chancery Court, 78
Chelsea Industries, Inc. v. Accuray Leasing Corp., 45–46
Chemco Leasing Spa v. Rediffusion plc., 29
circumstantial evidence, 118–20, 190n. 27
CISG. *See* United Nations Convention on Contracts for the International Sale of Goods
civiliter mortuus, 101, 184n. 5
civil law, 10–11, 29, 31, 148n. 12, 190n. 16
clauses: express satisfaction, 92, 94; exculpatory, 67, 68
Coase, R. H., 112
coding, 87, 172n. 99, 179n. 74
coherence theory, 134
Coke, Edward, 12, 22, 155n. 12
comfort instruments: in commerce and finance, 157n. 45; and contract intent, 28–32; defined, 28; enforcement of, 29–31; inconsistency of, 29. *See also* reliance theory
commercial law, 88
commercial practice, 42
common enterprise, 39
common law, 29, 20, 31, 33, 155n. 12; and assumpsit writ, 7, 78, 147nn. 2–3; and communal decisions, 132; and contractual consent, 101, 118; courts in England, 147n. 3; custom and trade usage as a source of, 60–64; doctrine of mistake, 69–70; and the element of intention, 1, 91, 145n. 8; and emancipation, 105; evolution of, 107; and the mailbox rule, 12; nature of the, 88; and performance, 98–99; and reasonableness, 62, 91; and subjective theory, 45. *See also* assumpsit; contract; law; mistake; seal
communal objectivity, 37, 94, 122
community standards: origin of use of, 23; Holmes on, 88–89; and intent, 37,

52–53; and judges, 132; Laski on, 122; and legal standards, 135; and the reasonable person, 52, 53, 85; and subjective satisfaction, 91–92
compensation, 87
competency, 109
conduct of contracting parties, 126–27
conflict of interest, 133
conscience, 22
consciousness, collective, 122
consensus ad idem, 12, 86, 122, 144
consent: apparent, 157n. 43; contractual, 71–72, 77, 101, 111–12, 175n. 145; and custom and trade usage, 64; implication of, 42–45; manifestation of, 122–23; and mens rea, 116; reality of, 109–10, 139; relational, 72–74. *See also* reasonable person standard; Llewellyn
consequential-based theory. *See* teleology
"Consideration and Form" (Fuller), 24
construction, 42, 67
constructive intention, 116
contract: bargain, intent, and reliance as pillars of, 25–26, 29–30, 41; basic assumption of a, 32; binding, 71–72, 144; boilerplate, 38–42; breach of, 10–11, 32–33, 66–68, 77–78, 99, 147n. 3; categorization of, 80; classes of, 150n. 31; classical, 56, 72–73, 150n. 33; comfort instruments and, 28–31; and conduct, 126–27; consensual, 77, 82–83; consent in a, 42–45, 71–74; court intervention and, 42, 43; defined, 32, 36, 39; dickered-deal, 38–42; dispute resolution, 138–39, 161n. 108; essence of, 8, 15–16, 123; evolution of, xiv, 7–9, 11, 72–73, 77, 82–83, 109, 142; externalities of, 12–14; form, 32–33; formalities, 48, 76, 108; freedom of, 11, 16, 19, 67, 147n. 2, 151n. 3; fundamental term of, 67; just, 82–83; language and intent, 55–60; lia-

bility, 26–27, 35, 65; negotiations, 48; non-sale, 99; obligation, 60, 77, 96; objective theory of, 81, 82, 85, 155n. 17; personal service, 165n. 180; and precontract, 48; presumption of intentionality and, 31–33; as promise, 7–11, 34; as reflection of intent, 40, 85; and reliance theory, 26–28; and revocation, 61–62; ritual, 76, 151n. 46; root essence of, 8, 15–16, 30, 66–68, 69, 80, 81–82; rules of, 42, 113; sanctity of, 7, 16, 71, 77, 147n. 2; satisfaction, 49–50; social, 84, 86; standard form, 38–42, 72, 108, 163n. 141; statements, 56, 169n. 35; symbols of, 86; trade, 60–66; transaction costs of, 112–14; unexpressed assumptions in a, 42; will theory of, 79. *See also* assumpsit; bargain; comfort instruments; contract law; contract theory; contractual capacity; enforcement; freedom of contract; intent; interpretation; language; law; law of satisfaction; liability; objective theory; promise; reasonableness; reasonable person standard; reliance; Roman law; rules of contract law; subjective theory; terms; tort; will theory
contract law: and agency, 124; default rules of, 14–16, 23, 37, 41–44, 82, 113; Eisenberg's responsive model of, 138; essence of, 8, 15–16, 123, 138; external forces of, 23–24; formality and, 11; and human values, 124–26, 129–33; inner experience of, 129–40; and judges, 129–33; move from subjective to objective view of, 20, 79–81, 136; nineteenth-century, 83; neoclassical, 150n. 33; and the reasonable person standard, 5, 147n. 36; rules, 42, 113, 134; socialization produced, 86; subjectivity and, 13. *See also* agency; breach of contract; contract; contract theory; form; objective theory; rules

of contract law; subjective theory; tort
contract theory: cyclical, 46, 136, 142,
   165nn. 81–82; and infancy law, 108;
   objective, 82, 104; and obligation, 103;
   rigid, 108
"Contract as a Thing" (Leff), 70
contract to bargain concept, 154n. 98
contractual capacity: and the dialectic,
   101–14; evolution of, 108; and infancy
   law, 86, 101–3
Corbin, Arthur L., 15, 157n. 42; on objective theory, 22; on the reasonable person
   standard, 51; on reliance, 26; on subjective theory, 45
courts: Chancery, 78; royal, 147n. 3. *See also*
   common law; interpretation
criminal law: evolution of, 77; and mens rea,
   115–21, 122, 136; and the reasonable
   person standard, 121
culpability (*culpa*), 8; in breach of contract,
   10–11; and consent, 116, 117–18;
   inferred, 118; as knowledge, 111, 117;
   promisor, 34. *See also* mens rea
custom: as an assumption, 42; in CISG, 127;
   defined, 61, 62, 64, 170n. 59; and good
   faith, 92; and intent, 56, 62, 113–14; and
   interpretation, 82; language as, 56,
   65–66, 170n. 63; as law, 62–63; and the
   reasonable person, 60–68, 124; as a tool,
   86, 124; and trade usage, 60–68, 82. *See
   also* community standards

D. & C. Builders Ltd. v. Rees, 111
debt: precedent, 147n. 3
deceit, 147n. 3
default rules, 14–16, 113; communal, 37;
   and court intervention, 42, 43; premised
   on use of objective theory, 23; and the
   reasonable person, 82; in the *Uniform
   Commercial Code*, 23, 41, 44
Del Vecchio, Georgio, 109, 129

Denning, Lord: on breach, 66; doctrine of
   presumed intent of, 80; *High Street House
   Limited*, 10; and the reasonable person,
   80, 111; restated the external focus of
   contract law, 24, 38, 162n. 123
deontological, versus teleological, philosophy, 17, 115, 124–26
deterrence, 115, 116
De Tourtoulan, Pierre, 85, 86, 89, 180n. 94,
   197n. 76
detriment, 147n. 3
Dewey, John, 52, 65, 130
dialectic: Barnett's theory of the, 43; as coding, 87; in contract law, 75–89, 142;
   coping systems and the, 115–27; deontological versus teleological, 17, 115,
   124–26; Durkheim and the, 82–83; and
   economic duress, 110; essence of the,
   82, 98; importance of the, 46–47; interpretation and the, 55; judicial mind and
   the, 88–89; Kant on the natural, 96;
   philosophical foundations of the, 79–85;
   psychological dimension of the, 85–88;
   religious foundations of the, 75–79; as
   synthesis, 136–38, 141–44. *See also*
   Hegel; objective theory; reasonable person standard; subjective theory
dickered-deal. *See* contract
Diplock, Lord, 36
disaffirmation, right of, 102, 103–4, 109,
   185n. 12, 186n. 42
discovery, 133
"Discretion and Judicial Decision"
   (Greenawalt), 134
discretion and subjectivity, 134–36
dispute resolution, 138–39
dissatisfaction, rule of, 95
distinguishing, 133
doctrine, as a concept, 17
doctrine of capacity, 42, 101, 107. *See also*
   law of incapacity

doctrine of commercial impracticability, 31, 32, 160n. 84
doctrine of consideration, 18, 147n. 3
doctrine of duress, 14, 176n. 18. *See also* duress
doctrine of economic duress, 46, 101, 109–11
doctrine of fair dealing, 14, 16, 28, 30, 42; Atiyah on, 8–9, 36–37; and objectivity, 140
doctrine of good faith, 14, 30, 42, 46, 86, 159n. 76; based on community standards, 94–95; CISG, 180n. 10; as implied terms of every contract, 108–9; and intent, 95; rejected, 92
doctrine of presumed intent, 80, 160n. 81. *See also* intent
doctrine of subjectivism. *See* subjective theory; subjectivism
doctrine of substantial performance, and satisfaction, 98–100
doctrine of unconscionability, 14, 30, 86; as implied terms of every contract, 108–9
double objectivity, 135
duality. *See* Gilmore; undue influence
due diligence, 120
Dugdale, Tony, 42, 163n. 143
Dunn v. Palermo, 107–8
duress: doctrine of, 14, 176n. 18, 187n. 72; economic, 46, 101, 109–11; and mens rea, 121, 187n. 61
Durkheim, Émile, 12; on free will, 117; and the just contract, 82–83; on obligation, 82; on the ritual contract, 76, 77, 82–83, 151n. 46
duty-based theory. *See* deontological
Dworkin, Ronald, 196n. 53

economic duress: doctrine of, 14, 176. 18, 187n. 72. *See also* duress
Egan, Thomas P., 157n. 41

Eisenberg, Melvin A., 9, 138, 140, 142
ejusdem generis, 162n. 123
emancipation, 105
empathy and legality, 139
enforcement: bargain, 157nn. 41, 42; of comfort instruments, 29–31; contract, 35, 106; Llewellyn on, 8; morality as a test of, 7
English law: and agency, 191n. 49; on breach of contract, 11, 92; on comfort instruments, 29; eighteenth-century, 7, 147n. 3; evolution of, 77–78, 108; fourteenth-century, 147n. 2; and good faith, 92, 159n. 76; and infancy law, 106; on intent, 59–60, 120; judge role in, 139; nineteenth-century, 10, 33, 36, 50, 98, 151n. 38; Sale of Goods Act in, 169n. 32; seventeenth-century, 147n. 3; sixteenth-century, 147n. 3; strength of, 139; thirteenth-century, 11, 191n. 49; twentieth-century, 24, 29, 36, 47, 48, 59, 61, 81, 111, 112, 134–35, 143
English Law Commission, 106, 172n. 99
ethics. *See* morality
evidence: and nonevidence, 139; state of mind and circumstantial, 118–20, 190n. 27; totality of, 119
evolution. *See* contract; Holmes; law
ex fictione juris, 93, 181n. 29
express satisfaction. *See* satisfaction
external(s): and contract intent, 112–14; as a distortion of reality, 37; dominion of the, 14–16, 153n. 87; manifestations, 94, 117; and objectification, 23; represented by internal, 21–22; subjectivity of the, 133–34. *See also* fairness; justice; reasonableness

fact patterns, 16–17, 132, 133, 134, 139, 140
fairness, 30, 37, 86, 94; of exchange, 83. *See also* doctrine of fair dealing

Farnsworth, E. Allan, 44, 182n. 39
fault concept. *See* culpability; mens rea
Ferson, Merton L., 12
Finnis, John, 7–8, 51, 106
"First Restatement (Restatement of Contracts and Mutual Assent, The)" (Whittier), 22, 30, 34, 75, 99
Fish, Stanley, 131
Fiss, Owen M., 89, 135, 179n. 90, 180nn. 91–93
Folk v. Central Nat. Bank & Trust Co., 63
foreseeability, 160n. 84
form, of law, 18–19, 24, 156nn. 33–34; contract, 72; internal repugnancy in, 28, 29, 32
form and substance, symmetry of, 17, 18–19
formalism, 103, 108, 109
forma non observata, infertur admullatio actus, 103
Forman v. Benson, 93
"Formation of Simple Contracts, The" (Ferson), 12
formula rules, 77
Foundations of the Metaphysics of Morals (Kant), 96
Frank, Judge Jerome, 94, 95, 96, 98, 181n. 32, 182n. 33, 183n. 60
fraud, 176n. 18
freedom of contract, 11, 16, 67, 86, 147n. 2, 151n. 39, 187n. 66; Braucher on, 102; expressed by will, 19; and infancy, 104; and intent, 112–14; and promise, 147n. 2; and reasonableness, 93–94, 110–11
freedom to contract, 8, 19, 104
free will. *See* will theory
French law, 12, 29–30
Fried, Charles: on blanket assent, 39; on promise, 7, 8, 34, 35, 96, 152n. 49
Fritzgerald, P. J., 115, 116
Frug, Gerald E., 85, 89, 136–37, 174n. 131
Fuller, Hoffman F., 69–70

Fuller, Lon L., 18, 19, 154n. 101, 163n. 148; "Consideration and Form", 24; on contract rationality, 70–71; reliance theory basis in, 26, 27
fundamental term of contract, 67

gap-filling, 70, 91. *See also* default rules
Gardner, George K., 33, 130, 139
German law, 8–9, 88; objectiveness in, 29, 30; symbolism in, 11
Gillespie Tool Co. v. Wilson, 100
Gilmore, Grant, xiv; duality of, 16–17, 34–35; on function of law, 179n. 85; on Holmes' thought, 16; on judicial mind, 88, 179n. 82; on the objective approach to law, 21; on syncretism, 34, 161n. 105
Glynn v. Margetson & Co., 68
Gobert, James, 120
Goldman, Alan H., 125
good faith. *See* bad faith; doctrine of good faith
Gordley, James, 75
Gottlieb, Gidon, 175n. 143
Granfield, David, 141
Greenawalt, Kent, 64, 82, 134
Grotius, 7
guaranty, 24
"guilty mind". *See* mens rea

Habermas, Jürgen, 49
Halpern, Sheldon W., 31, 32, 160n. 84
Hand, Learned, xiv, 95; announced the objective approach, 23
Hannah Blumenthal, 36
Hannen, Justice, 149n. 29
Harrison v. Commonwealth, 189n. 15
Hartog v. Colin & Shields, 47, 50
Haydocy Pontiac Inc. v. Lee, 105
Hedley, Stephen, 163n. 147
Hegel, Georg Wilhelm Friedrich, xiv; dialectic synthesis theory of, 136;

Phenomenology of Mind, xiii; on rationality of law, 71; three "spirits" of, 141

Helmolz, R. H., 188n. 1

Henderson, Lynne N., 139

High Street House Limited (Denning), 10

Hirst, Justice, 31

Hobbes, Thomas, 84, 142

Holmes, Oliver Wendell: on community law, 88–89; on conduct, 155n. 7; on default rules, 15; on evolutionary law, 16, 153n. 86; on the judge, 131; on language, 56–57, 65; on legal objectivity, 12, 54, 79; on morality and the law, 8; objectivity of, 129; *Path of Law, The*, 129; on private law, 88–89; on promise, 34

Hoosier Energy Rural Electric v. Amoco Tax Leasing, 53

Horwitz, Morton J., 13

Hotchkiss v. National City Bank of New York, 23

House of Lords, 59, 67

Howarth, William, 35, 161n. 117

human values: and contract law, 124–26, 129–33

Hume, David, 125, 183n. 50

imagery, legal, 87

impracticability. *See* doctrine of commercial impracticability

incapacity. *See* law of incapacity; infancy law doctrine

incompleteness: interpretive, 15; substantive, 15–16

infancy law doctrine, 101–7; and age of majority, 103–7, 184n. 7; flaws in the, 104–5, 109; and incapacity, 86, 101–3; and legislation, 106–7; objectification of, 103; purpose of the, 185n. 25; and reasonableness, 104–5

Ingram v. Little, 112

instrument. *See* form of law

insurance companies and breach, 113. *See also* corporate contracts

intent: actual, 3, 9, 11, 46–47, 55, 98, 119, 146n. 18, 160n. 81; actual versus apparent, 21–50; channels for, 18–19; and circumstance, 156n. 24; communal and detached objectivity and, 36–45; constructive, 116; criminal, 119; and custom, 56; direct versus oblique, 190n. 21; and freedom of contract, 112–14; and good faith, 95; implied, 48–49, 80–81; importance of, 164n. 156; and intention, 1, 118–19, 145n. 8, 154n. 101; intersubjective approach and, 49–50; and language, 43, 55; manifestation of, 33, 68–72, 91, 157n. 37; and meaning, 85; mutual assent and, 31, 69, 70; objective elements of, 19; objective implication of, 9, 10, 12; party-based, 36–37, 42, 69; as a pillar of law, 112, 151n. 41; presumption of, 31–33, 43, 67–68, 80; promisor-promisee objectivity and, 29–30, 33–36; promissory estoppel and, 27, 28; real, 69, 70; reality of, 101–14; and the reasonable person standard, 9, 13, 52, 54, 68–72, 122, 123; secondary, 43, 52; specific, 119; and state of mind, 118–20; subjective theory and, 19, 45–49, 64, 115, 188n. 1; symbolism of, 11–12; versus reliance, 9–10. *See also* Barnett; custom; dialectic; freedom of contract; intentionality; law; Llewellyn; mens rea; objective theory; subjective theory; will theory

intention. *See* intent

intentionality: and act, 117; and obligation, 1, 145n. 8; presumption of, 31–33

interactionism, 80, 177n. 33

internal as representation of the external, 21–22

internal repugnancy, 28, 29, 32

interpretation, 42, 46, 49, 53, 55–56; and custom, 67–68, 82; Fish's community of, 131; as defined by Fiss, 89, 179n. 90, 180nn. 91–93; is the law, 89; objective, 161n. 97; and operative meaning, 58; rules of, 42, 113, 133, 134; subjectivity of, 85. *See also* language; meaning
interpretive community, 135
intersubjective approach to contracts, 49–50

Jacob v. State, 62
James, William, 17, 132–33, 139
J. B. Lyon & Co. v. Culbertson, Blair & Co., 113–14
Jessel, George, 111
Jhering, Rudolph, 17, 24, 79
judge: and the law, 129–33, 142; and rules, 134. *See also* judicial mind
judgment: subjectivity of, 125, 133–36
judicial assault, on the infancy doctrine, 103–5. *See also* infancy law doctrine
judicial mind: Cardozo on the, 129; and the dialectic, 49; and human values, 129–33, 193n. 6; inner experience and, 140; intuition and the, 131, 132, 135, 194n. 21; objectivity in the, 130–33; Pound on the, 131; and process, 130; and the reasonable person, 88–89; subjectivity of the, 88, 125, 133–36, 143
judicial rule of interpretation, 133
jurisprudence: as a method of sociology, 17, 154n. 93; sociological, 175n. 4; of subjectivity, 141–42
jury: human values and the, 129–33; role of, 142, 176n. 25
just contract, the, 82–83
just result, 131
justice, standards of, 37, 86, 87; Kant on, 96, 97
Justinian, 76

Kant, Immanuel, 7; and agency, 192n. 75; conception of law of, 22, 96–98, 183n. 53; as an objectivist, 97; on promise, 125; rationality of, 125; as a subjectivist, 84, 125, 129, 155n. 8
Kelsen, Hans, 143
Kennedy, Duncan, 135
Kennedy Associates, Inc. v. Fischer, 54
Knapp, Charles L., 109, 154n. 98, 159n. 76
knowledge: actual versus imputed, 54, 61, 117–18, 119; not required, 116–17; presumption of, 43; and reason to know, 61; subjective, 43, 111. *See also* culpability
Kreis v. Venture Out In America, Inc., 55
Kronman, Anthony T., 192n. 80, 195n. 43

laissez faire, 11, 150n. 38
Langdell, Christopher C., 12
language: contract, 56–60; and context, 52–53, 65–66; as custom, 56, 65–66, 170n. 63; and intent, 43, 56–58; and liability, 56; limitations of regarding assent, 13–14; notational, 13–14, 152n. 62; objective meaning of, 30, 55, 56–58, 86; of the reasonable person, 65–66; shortcomings of, 38. *See also* intent; liability; meaning
LaRosa v. Nichols, 104
Larwin-Southern Cal., Inc. v. JGB Inv., 60, 95
Laski, Harold J., 121, 122, 191n. 50
law: basis in human nature, 129–33; canon, 75, 76, 77, 98; civil, 10–11, 29, 31, 148n. 12, 190n. 16; as a collective, 196n. 53; commercial, 88; common, 29, 20, 31, 33, 155n. 12; compliance goals and the, 97; corporate, 120, 121; criminal, 77, 115–21, 122, 136, 121; divine, 75, 76; duality of change in the, 61; essence of the, 138; as evolution, 16, 72–73, 77–78, 79, 86, 107–9, 170n. 59; generality of, 17, 18; and imagery, 87; inner experience

of the, 138–40; international customary, 171n. 70; and the judge, 129–33; natural, 7, 8–9, 51, 75–76, 78–79, 148n. 12; objectification of the, 16; "ought" of the, 130; private, 11, 88; psychology and the, 87–88; subjectivity of, 85, 89, 141; symbolic ceremonies in, 11–12, 151n. 46; techniques in, 198n. 18. *See also* agency; American law; Australian law; Canadian law; Cardozo; common law; contract; contract law; criminal law; dialectic; English law; French law; German law; Gilmore; Holmes; Kant; language; mens rea; New Zealand law; objective theory; philosophy; Roman law; spirit of the law; subjective theory

law of agency: and agent, 123–24; authority dichotomy in the, 115, 121–24; and contract law, 124, 191n. 49, 192nn. 60, 62–64, 75; essence of the, 123; and objectivity, 122, 123; reasonableness and the, 123–24, 124–27

law of incapacity (contractual capacity): and the dialectic, 101–14; evolution of the, 108; and infancy law, 86, 101–3. *See also* capacity

law of restitution, 188n. 1

law of satisfaction, the: and contracts, 91–100, 153n. 85; and Kant's concept of law, 96–98; and multiplicity of factors, 55; and objective theory, 91–93, 94–96; and presumption of reasonableness, 93–94; and the reasonable person standard, 54; and subjective theory, 49–50; and substantial performance, 98–100. *See also* subjective satisfaction

Law Quarterly Review, 35

laws of meaning, 23

Lawton, Lord, 24

lease, 24

leeways (Llewellyn), 131–32, 133

Leff, Arthur, 70

legal alphabet (Jhering), 24

legislative assault, 106–7

liability: basis of, 9, 56, 115–16, 117, 118; and custom, 65; expanded, 27–28, 147n. 36; test for, 33, 35, 41, 117; twin pillars of intent and reliance in, 27–28, 29–30; vicarious, 122

lifeworld, 49–50

Lipschutz v. Gordon Jewelry Corp., 61

livery of seisin, 24, 156n. 34

Llewellyn, Karl N., xiv; on contract and law, 171n. 79; on contract enforcement, 8; on the duality of assent, 38–42, 108; on judicial operating technique and socialization, 131–32; on leeways, 131–32, 133; on the reality of consent, 109–10; on rules and symbols, 13; on the subjective theory, 49, 138; on trade practice, 62–63, 170n. 64

Lloyd's Bank of Canada, 53

Locke, John, 77, 84

logic. *See* Aristotle

Luther v. State, 119

Macneil, Ian R.: on consent, 12, 13; on intent and the reasonable person, 69, 70, 71; on social adjustment, 71, 174n. 140; on the social purpose of contract law, 106; on tacit assumption, 73

mailbox rule, 12

main purpose rule, 66–68

Maine, Henry Sumner, 21, 107

Makousky, Inc. v. Julius Stern, 122

manifestation concept, 11–12; and agency, 124; and consent, 122; external, 94, 117; and intent, 33, 44, 46, 58, 68–72, 91, 157n. 37; objective, 86, 125–26; and the reasonable person standard, 68–72; and ritual contract, 76; and subjective satisfaction, 91–92

Mansfield, Lord: view of the contract by, 7, 103

Marshall, James, 119, 121, 190nn. 25, 27

Mattei v. Hopper, 92–93

May, Rollo, 178nn. 63, 66

meaning: and assent, 40, 46; and code, 172n. 99; communal intersubjective, 49, 167n. 207; conventional, 124; fair, 40; as a function of intent, 85; laws of, 23, 165n. 175; May on, 178nn. 63, 66; operative, 57; objective theory and, 43–44, 58; and the reasonable person, 22–23, 53, 65

Mehler, I., 102

mens rea: "guilty mind" as, 115; and criminal law, 115–21, 122, 136, 188n. 5; deontology and the purity of the, 124, 125; and intent, 188n. 4; and reasonableness, 116; subjectivism and 116–17; Thomas Aquinas on, 118; variations in, 189n. 6

Meredith Corp. v. Design and Lithography Center, Inc., 54, 168n. 22

Meyerson, Michael I., 174n. 138

Misano de Navigazione, SpA. v. U.S., 55, 93

misconstruction, creative, 38. *See also* language

mistake: common law doctrine of, 69–70; of fact, 117; of law, 117, 146n. 19, 176n. 18; mutual, 46, 47, 50, 160n. 92; subjectivity of, 166n. 205

M.J. Oldenstedt Plumbing, 25

modified subjective approach to contracts, 49–50

monopoly, 112

Moorcock, The, 80

morality: Hannen on, 149n. 29; Holmes on the law and, 8; objective, 8, 9; and the objective method, 7–19; subjective, 11–16

moral obligation: as contract basis, 7; duality of, 7, 148n. 4

More, Thomas, 82, 177n. 42

Morin Bldg. Products Co. v. Baystone Const., 93

mortgage, 24

motive, 118–19, 124, 189n. 5

Murray, Henry, 86

mutual assent, 38, 40, 86, 151n. 46; and intent, 31, 35, 69, 103; language and, 13–14, 59; manifestation of, 11, 22, 92; and rules, 12

Nagel, Thomas, 146n. 27

natural law, 7, 8–9, 51, 75–76, 78–79, 148n. 12

necessities doctrine, 103

negligence, 35, 113, 116

negotiation: bad faith, 113; precontract, 56, 124

neutral party. *See* third-party

Newman, Jon O., 131

New Zealand law, 120

Nimrod Marketing v. Texas Energy, 157n. 45

Nohcra Communications v. AM Communications, 182n. 34

non compos mentis, 101, 184n. 2

non est factum plea, 40

nudum pactum, 7, 10, 150n. 31

objectifying the law, 16

objective method of contract: announced by Hand, 23; defined, 9; impact of, 23; morality and, 7–19; standards of the, 17

objective rules, 9, 11

objective-subjective morality, 3, 11–13, 146n. 27. *See also* morality

objective theory, of contracts, 22–33, 43, 82, 104, 155n. 17; as a binary with the subjective, 141–44; and CISG, 127; compared to the subjective, 83–84, 92–93, 117, 138, 146n. 27, 179nn. 87, 90; defined by Slawson, 45; history of, 45, 81, 98–99; and intent, 19; and law of satisfaction, 91–93, 94–96; as party-based, 36–37, 44; and performance, 98–99; on promise, 36; rationalism of the, 97; rise of the, 164n. 158; Whittier's objection to, 22. *See also* dialectic; reasonable person standard; subjective theory

objectivism: Bernstein's definition of, 146n. 26; hard, 137; Holmesian, 54; and Roscoe Pound, 2, 146n. 14; subjectivism transformation and, 11–16, 136; and symmetry of contract doctrine, 17, 95

objectivity: and agency, 122–23; and bargain theory, 137; communal and detached, 36–45; and dispute resolution, 138; and dissatisfaction, 94–96; double, 135; and fairness, 140; Fiss' bounded model of, 89, 135; Howarth on, 161n. 117; and inner experience, 138–39; and the judge, 130–33; as myth, 85, 109; promisor-promisee, 33–36; pure, 109; relativeness of, 3, 146n. 27; role of in rule-making, 9, 11; Willistonian, 96. *See also* dissatisfaction; Durkheim; doctrine of infancy law; Law of Satisfaction; promise; reasonable person standard

obligation: background for contractual, 60; binding, 123, 144; defined by Finnis, 7–8; Durkheim on, 82; moral and legal duality of, 148nn. 4, 8; objectivity and, 9, 99; promise and, 96; vehicle for, 77

oportet facere, 106

Outlet Embroidery v. Derwent Mills, 44

pacta sunt servanda, 99

pareto optimality, 112, 113

parties. *See* reasonable person standard

paternalism, 189n. 11

Path of Law, The (Holmes), 129

Patterson, Dennis M., 15, 142

Perdue, William, 26, 27

perfect correspondence, 109

perfect tender rule, 98

performance, 54, 124, 183nn. 67, 72

Perkins, Rollin M., 117

per se rule, 102, 103, 106, 165n. 180

personology, 86

Phenomenology of Mind (Hegel), xiii

Phillip v. Gallant, 32

Phillips, Philip G., 172n. 89

philosophy: and the dialectic, 79–85; Greek, 69, 75; and the law, 79; and the reasonable person, 83–85. *See also* Cardozo; Pound

pleas, 40

pollicitatio, 80

Pollock, Frederick, 33, 155n. 12, 186n. 50

Porter v. Wilson, 103

Pound, Roscoe, 2, 77, 102, 144, 146n. 14; on deduction, 146n. 14; on judicial intuition, 131; on Roman law, 148n. 4; school of sociological jurisprudence of, 175n. 4

power: asserted, 33; predicted, 33

practices, 127

Pragmatism (James), 132–33

pragmatism and subjectivism, 143

precedent, 17, 87, 131, 192n. 80

precontract period, 48; negotiations, 56, 124

presentation, 14

prior dealings, 57, 86, 124

probable reality, 121

Problems of Philosophy, The (Russell), 83, 178n. 52

professionalism, 131

promise: actual, 33; apparent, 33; breach of, 10–11, 147n. 3; contract as, 7–11, 34; demise of, 80; Fried on, 7, 8, 34, 35, 96, 151n. 49; historic, 76; manifestation of the, 11–12; morally versus legally binding, 8–9, 125, 144, 157n. 39; parol, 147n. 3; power and, 33; principle, 183n. 50;

relationship to reliance, 10, 25; represents the will, 80–81; sanctity of, 7, 147n. 2; unreciprocated, 25–26; voluntary, 150n. 31. *See also* contract; Gardner; intent; Pound; Roman law

promisee, 26–27, 33

promisor-promisee objectivity, 29–30, 33–37, 161n. 109

promissory estoppel, 27, 28, 34, 157n. 42

promissory note, 24

promissory obligation, 1, 145n. 8

Prosser, William L., 51

prudent man standard, 125

psychology: and the dialectic, 85–88; folk, 118; and its hostile relationship with the law, 87–88; juridicial, 85. *See also* mens rea; state of mind

Pufendorf, Samuel, 8–9

"purity of heart", 121

R. v. Paquette, 121

R. v. Steane, 119

Raffles v. Wichelhaus, 33

rationality of Kant, 125

Rawls, John, 84

reasonable person standard: as agent of meaning, 22–23; and American case law, 53–55, 60, 61, 63; and assent, 40; broadened contract law, 5, 51–74, 147n. 36; created by will, 84; in criminal law, 121; custom and trade usage of the, 60–68, 124; defined, 9, 51–52, 82; and duress, 121; and emancipation, 105; and expert testimony, 63; externals and the, 15–16, 38; and freedom of contract, 93–94, 110; and infancy law doctrine flaw, 104–5; and intent, 32–33, 51–60, 122, 123; and the judicial mind, 88–89; language of the, 65–66; magic powers of the, 176n. 25; manifestation of intent and, 68–72; notion of reasonableness from the, 22,

99; and the objective theory of contracts, 23–25; objectivity and the, 9, 13, 149n. 22; parties and the, 53–56, 167n. 209; and performance, 124; philosophy and the, 83–85; and promise, 26, 36; purpose of the, 15, 164n. 156; relational consent and, 72–74; and the subjective approach, 55; in a tort, 25, 51, 52; totality of the circumstances and the, 56–60. *See also* duress; language; mens rea; promise; reasonableness; reliance theory

reasonableness: and intent, 37; and mens rea, 116; as morality's product, 172n. 94; presumption of, 93–94, 116; and the reasonable person standard, 22, 99; tools of, 124

Reid, Lord, 59, 67

reification, 174n. 131

Reiss, Stephen A., 121

reliance, reasonable: and liability, 27–28, 149n. 23; and the objective theory, 9–10; and promise, 10. *See also* reliance theory

"Reliance Interest:1" (Fuller and Perdue), 26

"Reliance Interest: 2" (Fuller and Perdue), 26, 158n. 57

reliance theory: bargain and, 25–26; contract and, 25, 26–27, 29–30; Denning's new era of, 10; and the reasonable person, 54; versus intent, 9–10, 54, 149n. 19. *See also* Roman law

religion, and ritual contract, 76, 78–79. *See also* dialectic

renvoi, 95, 182n. 45

representation, 21–22

respondeat superior, 121

"Restatement of Contracts and Mutual Assent, The" (Whittier), 22; and bargain, 30, 34; and intent, 30; section 75 of the, 34; subjective willfulness in the, 99

"Restatement (Second) of Contracts, The": on acts of contracting, 162n. 118; on agency, 122, 123; on the bargain principle, 25, 27, 157nn. 41, 42; on circumstances, 162n. 119; default rules in, 23; excuses impracticability, 31–32; and freedom of contract, 102; on good faith, 94, 99, 108–9; homage to Llewellyn in the, 39; intent in, 46, 47–48, 57–58, 166n. 200; on language and its shortcomings, 57–58; and law of meaning, 23; objectivity in the, 58, 61–62; on performance, 99–100, 180n. 12; on prior dealings, 57; on promise, 157n. 39; and reasonable persons, 53–54, 55, 61, 123–24; section 10 of the, 123; section 21 of the, 48; section 32 of the, 124; section 41 of the, 61–62; section 75 of the, 27; section 90 of the, 26, 27, 34, 149n. 24, 157nn. 39, 42, 158n. 57; section 200 of the, 33–34, 47; section 201 of the, 53–54; section 205 of the, 94; section 211 of the, 39; section 222 of the, 62; section 228 of the, 55, 180n. 12; subjective intent and the, 58, 92, 100; usage defined in the, 172n. 91.

revocation of offer, 61–62
Rich & Whillock, Inc. v. Ashton Development, Inc., 110
Ricketts v. Pennsylvania R. Co., 95, 98
rights, individual, 77, 120
Roman law: and consent, 11, 118, 176n. 18; and Greek tradition, 75, 79, 80; objectivism in, 151n. 43; obligation roots in, 148n. 4, 150n. 31; ritual in, 69, 83; symbolism in, 11; *stipulatio,* 24, 80, 156n. 33
Rose & Frank Co. v. Crompton, 29
Rosenthal, Peter, 191n. 48
Rousseau, Jean Jacques, 84, 142
rules, of contract law, 42, 113, 134; benefit, 103; capacity, 42; default, 14–16; dissatisfaction, 95; formula, 77; Gottlieb's aspects of legal, 175n. 143; importance

of, 194n. 10; interpretive, 124; judicial interpretation of, 195n. 43; mailbox, 12; main-purpose, 66–68; objective, 9, 11; perfect tender, 98; per se, 102, 103, 106, 165n. 180; strict construction, 42, 67. *See also* Llewellyn
Russell, Bertrand, 83, 84, 178n. 52

Sale of Goods Act, 169n. 32
Salmond on Jurisprudence (Fitzgerald), 115, 116
sanctity: of contract, 16; of promise, 7, 147n. 2
Sargentich, Lewis, 139
satisfaction: contract, 49, 180nn. 6, 12; objective, 94–96; and the reasonable person, 181n. 31, 182n. 40; subjective, 46, 91–96. *See also* law of satisfaction
Savigny, 60
school of sociological jurisprudence, 175n. 4
Schuler A. G. v. Wickman Tools, 59–60
seal, common law, 18–19, 24
sealed instrument, 150n. 35
"Second Restatement (Restatement [Second] of Contracts, The)." *See* "Restatement (Second) of Contracts"
security interest, 24, 87
Simon, Lord, 59–60
Simpson, A. W. B., 150n. 36
Slawson, W. David, 23, 45
Smith, Adam, 22, 77
Smith v. Hughes, 10, 36, 50
social contract, 84, 86, 143–44
socialization: and contract, 86, 106, 143–44, 174n. 140; and the judge, 131–35
Socrates, 82
Southern Pacific Co. v. Jensen, 131
specialty principle, 18
Speidel, Richard E., 41, 148n. 6, 163n. 148
spirit of the law, 148n. 4
standard form. *See* contract

standards, court-imposed, 15
stare decisis, 16, 17, 87, 130, 131, 192n. 80, 194n. 11; types of, 179n. 76
state of mind: and circumstantial evidence, 118–20; and intent, 120; in law, 116–17, 118, 153n. 87; proof of, 95, 101–2; subjectivity and, 124; third-party, 123. *See also* mens rea
statements, contractual, 56, 169n. 35
Statute of Frauds, 24, 42
Steller v. Thomas, 30
Sternlieb v. Normandie National Securities Corp., 104–5
stipulatio, 24, 80, 150n. 31, 156n. 33
Storer v. Manchester City Council, 24, 48
Story, Judge, 88
subjective satisfaction, 110–11
subjective theory, of contracts: as binary with the subjective, 141–44; in CISG, 126–27; compared to the objective, 83–84, 92–93, 117–18, 138, 146n. 27, 179nn. 87, 90; and conflict, 36; of contracts, 3, 43, 45–50, 146n. 19; and intent, 19, 45–49, 64, 115; modified approach of, 49–50; obsolescence of the, 42; and the reasonable person standard, 55; shortcomings of, 81. *See also* dialectic; objective theory; will theory
subjectivism: as arational, 139; doctrine of, 81; and freedom of contract, 11, 110–11; of Hume, 125; of mens rea, 116–17; transformed to objectivism, 7–19, 136
subjectivity: discretion and, 134–36; and evidence, 139; and intent, 10; of the judicial mind, 88, 125, 133–36, 143; and law, 141; and objectivity, 11–16, 136
substantial performance: doctrine of, 98–100
substantive reasoning, 109
Suisse Atlantique Societe D'Armement Maritime S.S., 67, 173nn. 113, 118

Summa Theologiae (Thomas Aquinas), 78
Summers, Robert S., 143, 198n. 18
Swift v. Tyson, 88
symbols, 86, 87
syncretism, 34, 161n. 105
synderesis, 22
symmetry, of form and substance, 17, 18–19, 95
sympathetic legal structure, 139, 177nn. 46, 51
synthesis: and the dialectic, 136–38; of law and subjectivity, 141

tacit assumption, 73, 157n. 58
Tate & Lyle Ltd. v. Hain Steamship Co. Ltd., 81
teleology, approach to law of, 17, 30, 88, 115, 121–22, 124–26
terms of contract, 67, 91, 162n. 140, 163n. 143
testimony, expert, 62–64
Theory of Communicative Action (Habermas), 49
third-party: analysis, 123; arbiter, 9, 110; determinations, 168n. 28
Thomas Aquinas: on the essence of contract, 30; on reasonableness, 22, 51, 78, 80; on state of mind, 118
Thornton v. Shoe Lane Parking, 108
tort: and contract, 34, 113, 147n. 3; and liability, 118, 147n. 3; reasonable person standard in a, 25, 51, 52
totality of the circumstances, 56–60, 110, 124, 126, 162n. 119, 169n. 32
trade practice, 62–63, 170n. 64
trade usage, 42, 56, 113, 124; and custom, 60–68, 82; and reasonableness, 62, 124
transaction costs, 112–14, 187n. 77
Turley, Justice, 62

unconscionability, 86, 139, 159n. 76

undue influence duality, the, 111–12
Unfair Contract Terms Act, 61
Uniform Commercial Code: article 2 of the, 41; on assent, 39, 41; defines course of dealing, 57, 169n. 46; default rules in, 23, 41, 44, 180n. 5; excuses impracticability, 31–32; and externals, 15; firm offer rule in the, 149n. 19; on good faith, 94; and intent, 59, 170n. 51; liability test in the, 41; Llewellyn's duality in the, 41; meeting of the minds in, 150n. 34; perfect tender rule in the, 98; and performance, 98; prior dealing defined in the, 57; and reasonable persons, 61, 180n. 5; role of the, 144; section 1–205 of the, 60, 169n. 46; section 2–207(2) of the, 71; on terms, 71–72; and trade usage, 60
United Nations Convention on Contracts for the International Sale of Goods (CISG), 12, 126–27, 180n. 10, 193n. 83
United States v. Thompson, 119
Upjohn, Lord, 67
Upton-On-Severn Rural District Council v. Powell, 47, 166nn. 193, 194
usage, 86, 92, 124, 127, 172n. 91. *See also* trade usage
utilitarianism, 125
Utopia (More), 176n. 42

Vaisey, Judge, 29

values: community, 135; human, 124–26, 129–33; institutional, 130; judges', 135, 193n. 6
Vorster, J. P., 35–36

warranty, 147n. 3
Weisz Trucking Co., 55
West, Robin, 139
"What Price Contract?" (Llewellyn), 49
Whittier, Clarke B., 22, 155n. 13
Wiesner, Don, 93
Wigmore, John H., 115
Wilberforce, Lord, 59
Williams v. Roffey Bros., 143
Williston, Samuel, 150n. 33; 157n. 42, 158n. 54; formalism of, 103; and infancy law, 104, 105; and objectivity, 96; on promise, 34, 157n. 42; on the subjective theory, 45, 165n. 177
will theory, of contracts, 11, 12, 13, 77, 103, 112, 151n. 49; and breach, 92; defined, 19; Durkheim on free, 117; and the external, 14, 15, 183n. 49; and promise, 80–81, 125, 151n. 49; reasonable person created by, 84; role of, 46; shortcomings of the, 79–80. *See also* assent; intent
Wood v. Lucy, Lady Duff-Gordon, 13
writs: assumpsit, 7, 78, 147nn. 2–3 history of English, 147nn. 2–3; types of, 147n. 3

Young, Robert L., 50